BOOKS BY

Relman Morin

EAST WIND RISING:
A Long View of the Pacific Crisis
1 9 6 0

CIRCUIT OF CONQUEST
1 9 4 3

East Wind Rising:

A LONG VIEW OF THE PACIFIC CRISIS

EAST WIND RISING

A LONG VIEW OF THE PACIFIC CRISIS

Relman Morin

ALFRED A. KNOPF : NEW YORK

19   60

L. C. catalog card number: 60–7298

© RELMAN MORIN, 1960

THIS IS A BORZOI BOOK,

PUBLISHED BY ALFRED A. KNOPF, INC.

FIRST EDITION

THIS BOOK IS FOR

D. W. L.

Contents

East Wind Rising:

A LONG VIEW OF THE PACIFIC CRISIS

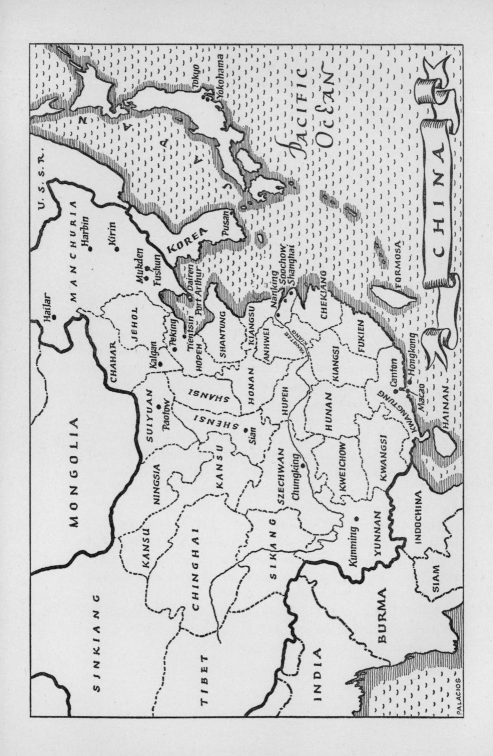

Chapter I

THE HOUSE
OF ASHES: 1950

ON THE MORNING of that strange incident, there was a grayness over Tokyo and a thin rain was falling. Veils of mist hung in the trees that screen the Emperor's palace, as though snagged in the branches. A skittish wind rippled the water in the moat and spattered the gray stone walls with raindrops. It was a very Japanese morning, green and pearly, like the pastel shades in a Japanese print. In this light even Tokyo—poor, shabby, broken-nosed Tokyo—was beautiful in a haunting, melancholy way.

I parked the jeep, locked it, and walked upstairs to the office. The elevators observed Sunday, which was probably a good thing for underexercised colonels. Pausing unconsciously at the door, I felt the familiar tingle of anticipation. What would the day bring? It was wartime.

The Japanese office boy, nicknamed "Mike," looked up from his grammar, still frowning with concentration. He was studying English. He rose from the chair and bowed—a slight bow, not a deep one. Occupation or no, he clung to his customs, but modified them for Americans.

"Was it a busy night?" I spoke slowly, spacing the words to help him understand them.

He struggled, but couldn't quite get it.

"*Isogashii?*"

His face brightened. Now he had it. "Not busy," he said. "War quiet."

"There ain't no such thing," I said. "Let's see the clip boards."

To practice his English he named each as he handed it to me: "outgoing cables . . . incoming messages . . . Peiping Radio . . . San Francisco broadcasts." He mangled the last.

He was right about the war. Only a few reports had come in from Korea overnight. The story was still the same—retreat. All too accurately Peiping Radio observed: "The Americans are buying time with land." And running short of land. The lines on the big map of Korea had contracted again. Every day we changed the pins and the strands of yarn, blue for us, red for the Communists. The lines were drawing down toward the lower right-hand corner of the map. Soon that corner would be known as the "Pusan Perimeter."

July 1950.

A few weeks earlier the North Koreans had struck across the 38th Parallel. Now they were driving down the peninsula, racing time and Douglas MacArthur.

Hospital planes had landed in Japan with the first wounded. A Negro infantryman lay in the stretcher, softly humming. A bearded GI, both legs in splints, called gruffly for water. A slight, blond boy, unnaturally pale, stared at nothing, whispering: "He was covered with worms. He was just laying there, all covered with worms. Oh, Jesus, the worms were—"

A few weeks before, they had been Occupation troops on soft duty in Japan. Now they were being "blooded." The word is used more often by officers at headquarters than men in the field.

The first war correspondents had already died. Bill Moore was missing. A transport plane blew up near Oshima Island. Another piled up on a mountain. Good friends aboard both. The casualty rate for correspondents was running ahead of World War II. Strange. The big war was only five years behind, and here we were, doing business at the same old stand, writing about combat, trying to get on paper the essentially untranslatable feelings of the soldiers. Nobody can do that. There are no words for sweating, animal terror, for heartbreak and shock. We called ourselves "retreads." Each of us claimed to have coined the phrase "This is where I came in."

My wife had walked out to the steps of the airplane ramp. She said: "All the best of luck." Then she walked away with a starched smile still stuck on the corners of her mouth.

Somewhere over the Aleutians, while the plane droned on through the night, the excitement had begun. Back to the Orient. Back to a different yet wholly familiar world. Pictures came crowding in like a montage: the Forbidden City; Mongolian bandits riding in the sandstorm; the girls on Oshima Island with camellia oil perfuming their long black hair; the house of the headless corpses; opium fumes in the gambling dens; a temple bell tolling; the secret message in *gamelang* music; a homecoming for me in the Far East.

The wars of those years seemed far away, but were not. The civil wars of China, the wars called "Incidents," the Pacific War, and the Communists' final triumph in Peking were all links in a chain. The Korean War was no isolated event. It descended in a direct line from those obscure conflicts of the 1930's.

I had seen them more than twenty years before when I came to China as a student. The Communists already were well organized then, and I went to their meetings in Shanghai. From Mongolia to Singapore (with the infallible aid of hindsight, of course) I had seen the picture taking shape.

That was in the day of the Old China Hand. You went to "tiffin," signed "chits" at the club, listened to the *taipan* talking to his *comprador*. U.S. marines patrolled in Tientsin. The gunboats of many nations rode on the Yangtze River, guaranteeing "extrality"—immunity from the Chinese government, police, and courts.

High noon for the white man in the Orient.

High noon for the missionaries in the lush field.

High noon for the war lords. They were busy as atoms, forming and re-forming in changing combinations against the government, against each other, against newcomers. They were always amenable to the "silver bullet," a bribe, no matter who offered it.

The Nationalist government—Chiang Kai-shek, his wife, her relatives, the Kuomintang party, and the hangers-on (not necessarily in that order of importance)—were riding high then. They seemed to have the future well in hand. "Let China sleep," Napoleon had said. But in the 1930's China was wide awake and stirring. The Chinese I knew best, university students, were on fire with visions of democracy, schools, factories, hospitals, a better life for the millions of patient peasants.

Some of them were Communists. They took me to their meetings in Shanghai. Their main base, though, was in Kiangsi, deep in the hills of south China. They were a small and harried group then. The Chinese Communists did not seem dangerous now that the Chinese Revolution was "over."

People worried more about Japan across the Yellow Sea. "We will have trouble with Japan for fifty years," the university students would say, "or however long it takes until China is strong." Japan had signed the treaties renouncing war and agreed to the naval ratios. Conservatives dominated the government. "But look out," said the foreign merchants and diplomats, "if the army takes over."

To the south, the massive colonial structure built by the British, French, and Dutch seemed as solid and durable as the Marble Arch in London. Nationalist movements had developed, but they had little strength, and no real leaders had appeared. Who could picture naked Malays or Indonesians driving white men supported by modern arms out of the Orient? Who cared, or even knew, that a thin-faced zealot, later to be known as Ho Chi-minh, had tried to see Woodrow Wilson at Versailles in 1919 to plead for the people of Indochina? He got no help in the Hall of Mirrors, but the reception would be better in Moscow when the time came. Nobody understood that the hour was so late. Certainly not the planters and traders and *fonctionnaires* and newspapermen in that part of the world.

In the middle 1930's I had come back to Japan again, this time as a correspondent, and watched the forces that brought on the Pacific War develop, slowly at first and then with gathering speed. The work had taken me all over Asia—to China again, Korea, Manchuria, Mongolia, and through the golden tropics. How incredibly remote that world seemed now. How little we had understood.

Now it was 1950. On the long flight out I thought back to those years and saw the story as a whole—a connected, inexorable sequence of events. The Pacific War, the end of colonialism, the Communist sweep in China, and now the Korean War—all were linked in the plastic flow of history, parts of a whole.

I finished reading the files that Sunday morning in Tokyo. Now was the moment for something that caught me in the throat whenever I thought of it. I said I would be back in a little while.

"Going out for coffee?"

"No," I said. "To a house."

"The girls don't work on Sunday morning."

"This is a special house. Maybe I'll let you in on it later."

I started walking, slowly at first. I wanted to get the feel of Tokyo again.

❦

Long years had passed, a full decade away from Tokyo. One year roving in Southeast Asia. Then, after Pearl Harbor, long months as a prisoner in Saigon. They ended when the famous "exchange ship" took us home. Then the Second World War. Vivid, terrible years.

But now that I was back in Tokyo in 1950, they seemed unreal. Or, rather, as though the things that had happened in those years belonged to a different world and another time. Walking along the street, hearing the language and seeing the people, I had the illusion of never having left Japan. The two edges of time, the then and the now, overlapped, melting into each other. Many times in the most unlikely places I had dreamed of walking around in Tokyo. These were the same streets as the streets in the dream, and the fragments of conversation were hauntingly familiar. Memory and dreams. Perhaps they come together somewhere in another dimension. Who knows?

A gust of wind shook the trees in Hibiya Park and brought down a shower of drops. Across the street a brown staff car rolled up to the front entrance of the Imperial Hotel. An American officer strode briskly into the lobby.

Occupied Japan. The U.S. army had dotted the cities with PX's, snack bars, clubs (a club for every rank), movie theaters, and all the comforts of home. Japanese cooks broiled Kansas City steaks, Japanese bartenders mixed the Martinis. Japanese dance bands played *The Third Man* theme. Military residential districts looked exactly like American suburbs, especially at night when American cars, bumper to bumper, lined the streets.

Who could have pictured the *Sui-ko-sha*, the Navy Club, as a billet for American businessmen and correspondents? It is an old building on a hilltop in Tokyo, architecturally a Japanese version of Victorian, with rooms of many shapes and sizes. Before the war Japanese officers seldom invited foreigners there, except on formal occasions. To them it was almost a shrine. The strange aura of mysticism that hung like incense over the Japanese armed forces had been especially noticeable in the blocky old place.

Now it was a hotel, more or less. Jeeps jammed the courtyard.

In the bar, peanuts and pretzels came with the drinks. Canned radio shows from America, slot machines, drunken arguments, and discussions of the latest Big Deal gave it an authentic homeside atmosphere. Sometimes, moving through the high-ceilinged rooms and up the wide staircase, I felt like a carpet-bagger in *Gone with the Wind*.

The little Japanese waitresses all seemed inexplicably buxom, until someone discovered they had taken to wearing falsies. "In less than a week," said Hal Boyle, the columnist, "you can spot the difference between Goodrich and Firestone."

Two legends had grown up about the Navy Club: one, that the details of the attack on Pearl Harbor had been worked out in these rooms; the other, that the dark stain on a rug marked the spot where a Japanese admiral had committed *seppuku*, the ceremonial suicide, just before Japan surrendered. The latter story fascinated lady visitors. "You really mean he did it right here?" said a wide-eyed WAC. "I'd love to snip off a piece of that rug for a souvenir."

As a study in behavior, the Occupation was a fascinating spectacle. On the whole, Americans behaved very well in the unusual situation. Some of them saw to it that the children of their Japanese servants had orange juice and vitamins. Many traveled and discovered the beauty of Japan. Others established the familiar orbit, home-office-club, and never left it. Officers without their families, no doubt pillars of the community at home, quietly acquired Japanese mistresses. A few became arrogant, or at best condescending, toward the Japanese. It was curious to see American men and women, brought up in a democratic tradition, subtly and perhaps unconsciously develop a master-race posture. They were like the Old China Hand of the generation before. Strangely enough, American women seemed more prone to this than their men. Perhaps the American woman is a natural bully. At any rate, a great many military wives tyrannized their servants and took advantage, generally, of their position as wives of the conquerors.

Otherwise, the Occupation was by no means harsh or op-
pressive. Murder, rape, and robbery occurred, to be sure, but
the rates were expectable for soldiers surrounded by civilian
communities, especially defeated foreign civilians. However,
when the Korean War began, the incidence of soldier crimes
dropped radically, and for good reason. Instead of being ordered to the stockade, the military prison on the outskirts of
Tokyo, the soldier was sent straight to Korea. "Overnight," the
commander of the stockade told me with a grin, "we got the
best-behaved army in the world." But even before that the
American Occupation had been a picnic for the Japanese compared to what Chinese or Russian troops would have inflicted
on them. They knew that.

Nevertheless, to a people who had never experienced defeat,
who sincerely believed that a mysterious power made Japan
invincible, the Occupation must have been a shocking experience. As children, they had been taught that *Yamato-damashii,*
the Spirit of Japan, a mystic but to them a very real force,
would overcome any enemy, regardless of his size or strength.
Now they were a defeated nation. Had *Yamato-damashii,* after
all, been a myth?

It was impossible to know their feelings. Neither by word nor
deed nor by a fleeting expression did they show them. Did they
hate Americans? Would they understand, much less ever for-
give, Hiroshima?

They obeyed and endured, and that was all you could know.
In a storm the bamboo bends to the ground, but never breaks.
When the wind dies, it springs up again. So with the Japanese.
Moreover, they had always lived close to natural calamity—
earthquakes and typhoons. It occurred to me that perhaps they
brought the same resignation to the calamity of defeat and
Occupation.

For example, a newspaperman invited me to dinner. On the
way to the restaurant he remarked, almost too casually, that
I might find his wife somewhat changed. "She was in a shelter

during an air raid," he said. "Some other people were—ah,
burned to death in there. My wife barely escaped. She has been
rather nervous ever since. I hope you won't be disturbed."

From his manner, he might have been describing a traffic
accident, not an act of war.

Another friend, I discovered, no longer lived in the rather
splendid family home that I had known before the war. He
now dwelt in a small cottage near one of his married daughters.
He said he had "lost" the big house during the war. There was
just a moment of awkward silence, and no explanation. Then
his daughter said, gently: "I am grateful that it brought him
closer to me." She smiled.

These were not intimate friends who might be expected to
display their deepest feelings. Another incident, however, was
different.

Soon after I returned to Tokyo, a lady called at the office.
She was formally dressed in a lovely old kimono and was
carrying flowers. She was the old cook, the "Number One" in
my house before the war. Except for a slight stoop, she had
changed very little. Her dark brown eyes were still bright and
mischievous, and her cheeks were like ivory. She used to run
the house pretty much as she pleased—"squeezed" a bit on the
food bills, tyrannized us, and made us supremely comfortable.
She was a wicked and delightful old lady.

"Are you well, *Danna-san?* Yes, I see you are." That was all
for me. "And Mary-*chan?* She is eleven now."

"Ten," I said.

"Eleven," she retorted. "She was born in Japan." In Japan
you are considered a year old at birth.

"Mary's a big girl," I said. "As tall as you."

I showed her a snapshot. She put on her glasses and peered
at it, murmuring, and wept a little. Then, without bothering
to ask for the photograph, she tucked it in her *obi.*

"How is your son?" I asked. "Well, I hope."

She hesitated. He had been hurt, but he was getting better.

"Hurt in the war?"

"Not in the war, *Danna-san*. Only a short time ago."

She said some soldiers attacked him in the street one night, robbed him, and left him unconscious. She did not say they were Americans, but there were no other soldiers in Japan then. "*Shikata-ga-nai*," she said. "It can't be helped."

You can't generalize. There may be millions of Japanese who hate the United States now. It would not be strange if they did. A war is not a football game, and there is no rule that compels you to be a good loser. As for the Occupation, some Japanese claimed to have found much good in it. They professed gratitude for the Occupation policies and admiration for the United States.

Not all of these professions, in my opinion, rang true. Is the question of any importance? It is if it affects Japanese policy. Japan is still, potentially, the most powerful nation in the Orient. Therefore, China and the Soviet Union are bending every effort to draw Japan into the Communist orbit. Wherever they can find a residue of hatred for America, they try to fan it into flame. They certainly will never permit the memory of the atom bombs to die. They have had considerable propaganda success in campaigning against rearming Japan and establishing missile bases on the islands. "Why should you fight America's battles?" they say.

As against the pull of China and the Soviet Union, there are factors of self-interest to the Japanese, primarily trade and strategic considerations. As long as Japan finds her best interests served by aligning herself with the West, there is little danger. Should the position change, however, the bitter memories of the war and the events that led to it will spring to the surface. The Japanese, naturally, do not hold themselves *solely* responsible for the Pacific War. In any case, with all her latent power, Japan is a country to watch, now more than ever.

After the cook left that day, I had an almost uncontrollable urge to rush out and see the house where we had lived. I could

hear the floors creaking and the hissing water heater threatening to blow up, and saw again the Rube Goldberg contrivances
in the kitchen and the bathrooms. Some were Japanese, some
foreign, some a mixture of both. The cook worked simultaneously on a *hibachi,* which burns charcoal, and a gas range. She
would flip a lamb chop with a fork or with iron chopsticks, depending on which utensil was near at hand.

You would hear her in the kitchen, mercilessly questioning
the tradesmen and delivery boys. She found out what every
foreign family would be having for dinner that night, who was
pregnant, the family fights, how the bachelor officers at the embassy were spending their evenings. Her intelligence system
worked like a vacuum cleaner, sucking in gossip about the
foreign colony in Tokyo.

Off the kitchen were three Japanese-style rooms where she
and the two maids slept on mats on the floor. One of the delivery boys (I never discovered which) occasionally visited the
older maid at night. This had an unsettling effect on the cook,
even at her age. At breakfast one morning the magpie chatter
and giggling seemed unusually brisk in the kitchen. I asked the
younger maid what was going on there.

"Oba-*san* is teasing Hatsu-*san*," she said. The corners of her
mouth twitched as she tried not to smile.

"What about?"

"I don't know," she said primly. "I was asleep."

Their rooms were unheated except for the *hibachi.* On winter nights, with charming eagerness they would ask if they
might come into the living room. They would then sit on the
floor, around the old pot bellied stove. The cook would tell
stories about the village where she was born and about her
husband, who was gone now, and the maids would ask questions about American movie stars. They would go on talking
until the coals in the stove faded to an orange glow. Warm,
happy evenings.

On the first free day, that rainy Sunday morning, I set out to find the old house again. It was on a hill, set back from the street, about three miles from the office.

A Japanese boy and girl came out of the park and signaled a taxi. The driver passed without seeing them. As they started walking, the girl slipped her hand inside the pocket of the boy's raincoat. He glanced at her and smiled.

To me the simple gesture was almost dramatic. It symbolized one of the great changes that had taken place in Japan. Before the war an unmarried couple, as I judged these two to be, would seldom be seen walking together and holding hands in the park. Very few Japanese fathers, not even those who had been educated abroad and wore Western business suits to the office, ever gave their daughters that much freedom. What we consider a normal boy- and-girl relationship hardly existed. Boy simply did not meet girl—nice girl, that is.

He visited the geisha if he could afford it, or went to the unadorned prostitutes in the Yoshiwara, and nobody thought anything about that. To have asked the girl next door for a date, however, would have startled both her parents and his.

The young woman was supremely unimportant. She lived only to serve. If she came from a poor family, her father might, for cash, article her to the geisha syndicate or to a factory. In marriage she had no legal status. She could be divorced by the recital of a brief formula and without going to court. Regardless of the cause of the divorce, she was not entitled to alimony, a division of property, or the custody of her children. The man came and went as he pleased. If he spent the night with another woman, it was none of his wife's business. She was expected to be content with the simplest kindness from him. Her friends counted her a happy woman if she said: "He is kind to me."

Imagine the impact, then, of the American GI. Naturally, he romanced the Japanese girl. He took her to the movies and to dance halls. He bought groceries from the commissary. On payday he took her to the PX and let her select a "present-o." She became his "moose" (the GI contraction of *"musume,"* Japanese word for "maiden"). The arrangement surprised and delighted them both.

Very soon Japanese young men imitated the soldiers. They could not buy presents very often, but they could offer romance. Instead of taking the girl for granted, they set out to "win" her, American style. Japanese couples walked the streets, holding hands, and embraced in the parks at night. "Student marriage" became, not common, but by no means rare.

Who can say? This may be the only enduring product of the Occupation. American political theory, the decentralization of authority, swims upstream against centuries of Japanese tradition. With a sneer, a Japanese politician spoke to me of "our so-called democracy now." Land reform has given ownership of the earth to the peasant, something his ancestors probably never knew, and given him a new importance in his village. That may remain. But breaking up the great industrial complexes and encouraging a labor-union movement—these American economic ideas, in my opinion, have small chance of survival. As for erasing Japan's great military tradition, this is not so ardently desired now as it was a few years ago. The gigantic shadow of Red China stretches across the Orient today. So, the Japanese military spirit and competence are almost as important in American thinking today as twenty years ago—but for quite different reasons.

A boy and girl holding hands represented a genuine social change. But in politics and economics Japan was still Japan, so far as I could see.

What about the Emperor?

Without realizing how far I had walked, I now found myself at an intersection near the palace. At this intersection, before the war, a girl conductor on a streetcar would sing out in a high-pitched voice: *"Kyujo-mae-ni."* It meant the car was approaching the palace. People would rise from their seats, bowing deeply. I would usually raise my hat. In summertime, however, when I would go out hatless, there would always be a brief and difficult dilemma. Americans expect a foreigner to take off his hat for the "Star Spangled Banner," and in a foreign country one feels compelled to observe national amenities. But, being without a hat, what does one do? Once I rose and bowed with American awkwardness. Two white men in the car stared in stark astonishment. After that, I would simply get off the streetcar before the girl squeaked: *"Kyujo-mae-ni."*

Now the Emperor visited factories, called on General Mac-Arthur, and appeared in public frequently. (He seemed to enjoy it, too.) No more pulling down the blinds in the windows of your office or waiting in a blocked street until his automobile passed.

Yet in the people's faces the same expression of reverence glowed. Perhaps there was less awe and more affection now. But, in any case, the enormous spiritual force flowing out from them to the Emperor was still there, unchanged by defeat and the Occupation. It is a factor the Russians and Chinese must reckon with in their timetable for the Orient.

A step or two more brought me to one of the main avenues of Tokyo. Across the street stood the South Manchuria railway building, symbol of a crumbled empire. The Sanno Hotel, like the Imperial, had become an officers' billet. An ugly, fire-blackened scar marked the spot where the Tokyo Club had been.

I could almost hear the billiard balls clicking in the noontime "snooker" game, and smell the odor of stale beer from the bar. I thought of Admiral Nomura, the ambassador who, with Kurusu, had been in Washington, negotiating with Roosevelt and Cordell Hull at the moment the Japanese attacked Pearl

Harbor. When he was appointed, about eighteen months before the attack, I had interviewed him at the Tokyo Club.

Nomura was big, wrinkled, gray, and a little paunchy. He wore gold-rimmed spectacles and had a benign, grandfatherly manner. He spoke English, but not fluently. I often wondered in later years how much may have escaped him in his discussions with Roosevelt and Hull. How much history may hang on that simple linguistic failing? We sat in the deep, black leather chairs through a long afternoon, talking about the disagreements between the two nations. Nomura could not understand the depth of feeling in America. "Why," he asked, "since you have so little at stake in China and we have so much?" A formula for compromise must lie somewhere. I tried to get him to spell out his ideas for it. But he only chuckled and recalled what William Jennings Bryan had said, as Secretary of State, to an earlier Japanese ambassador: "Nothing is ever final between friends."

Now I came into the district where we had lived. A few more blocks, now, to the house. Unconsciously I began to walk faster.

Up the hill . . . Past *Roppongi,* the Six Corners . . . From there you could see the barracks where the bloody "February 26 Incident" began on a snowy night. It was an army revolt against the too conservative—or, as they called it, "immoral"— policy of the government, a very big milestone on the road that led Japan to Tojo. . . . Past the restaurant where we ate eels (eel meat, they say, is better than antihistamine for avoiding colds) . . . Past the shuttered, forbidding Soviet embassy . . . Around another corner and into the street that leads to the Nagai compound . . . I knew every inch of it.

Oh, but it had changed! I recognized it only by relating it

to the pattern of the other streets and because I could see the brow of the hill ahead. Fire must have come through here like a scythe. The little shops, flimsy as matchboxes, were gone, and unfamiliar matchboxes lined the street. The fishmonger, the mason and his stone lanterns, the man who stocked such unlikely combinations as secondhand books and baseball equipment, the sweet old couple who sold crockery—all of them were gone.

Well, the house would still be there. I wondered who would be living in it. No doubt, the army. Such a pleasant compound would be requisitioned for officers with families. High-rankers, too, without question. "R.H.I.P.," as the GI's say—"Rank has its privileges." I would ring the bell and explain to whoever answered: "Haven't seen the old place since before the war . . . Sort of a sentimental journey . . . Does the window in the upstairs bedroom still rattle when the trains go by?"

A compound, I should explain, is a cluster of buildings surrounded by a wall or a hedge. Ours was like a park. Six houses in the form of a crescent looked out across a wide lawn. There was a round flower bed in the center. Shade trees bordered the driveway leading to the street. The landlord, Mr. Nagai, lived in the biggest house. He was a rich man, a retired diplomat. All his tenants were foreigners. He could have built several more houses on the grounds, but he liked the openness. This way, too, there was room for a tennis court between the points of the crescent.

A police box stood at the end of the driveway where it came into the street. It served as a substation for the whole district, not just the compound. In the last year or two before Pearl Harbor, when the Japanese began seeing a spy behind every tree, the policemen kept a record of everyone who came and went. They noted the number on an automobile license plate, particularly a diplomatic plate. If you had a guest from one of the embassies for dinner, the policeman would be in the kitchen early next day, quizzing the servants. He couldn't have learned very much because none of the servants in the compound, so far as we knew, understood enough English to have overheard what were called "dangerous thoughts."

I came up the street and found the police box. It was the only familiar object along the block, the only thing left. It looked a little seedy. (Showing its age, I thought, like the rest of us.) The cement walls were chipped and blackened. I went to the window. A film of dust, streaked with rain, covered the panes. Old newspapers littered the floor. The telephone had been taken out. The station was empty. Strange.

Then I turned into the driveway and stopped short, puzzled. Weeds and high grass lined both sides. The tall stalks bent over in an arch. Just ahead a thick stand of bamboo pressed against a rickety fence and had dislodged some of the boards. One of them, hanging loose on the nail, swung in the wind like a semaphore. Neither the bamboo nor the fence had been there before.

A few more steps brought me to the place where the driveway divided, one branch leading off to the right toward our house. Here there should have been a clear view of the compound, past the houses, across the lawn, all the way to the tennis court. Instead, another wall of weeds blocked the view.

For a moment I thought I had come in from the street at the wrong place. This could not be the compound. Nothing about it was right. Yet behind me there was the police box, undeniably the same cement cubicle, standing in the same place, exactly as before.

I stood there, trying to get my bearings. Where were the trees? They should be visible above the high grass and bamboo. Where were the upper stories of the houses? It was like a dream—eerie, mocking, unreal. My cheek stung where a weed had whipped it. My clothes were wet and cold from rain. These sensations were real; yet they seemed parts of a dream.

Just another step, I thought, would bring the open lawn and the houses. Then the curtain would part and everything would be the same as it had been ten years before. I pushed into the thick weeds and struggled forward. A yard, ten yards. Nothing but bamboo and the wet, rustling underbrush.

My foot struck a solid object. Standing in the weeds was an L-shaped fragment of concrete. Fire had scorched it. For a moment it meant nothing. Then I understood.

This had been the corner of a foundation for a house.

I stared at it and then closed my eyes. Now the eerie, nightmarish sensation welled up more strongly than before. As if I were looking at a double-exposed film, I saw the house as it had been and, in the same image, the scarred remains shrouded in weeds. It took a long time for me to accept.

The wind moaned. The bamboo shuddered, spattering raindrops. Silence closed over again. Suddenly I felt tired.

An old Chinese poem tells of a man who returns to his village and searches for his home:

> *I have been away such a long time*
> *That I do not know which street is which.*
>
> *How sad and ugly the empty moors!*
> *A thousand miles without the smoke of a hearth.*
>
> *I think of the house I lived in all those years.*
> *I am heart-tied and cannot speak.*

The blackened fragment alone remained.

Let it be a gravestone for all those who died in the war. Let it be an ugly monument to folly, ambition, and racial hatred. Let it mark the tragedy that need never have come in the Pacific.

Chapter II

SEGREGATION
IN CALIFORNIA

"SOMEDAY there will be war with Japan."

The immediate causes of the Pacific War developed in the 1930's. (Mark that word "immediate.") Before then the civilian governments had largely frustrated the Japanese Army's and Navy's ambitions in Asia. Then, about ten years before Pearl Harbor, the militarists succeeded in seizing power in government. Almost immediately they started operations in Manchuria and China proper. Later they prepared to move southward against the European colonies. The United States took the lead in blocking, or at least retarding, these operations. American policy is reflected in the Stimson notes, President Roosevelt's "Quarantine Speech" in 1937, and finally in economic reprisals. So, the 1930's fostered the immediate causes of Pearl Harbor.

But the story is not as simple as that, not as one-sided or by any means as recent in origin. Long before 1930, by word and deed, Americans helped prepare the ground. Discriminatory laws against the Japanese in the Pacific Coast states alarmed a President. A Secretary of State said: "I dislike to think" of the effects of the Exclusion Act passed by Congress to choke off Japanese immigration. A Secretary of the Navy reports that as far back as 1913 two admirals tried to persuade him that the

United States must fight Japan. Labor unions, politicians, and journalists fanned the flames for selfish purposes. Most important, millions of Americans permitted the most virulent of all poisons—race prejudice—to condition their opinions and distort their judgments as they looked across the Pacific. In California, as far back as I can remember, people said: "Someday there will be war with Japan."

The roots of Pearl Harbor are wide and deep. Some grew out of Tokyo, Manchuria, and north China. The seeds of others were planted in Washington and the capitals of the Pacific Coast states. Still others began in a few poor parcels of land that have no name.

In the early 1920's there was still open country between the western edge of Los Angeles and the little towns on the seashore. Dwellings stopped at a fairly distinct line. Real-estate agents hopefully subdivided the flat stretches beyond, as far as the Baldwin Hills. From the hills to the beach lay about ten miles of open fields. Eucalyptus and pepper trees lined the country roads between the main highways. Wooden pumps sucked oil from the ground, their massive arms swinging in a slow, elephantine rhythm. Two cement numerals, "57," set in the face of a hill, advertised pickles. You could hunt rabbits around there.

A heavy stench hung over this land, a compound of oil seepage, salt water, and rotting vegetation. It was swampy land, unfit for large-scale ranching and unattractive for real-estate development.

Here the Japanese lived and raised vegetables. They lived in shanties without water or electricity. They covered the boards with tar paper that ripped when the wind blew strong from the ocean. No curtains covered the windows. Sometimes the pale gold light of a lantern flickered inside at night; mostly, though, the shanties were dark.

The Japanese worked like ants. They worked in the summer heat and the chilling winter rains, on Sundays and holidays. They went out at sunrise and remained through the brief California twilight, bending low over the vegetables, tending them with knowing hands.

"They live like animals," people said. "They don't know anything better."

The woman worked in the vegetable rows with her husband. She probably came to California as a "picture bride," married by proxy in Japan to a man she had never seen. Often she worked carrying a baby on her back, papoose fashion. The baby's head would fall back limply and bob around with every move the mother made. Sometimes the woman hitched herself to a wooden "trough plow" and pulled it, while the man guided the blade.

They were displayed for tourists, like animals in a zoo. "Would you believe it in this day and age? You won't see anything like this back in Iowa."

We used to bicycle past the fields and yell: "Hey, Itchy Scratchy, get a horse." "That ain't a horse, that's his wife." They seldom so much as glanced at us. So then we would throw stones and ride away fast, looking back to see if they were pursuing.

Working incessantly, they prospered little by little. They brought the produce to town in pickup trucks instead of pushcarts. The flower shops on San Pedro Street grew bigger. It became rare to find a white man selling fruit and vegetables in the markets. The proprietors were all "Japs."

"What can you do?" women said. "Their vegetables are better and cheaper. You certainly aren't going to pay more just to trade with an American."

"They work eighteen hours a day, seven days a week," the men would say. "How'd you like it if I worked like that? Well, you watch—one of these days the damn Japs will take over all of California."

Californians resented the competition. Far worse, they believed, and were encouraged to believe, that Japan had plans to invade the Pacific Coast. When the attack came, every "damn Jap" had a specific sabotage assignment, people said. There were innumerable stories. A Los Angeles newspaper reported that police found "quantities of high-powered radio equipment" in a Japanese rooming house. The opposition newspaper, as opposition newspapers delight to do, debunked the story: a gardener had been buying separate parts and building his own receiving set; he was too poor to afford an ordinary radio.

"Little Tokyo," the Japanese quarter in Los Angeles, was believed to be the center of a spy web. It huddled in the old part of the city, not far from the original Plaza. The alleys smelled of rice wine, flowers, straw matting, *sukiyaki,* and the tiny pyramids of incense that predated deodorizers. There were curio shops, wholesale florists, a newspaper office, and a branch of the Yokohama Specie Bank in the district. A sign with three *katakana* characters, *ho tay ru,* marked the hotel.

At night "Little Tokyo" looked deserted. On Main Street there were burlesque shows, shooting galleries, and dance halls. Mexicans and Filipinos fought over the taxi dancers. The Negro quarter on Central Avenue had its own noisy night life. But the Japanese quarter was dark and still. Occasionally the mournful twang of a *samisen* came from an upstairs restaurant. The sound of voices speaking staccato Japanese crackled in the hotel. Otherwise it was dark and silent. Bad sign.

They worked, saved, stayed out of trouble. A Japanese name seldom appeared on the police blotter. During the Depression they were not seen in the bread lines; evidently they supported their unemployed with their own means. In the charity drives "Little Tokyo" always met the assigned quota. On all counts they qualified as good citizens. But in the climate of the times this only made them more sinister.

Certainly they were not wanted as neighbors. Zoning laws restricted them to designated areas to protect property values elsewhere. "I would rather have a good, clean Nigger family next door any day than a damn Jap," a man said. "At least the Niggers get dressed up on Sunday."

An undistinguished suburb named Rose Hill was developing on the outskirts of the city. One morning the newspapers published a photograph of a bosomy woman standing in front of a sign: "Japs, keep moving! Don't let the sun set on you here. This is Rose Hill!" The news story reported that a Japanese family had tried to buy a lot there.

Most probably it was merely a real-estate salesman's idea of publicity. The echo of Rose Hill came a few years later. In the uproar in Japan over the Exclusion Act, Tokyo papers reprinted this picture. The sign and the bosomy woman became symbols in Japan of, not one small community, but the whole United States. A Japanese cartoonist had no difficulty in converting the figure of the woman with her upraised fist into a parody of the Statue of Liberty. What is the message on the statue?

> *Give me your tired, your poor,*
> *Your huddled masses, yearning to breathe free.*

Not in the California of the 1920's. "Keep moving, Japs!"

Race prejudice, particularly if you grow up in an atmosphere of it, is an odorless, colorless poison gas. You are not aware of breathing poison. You don't question the legends. Catholics take orders from the Pope. The Jews are out to control all the money. Every Negro wants to marry a white woman.

The Japs are planning to invade California. Someday there will be war with Japan—it's inevitable.

Perhaps it was. There is a theory that if you fear something

deeply and think about it long and hard, it will materialize. In
these circumstances it is a wonder that the war did not come
sooner. I often question whether it would have come at all had
we known the history and reason for our prejudices in California.

†

The history began with Chinese labor during the railroad-
building days in the West. Coolies were brought over in boat-
loads at so much a head. When the roads were finished, the
Chinese came into the labor market. They were willing to
work long hours for low wages. Labor unions immediately perceived the threat. (Some Chinese were taken all the way to
North Adams, Massachusetts, to break a strike in a shoe factory.) Riots broke out in the Chinese quarter in San Francisco.
Western congressmen, responding to the clamor, began demanding laws to bar Chinese immigration. The United States
government blandly violated its treaties with China. The door
closed. China protested, but the monarchy, already collapsing,
was powerless.

A few years later Japanese immigration began. The agitation on the Pacific Coast now centered on the Japanese laborer. Again San Francisco was the scene. Again the fear that
Oriental labor would damage the American standard of living
was the cause.

In 1906 this hostility created an incident which has a peculiar echo today—segregation in the San Francisco school system. The school board removed ninety-three students of Oriental parentage from the regular schools and put them in a
separate institution. Of the total, twenty-five were American
citizens, having been born in the United States. The board said
it acted in response to demands from white parents, but the

resolution added: ". . . also for the higher end that our children should not be placed in any position where their youthful impression may be affected by associations with pupils of the Mongolian race."

Japan reacted fiercely. Alarming cables about the violent feeling came from the American embassy in Tokyo. Theodore Roosevelt answered with a conciliatory message that calmed the storm to a degree. He wrote privately to his friend Baron Kaneko: "The movement in question is giving me the greatest concern."

A correspondent for *The Times* of London cabled from San Francisco: "The whole agitation against the Japanese here is causeless . . . artificial and wicked . . . The people have been worked up to a high pitch of excitement by politicians who believed that by raising the Japanese issue they could increase their own popularity."

But "those infernal fools in California," as Roosevelt was now calling them, refused to be silenced. The Building Trades Council and the Asiatic Exclusion League harshly condemned the President. The California Federation of Labor sent a resolution to Congress. Concealing the unions' interests behind emphasis on the schools, it said: "We insist upon, and shall, to the limit of our own power, maintain our right to safeguard the pupils in the public schools."

The San Francisco *Chronicle* hinted darkly that California might have to secede!

There was more, and worse, to come.

As a result of the segregation incident, Washington and Tokyo worked out a face-saver, the "Gentlemen's Agreement." Japan agreed to prohibit laborers from migrating to the United States. The ninety-three Oriental children went back to the regular schools in San Francisco. For a time quiet returned.

The "Jap problem," however, was an issue much too good for politicians to resist. Within two years bills were in the California legislature to segregate the schools and to prohibit Orientals from owning land.

Roosevelt succeeded in getting them pigeonholed.

Four years later Woodrow Wilson had to contend with them. Using Roosevelt's maneuver, he sent Secretary of State Bryan to California to head off the legislation. Josephus Daniels, Secretary of the Navy, wrote that Bryan had little hope of succeeding. He did not succeed.

An Alien Landholding Bill became law in May 1913.

War talk started again. Daniels's description of the picture in Washington indicates that there were officials in the capital who wanted war. He cites the unauthorized actions of an army-navy organization, the Joint Board, in preparing for war. The Board, he says, "leaked" the news of this to the papers. Wilson angrily disbanded the Joint Board.

And personal equations always play a part. In the section of his story called "The Yellow Peril" Daniels wrote:

"All that Spring and Summer when negotiations were going on growing out of the California land law, Admiral [Bradley A.] Fiske, aide for operations, was incessantly talking to me about the danger of war with Japan. He and Richmond Pearson Hobson, who was a member of the Naval Affairs Committee, were obsessed with the Yellow Peril. They sat up nights thinking how Japan was planning to make war on America and steal a march on us by taking the Philippine Islands and going on to Hawaii. Hobson made speeches about it which the President regarded as in bad taste at a time when critical matters were at issue between two countries. Admiral Fiske, I think, fanned the fire with Hobson and confined himself, so far as I know, to trying to convince me that the war with Japan was inevitable and that we ought to carry out the recommendations of the Joint Board. He was so obsessed with this plan that he took much of my time with his arguments."

Daniels says he gently ridiculed the admiral.

Perhaps Fiske and Hobson sincerely feared an attack by Japan. If so, something was wrong with their logistics. Even in 1943, with faster ships, long-range aircraft, floating bases, and so on, the task of sustaining an attack across thousands of miles of ocean was still staggeringly difficult. With the equipment of 1913 it was all but impossible. The man on the street could not have been expected to know that. But Fiske and Hobson, as technicians, must have understood it perfectly.

In any case, the refrain had begun: "War with Japan." Newspaper editorials warned of the "Yellow Peril." A 1916 movie pictured the Japanese attacking California. A book, *The Great Pacific War*, visualized a series of titanic naval battles, and a magazine review of the book said: "American sea-dogs believe this is pretty much the way it will go."

Long ago the war drums sounded.

❦

Not long after the end of World War I a climax came. Now the question of Japanese immigration coincided with fears of a flood of people from Europe. Millions there clamored for entry to the United States. A Commissioner of Immigration in New York said: "The world is preparing to move to America."

The old specter of a glutted labor market rose again. To Californians it was a familiar bogey. Suddenly it confronted Americans in every state. Congress responded with laws setting up the quota system for immigrants from the various nations.

The quota for Japan would have been small, an estimated three hundred yearly or less. The Western states, however, called for total exclusion. They asserted that Japan had consistently violated the "Gentlemen's Agreement" banning laborers by means of the "picture-bride" system—the marriage by proxy which opened the way for Japanese women to come in. This was one of several accusations. To head off exclusion, Japan agreed to apply the "Gentlemen's Agreement" to laborers' brides. Henceforth, passports would be denied them, too.

Meanwhile, the chairman of the House Committee on Immigration, Representative Albert Johnson, of Washington, was writing a bill providing for total exclusion. The Syracuse *Post-Standard* said of Johnson: "He has the antipathy of the Pacific Coast states to the Japanese, but he is writing a bill for all states, not for the Pacific Coast alone."

As the bill moved through Congress, newspapers frankly set forth the reasoning behind it.

"The industry, thrift and ability of the Japanese have already put many American farmers and small tradesmen out of business," said the Chicago *Tribune*. "Do we want this to continue?"

"There are strong economic and racial reasons why they should be barred," said the Los Angeles *Times*.

But the Springfield (Massachusetts) *Republican* expressed resentment. "A small minority of Pacific Coast and Rocky Mountain senators and representatives are imposing their will on the enormous majority of the American people," the paper said.

In Japan, newspapers covered the story in great detail. One of the most influential, *Asahi*, pointed out that in ten years the white population of California rose by about one million, while the increase in people of Japanese parentage was thirty thousand. The paper asked: "Where is the cause for alarm in California?"

A magazine, *Yorodzu*, observed that "no sooner had the farming and other industries in the coastal regions become prosperous than the anti-Japanese agitation began."

The papers all recalled that Japan had given money to the victims of the San Francisco earthquake. A cartoonist depicted

Uncle Sam taking a bag of gold from Japan with one hand and slapping her face with the other.

A clergyman, Reverend Mr. Tamura, was quoted as saying: "It is foolish to talk of adopting resolutions of protest. The time will come when America and Japan will have to fight it out if America continues her present attitude against the colored races."

Secretary of State Hughes opposed the bill, both on legal grounds and as unnecessary. He calculated that only two hundred and forty-five Japanese a year would come to the United States under the quota system.

However, it was the Japanese ambassador, Masanao Hanihara, who unwittingly tripped the trigger. In one of his communications to Hughes he wrote: "To Japan, the mere fact that a few hundreds or thousands of her nationals will or will not be admitted into the domains of other countries is immaterial so long as no question of national susceptibility is involved. The important question is whether Japan, as a nation, is or is not entitled to the proper respect and consideration of other nations." Then the fateful sentence: "I realize, as I believe you do, the grave consequences which the enactment of the measure . . . would inevitably bring."

A senatorial clique seized on this sentence as a "veiled threat." The proper answer, they said, was to pass the Exclusion Act.

In vain Hanihara protested that he intended no threat. He said that he did not question "the sovereign right of any country to regulate immigration of its own territories." The two offending words, "grave consequences," had to be considered in the context of the whole message, he said.

It was too late. The damage was done.

In his careful study *The Far Eastern Policy of the United States* Professor A. Whitney Griswold assessed the damage: "It seems safe to say that the American people have never resented any policy pursued by Japan in China or elsewhere as deeply, as unanimously, and with as poignant a sense of injustice as the Japanese have resented the statutory exclusion of 1924."

When the news reached Japan, a volcano of anger erupted. The Associated Press correspondent reported "nation-wide demonstrations and mass prayer meetings at all the Shinto shrines throughout the country." He sent a photograph of a crude sign, written in English, on a Japanese store front— "Yankee, don't come here. I sell no American goods."

The Rose Hill photograph now had its counterpart.

But there was exultation in California. A San Francisco newspaper editorial said: "That American farmers cannot meet the low-standard Japanese competition is true. That the 'Gentlemen's Agreement' has been made a laughing stock across the Pacific is true. That the 'picture bride' evil, in all its ghastly insincerity, was a menace and a subterfuge of a colonizing empire is true. That the Japanese in America have remained loyal to Japan and have sought merely to exploit America is true. That inter-marriage of the two races is biologically dangerous is true.

"Now we look forward to an era of purgation."

If the syntax is weird and tortured, it is no worse than the thinking it reflects.

Some twenty years later the most decorated unit in the U.S. army was composed of *nisei*, American-born Japanese.

In Japan the Exclusion Act became known as "the slap in the face," a mortal insult. I found the bitterness still simmering when I went to Tokyo as a correspondent more than ten years later. With clear prescience Secretary Hughes had written Senator Lodge: "I dislike to think what the reaping will be after the sowing of this seed."

Some of the harvest already has been gathered. More, I fear, is still to come.

In the 1930's the Japanese militarists made effective use of the California story. They recalled it in order to becloud the real reasons for the deterioration of relations with the United States. The average Japanese could not understand that Americans opposed his government solely because of the aggression in China. He was told that American hostility to Japan went back long years before that. The military merely reminded him of "the slap in the face" and the actions that preceded it. He read the Stimson notes and the "Quarantine Speech" against the background of the previous decades.

The Pacific War is past. Still ahead is the struggle for Asia. Recalling colonialism and Western exploitation in the Orient is only one arrow in the Communist quiver. The white man's assumption of racial superiority and the memory of discrimination are also deadly weapons. It is no exaggeration to say that much of our trouble in Asia today goes back to thoughtless cruelties—kicking a ricksha boy, abusing a servant, making it plain that the Oriental was an inferior.

Much of the story of the Far East in the past one hundred years or more turns on two words—human dignity. Nationalism, the desire for self-development, and Communist maneuvers all played a part. But the most powerful force was the determination of the Oriental to be accorded human dignity. This is the significance of the California story.

Chapter III

CHINESE ADVENTURE

It was a warm May morning, too sunny and blue for us to stay in class, so we cut Geology IV and sat under a tree near the library. Graduation day was a month away. Tsui stretched out on the grass and closed his eyes. I thought he was asleep. Suddenly he sat up and said: "What would you think of spending next year in China?"

His name, in the Chinese manner which puts the family name first, was Tsui Sik-leong. Like Jones John. However, he called himself Sik-leong Tsui, Western fashion. When people from China were introduced to him, they often addressed him as "Mr. Sik" and said it was an unusual name. Tsui would agree blandly and suggest that his ancestors, who were Hakka, might have tampered with it.

The Hakka are the rebels of China—the individualists, the dissenters, the never reconstructed. They fought and connived against every foreign race that conquered China, forming secret societies and revolutionary groups and raising hell, in general, against imposed authority. Hakka blood ran hot in Tsui.

His parents had emigrated from a village in south China to Hawaii. His father became a clergyman. Tsui and his twelve brothers and sisters were born in Honolulu.

He was small and handsome, with skin the color of old ivory, and wide, glowing eyes. He assumed an air of Confucian graveness that was convincing until you caught the expression in his eyes. They often glittered with amusement while his face remained a blank. He liked practical jokes, and I thought his question was leading up to one now. You always played along, waiting to see what would happen.

"It's a good idea," I said. "When do we go?"

"You think I'm kidding. Listen, I've got a project." He opened his notebook and showed me the draft of a brochure for an Oriental Study Expedition. It would take ten freshly minted college graduates to China for a year. They would work in Chinese universities, each doing research in a specific field.

"Here's the point," he said. "The revolution over there is—"

"What revolution?"

"It's been going on for years. Now it's about over. The new government is just getting under way. This is the beginning of something so big that nobody fully understands what it means or where it will go."

"It's all news to me," I said.

"No wonder," he said. "The newspapers and magazines have done a crummy job of reporting on it. So much the better for us. We each take a field—government, education, banking, foreign relations, and so on—and work over there for a year. Then we write the findings, and, bingo, out comes a brand-new book on China at the biggest turning point in history. How about that?"

"Well, two things," I said. "How long does it take to learn Chinese? And what do we use for money?"

"Never mind about the language. They speak English in the missionary schools. Besides, we won't be working much in classes. As for the money, I figure one thousand dollars apiece will do it."

He knew the price of a steerage ticket to China on the Japanese ships. We would stay in dormitories with the Chinese students, travel third-class on the trains, and save money on food by eating Chinese meals.

"Chop suey three times a day?"

"Sure, why not?" he said. "You'll eat worse things than chop suey over there."

He said he had already talked about the project with some of his friends in college. Pomona College is a liberal-arts school, but he had approached students who were beginning to specialize. "You're going into newspaper work. Okay, you can study newspapers over in China. Find out how much the foreign language and Chinese papers influence public opinion. Also, you can send stories back to the papers here. Maybe pick up a little change."

"The only hitch is that I couldn't raise a thousand dollars," I said. "Right now I couldn't raise ten."

"None of us can," Tsui said. "But we're going to find people who will put up the money."

When he left, I went into the library, opened an atlas, and looked at a map of the Pacific. Yokohama. Hong Kong. Peking. (So that's where Peking is!) I was so ignorant that I searched the Moluccas, trying to locate Formosa.

I suddenly realized that I knew very little—next to nothing, in fact—about the Far East. No history, no economics, nothing whatever about the literature, art, or religions of the Far East. The American student in that day swallowed massive doses of European history—such vital information as the minor details of the feudal system in England, for example—but almost nothing about the breakup of China or the effects of long isolation on modern Japan. This seems strange because, in the West particularly, "the dawn of the Pacific Era" had become a cliché. Great new centers of commerce and the new patterns of politics and strategy were developing swiftly in the Orient and the Western states, analysts said. We were badly prepared for these changes. To many Americans the map west of Hawaii was a total blank.

I began looking at Orientals with a new curiosity, especially at the Japanese. What were the thoughts of the stolid little gardener edging your lawn for ten cents an hour? Was he really a spy? Did he, too, expect war one day between the United States and Japan? In Little Tokyo there was a lunch counter run by a Japanese and his wife. I attempted some research there under cover of the pie and coffee. First I asked them how to say "thank you" in Japanese and how to count to ten. Having then, as I thought, put relations on an easy basis, I asked some of the questions which were troubling me. They never answered. Mama-*san* would only smile and change the subject. "Now I teach you 'good morning' in Japanese. It is easy. You say *O-hayo*, like Ohio, where is city of Corumbus. Only you must say *O-hayo gozaimasu* to be porite."

Californians wrote with warmth and humor of the Chinese, the *paisanos*, the Filipinos, and the Serbian fishermen. In novels and short stories they were usually sympathetic characters. One of the best writers, Harry Carr, was drawing affectionate sketches of the Mexicans. But no one had anything good to say for the "damn Jap." He remained unknown, therefore suspect.

Weeks passed without word from Tsui.

Suddenly, in July, an alarming development seemed to threaten his whole plan. "Russia Threatens China," said the headlines: "U.S. May Intervene." Trouble had broken out in Manchuria. Where was Manchuria? Again I opened an atlas. There it was, in the north, outside the Great Wall. As for the issue between Russia and China, the news reports were hard to understand—something about a railway. In a day or two the story disappeared from the papers. Actually, the events were far more important than Americans realized, but in the reporting of that day the background and significance were not made clear.

"Don't worry about the trouble in Manchuria," Tsui wrote. "It won't affect the parts of China where we are going."

He said the necessary money was nearly in hand. He felt sure he would get it. The summer of 1929. The banks had money, business had money, everybody had money. The stock market climbed in delirious spirals. Everything was booming.

A chicken in every pot. Two cars in every garage. Nothing was impossible in that fine, dizzy, champagne summer.

Then his telegram came. "Dough in hand. October sailing date. Counting on you."

The ship sailed from San Francisco on a gusty day. I was hot with fever from a typhoid shot and cold with misgivings. The whole project seemed idiotic, worse than a waste of time. Why leave the known to go roving into the unknown? Why, when the moment came, did I do so?

The ship passed through the Golden Gate and lifted joyously in the first long swell of the open ocean.

"I've got a funny feeling," Tsui said. "I think this is going to lead to something. Maybe a lot more than we figure now."

"I've got a funny feeling, too," I said. "I think I'm going to be seasick."

Chapter IV

BURIAL AT SEA

THE *Shinyo Maru* came through Kaulakahi Channel, skirting the cliffs of Kauai. As she cleared the island, her black bow swung northwest. Ahead now lay the open sea.

It was late afternoon. Long, slanting shafts of sunlight touched the clouds with rose and gold. Kauai and her sister island, Niihau, began to sink on the horizon, melting into a blue haze. The scent of Hawaiian flowers, *pikaki* and ginger, grew fainter. The sea gull that had picked up the ship off Konole Point, hovering hopefully over the stern, uttered a last disconsolate squawk and wheeled back toward land. A hush settled over the ocean.

The decks were almost deserted. An hour or so before, people had lined the rails and milled around, caught in the excitement of sailing. The Hawaiian troupe on the dock sang "*Aloha Oe*" in glorious voices as the ship pulled away, and people wept openly, as they always do, and dropped *leis* into the water to make sure of seeing the islands again. Now the islands were almost lost in the hissing white wake of the *Shinyo Maru*.

Two slightly alcoholic American couples on the upper deck finished a flask, and the women said they must go below and unpack.

"Yokohama, here we come."

"What does *maru* mean, anyhow? Ever notice that all Jap ships are something-*maru*?"

"*Maru* rhymes with barroom. Let's go see if the barroom on this *maru* is open yet."

"Nobody dresses the first night out, so I think I'll wear . . ."

Their voices died away. Silence settled over the ship. I stood leaning against the stern rail, watching the sunset and the high-arching sky. The air was soft and warm. Silence and the hypnotic swell of the waves cast a spell. Time stopped. Suddenly this moment became the whole past and the whole future, the eternal Present.

It is always so in the beginning of an ocean voyage. The mystery always repeats itself. At the instant when the lines are cast off, the ship becomes a world in itself, apart from the world on shore. Then, imperceptibly at first, a gulf widens between them. The outlines of shapes on land begin to blur and the colors change. Something has ended, completely and irreversibly. A strange feeling of clairvoyance comes with this moment. It is not exactly seeing or touching the future, but a kind of reaching into it, an acute awareness of things that lie ahead.

One night years later I was going down the Hudson on a ship bound for England. It was wartime. Even in the "brown out" New York glittered in the dark sky like a huge jewel box. An icy wind was stinging my face and pinching my ears. The wind, the cold, the lights, and the needle-point spray were all sharply real, demanding attention. Yet suddenly—I think when the ship came into the open Atlantic—some other consciousness intervened. An indescribable sensation, a mixture of fear, excitement, horror, and sadness, swept through me with such overpowering force that it blotted out the reality of the ship, the cold, and the dark water. It seemed utterly without cause, unrelated to any sensory perceptions of the moment. When I was in Italy during the fighting, this sensation came back. Beside a stone barn I looked inside a knocked-out tank and saw what happens to men when a tank burns; one alone had managed to get out, and only a charred torso remained. That night a shell caught a fighter bomber above the beach.

Flames spurted from the wing. The plane shot upward in an impossibly steep angle, then nosed over, heading straight to earth. In that instant the plane, the gutted tank, the landing at Paestum, all the indelible pictures of the fighting there, fused into a montage of feeling.

It often happens when a ship sails—some knowledge, some certainty seems to lie just beyond a curtain, and shadowy forms appear. But on that first voyage in November 1929 it was a brand-new experience for me.

What were we getting into? A year in China. A year's work in some Chinese schools. More campus life. Another ivory tower—different, perhaps, but still an ivory tower. Only that? The strange feeling, tantalizing and touched with foreboding, suddenly faded.

The sun sank into the Pacific. The western sky glowed like a rose-and-gold orchestra shell. The ocean turned to molten bronze. Then darkness came racing out from the east.

Above, on the promenade deck, a man and woman came to the rail and stood watching the sunset. In spite of the first-night-out tradition, they had dressed for dinner. The man had squeezed into the tropical costume, a white, tight-fitting "monkey jacket." The woman's gown hung like a gunny sack, with loose, ambiguous lines. The skirt fell an inch or so below her knees—that is, so long as she was standing. When she sat down, it would climb well above them. This was the Age of Knees and Thighs, before the Age of Big Bosoms.

A steward brought a tray of cocktails. Almost before he turned his back, the man and woman were calling for a second. Other people joined them, and the steward barely kept pace with the emptying glasses. Prohibition, of course, did not extend to ships at sea. However, it had become such a national obsession that Americans drank feverishly even when liquor was readily available and talked of it even more feverishly.

"Man, it's great to taste the real stuff again after the rotgut they sell you at home. . . ."

"I've got a pretty good bootlegger. Oh, he charges me plenty, but at least I don't have to worry about waking up blind on the morning after. . . ."

"Hell, I get mine from a cop on the liquor detail. . . ."

"The only really safe thing is alcohol and a mix. . . ."

"Fellow at the office always makes it a point to show up real late at parties, and when they ask him how come, he always says—he's a card, this fellow—he always says he wants to give the gin more time to age. Haw, haw . . ."

They talked about the Stock Market.

"I see by the paper there was some pretty heavy selling last Thursday and Friday. . . ."

"It doesn't mean a thing. Probably just some of the big boys driving prices down to make a killing. . . ."

"I'm in it up to my neck, and I got a great kick out of my wife. Broker told me the other day she bought quite a chunk of oil—not much margin, of course—and I couldn't figure where she would have got hold of that much money. Well, sir, it turned out she put her furs and jewelry in hock. . . ."

"Friend of mine paid twenty per cent interest on some borrowed money the other day and got it all back in a week, plus plenty more. . . ."

"Sometimes it all seems completely crazy, but, the way I figure, we're on a permanent plateau. . . ."

And Politics.

"Al Smith was all right, but, hell, Hoover's a businessman, and you don't have to worry with the Republicans in there. . . ."

"The Democrats are finished. You stop to think, they've only elected one president in nearly forty years. . . ."

"Yes, and he was a mistake. I've always said Wilson should have been impeached for some of his crackpot ideas. It's not our funeral if people in Europe or anywhere else want to have a war. Let 'em settle their own problems. . . ."

And a National Idol.

"I simply swoon when he sings 'The Vagabond Lover.' . . ."

"So do I, but the men hate him. George—that's my husband —swears he's going to smash the radio. . . ."

And the Best-Seller.

"I'd be afraid to go out on the street wearing a green hat now. . . ."

"I felt sorry for her. But then George read the book and he said she was nothing but a nymphomaniac, and I hadn't thought of her that way, and . . ."

In the lounge the Filipino band, decked out in white trousers and striped blazers, assaulted a song—"Running wild . . . I've lost control."

1929. November. A decade was ending, and more than that. The last carefree age the world would know for many years was dying. Who could have foreseen the malignant forces already moving? Who would have believed that bread lines would soon be forming in the streets of American cities? "Brother, can you spare a dime?" Or that other men, unhinged with ambition, would soon be spreading death across the world, saying: "The Democracies are decadent."

The frivolous era was passing, and we were moving into the shadows.

"Running wild . . . I've lost control."

From below decks came the frantic clash and clangor of a brass cymbal. That would be Leong Tong signaling the dinner hour. Dinner in steerage! Steerage passengers lived a communal life, just at the ship's water line. It was the cheapest passage across the Pacific, designed primarily for Orientals. During the first few days of the voyage the other passengers, both in the hold and on the upper decks, stared at us in open curiosity. We "lost face." Then they learned we were students and commended us for traveling steerage. In general, poor people were distinctly unpopular in the 1920's.

In the hold that night people from all sides were converging on the long wooden tables. It looked like the rush in the subway at six o'clock, but with a curious difference. There was no jostling or pushing. Each person, without actually pausing, made way for the other. Later I discovered that this is a characteristic of Chinese crowds. No matter how jammed the street, a coolie balancing a long carrying-pole can always go through. A ricksha somehow navigates the thickest mass in an alley. I have seen Chinese swarm over every inch of space on the sides and tops of the cars in a freight train. Yet if one more could get a foothold, there was always room for him.

This kind of courtesy—the natural consideration for the other person's need for space—has become instinctive in the Far East. (Orientals can be brutally callous in other ways.) It probably came from plain necessity, the result of the terrible overcrowding. In China and Japan and Java and certainly in India there are just too many people for the amount of available space. Two people are always occupying or moving toward the same square foot of space. Hence, courtesy in public has become almost a reflex. It lies beneath the almost disinterested kindness that astonishes white men so much at first. It is the lubricant that makes life bearable in an overcrowded land.

Consequently, living in steerage constituted no problem for the Chinese and Japanese on the ship. We quickly adjusted to the cramped quarters, the steamy air, the eternal necessity to wait. No doubt our own forebears, for the most part, came to America in circumstances pretty much like these. How did they make love, I wondered, in the midst of so many people?

Each cabin held ten bunks or more, set in tiers against the bulkheads. Being ten together, we had a cabin to ourselves, but there was too little floor space for all of us at the same time. At first we went to bed at night and rose in the morning in relays. Then, like the other passengers, we went out in the corridors to dress and undress. Without a sign of embarrassment the men stripped down to their underwear; the women, wriggling like escape artists in a vaudeville act, contrived to undress inside their kimonos.

Everything in steerage operated on the cafeteria principle. There were queues for the removable copper washbasins, queues for hot water, queues for the baths; we learned how to wait.

There was no queue, however, for meals. Leong Tong and his aides brought the food to long wooden tables which were innocent of linen and rubbed smooth from years of use and many hands. In front of each place, depending on whether the food that day was to be Japanese or Western, chopsticks or cutlery weighted down a paper napkin. Most of the time the dishes were Japanese—rice, fish, thin, crackly squares of blue-green seaweed, and *daikon*, a giant radish pickled to be sweet or pungent. Frequently the main dish for breakfast was *miso-shiro*, a thick bean soup with a smoky flavor. The Japanese insist that it dispels a hangover.

Leong Tong, the steward, was a Chinese, plump and prosperous-looking, with a round, glistening face. He wore white coats which were a size too small, so that he invariably looked like something half squeezed from a tube. He had a calm, knowing manner and massive dignity. So far as I could tell, he spoke Japanese and Chinese equally well. But his English, usually so fluent, would fail at odd moments—no doubt when it was wiser not to understand. For example, he readily told of his wife and family in Canton, and how, although Chinese, he happened to have signed on a Japanese ship. "Work cheap in galley first, then catch this job. Maybe topside steward bime-by." But when I asked what he thought of Japan and how the Japanese treated him, his face went blank and he said he did not understand. From time to time he smuggled desserts from first class to our table, beaming as he passed them around and murmuring: "You like 'um? Allasame Mock Hockins, yop?" He meant the Mark Hopkins Hotel in San Francisco.

He did not assign the tables, but we went to the same one each day and gradually it became ours. Even when we were late, we found it unoccupied. A Russian bound for Shanghai, a Filipino boxer and his manager going to Manila, and a loquacious Japanese, a Member of Parliament, became regulars at the table. The Member of Parliament, like politicians the world around, talked with everyone in steerage who would listen, including the sailors and even the Chinese. Who knows whence a vote may come someday?

The Russian said he had escaped across Siberia during the Revolution and settled in Harbin. It is not unlikely; China swarmed with White Russians in those years. Harbin is (or was) a lovely old city in Manchuria, originally built by Russians. It was like a European oasis on the dreary northern plain. Wide, tree-lined avenues connected the squares in the center of the city. The gilded minarets on the churches turned to red-gold in the late afternoon sun. At night balalaikas tinkled in the little cafés, and anyone, even the wife of a consular clerk, could afford to hire a complete Russian orchestra for a party.

At that time Harbin was the control point for an unusual railway, the Chinese Eastern. The Chinese and Russians jointly owned and operated it. Russians held most of the administrative posts. The railway served, not only as a Soviet foothold in Manchuria, after Moscow had renounced her other concessions in China, but as a valuable channel for propaganda.

The Russian on the ship had been a clerk in the Harbin office. He enjoyed describing his life there. All the White Russians were poor, he said, hence none was really poor. They had picnics on the Sungari River, with the beautiful Dossias and Olgas, who also were poor and expected nothing but a little vodka or *kvass* and conversation.

One night, after another anecdote, the Russian paused, twisted the long holder on his cigarette, and struck a match. "Then a new manager came from Moscow," he said. "He brought new regulations. Phtt! Only Communists could work on the railroad. Of course, if we wished, we could apply for membership in the party. Some did and kept their jobs. Some left. I did not stay." He shrugged his thin shoulders. Sadness came into his face.

"Wouldn't it have been simpler to join the party?" someone asked. "You could pretend to be a Communist."

A curious expression, a mingling of pain and scorn, twisted the Russian's face. "Perhaps," he said. "But I would rather starve than join them. And I almost did."

The Filipino boxer seldom spoke. He ate his meals in silence. If anyone spoke to him, he answered in a monosyllable, glowering. Now he suddenly burst out: "What the hell difference does it make how you pick up a buck? Everybody's gotta eat."

"True," said the Russian. "But sometimes you have to choose between your stomach and your soul."

"No contest," said the boxer. "Always eat."

"In Japan," said the Member of Parliament, "we are very worried about—ah—Marxism."

The Russian smiled knowingly. "In the universities?"

"Yes, mostly the universities. The students talk about it. They hold meetings. It has become popular with the *mo-bo*— pardon me, that is Japanese slang for 'modern boy.'"

"You will find the same in other countries," said the Russian. "It is no accident."

In mid-ocean a fearful storm swept up from the south. For three days the ship heeled over to starboard. Tremendous gusts of wind pushed her over until the angle was so steep you could hardly walk. Then, painfully, creaking and cracking in every joint, she would struggle to right herself. Through the howling of the wind you could hear dishes and glassware shattering.

The hold was like a pesthouse. Meals ceased. Sleep became impossible. The passengers lay in the bunks, retching and struggling.

On the third day the wind died down and it was possible to go on deck.

The sea was a devil's playground. Thick, dark clouds hung curiously low over the water. The *Shinyo* seemed to be moving through a vast, murky room. Towering waves bore down on the port side. They moved with terrible majesty, like great black beasts.

In the hold a woman died.

She was old and alone. Nobody knew much about her. Nobody could say when death came to her. No doubt she had been frightened and filled with longing, lying in the bunk. Nobody could say . . . An old woman, nameless and faceless among the many in steerage. Leong Tong told us what little information there was. From some letters and her passport, it appeared she had lived near Fresno, California, for almost thirty years. They found a snapshot of a lunch counter with a wooden-faced Japanese staring from behind it. Evidently the woman and her husband had had some lettuce property, too. He had been killed in a traffic accident. She had sold out and taken passage for Japan. She had a sister there, also a widow. That was all.

For once Leong Tong's varnished impassiveness cracked. The mask softened. He sighed and said quietly: "Must put 'um in sea."

A tingle of horror went through me. "You mean bury her at sea?"

He nodded.

"But why? Why not take her body home for burial?"

"No can," he said. "No can wait so long for Yokohama."

Around ten o'clock that night the ship's engines slowed. At quarter-speed the ship was unusually quiet.

Silently, people began moving toward the stern. They clustered on the ladders leading to the upper decks, climbed up on the rails, and stood in a half-circle around the shapeless form laid out on deck. The light was deceptive. The woman's body had been sewed inside a weighted sack and placed on a long wooden board. A priest stood beside it now, white-robed and still.

The storm had gone. Hardly a whitecap whispered in the ocean. A waning moon kept scudding in and out of the broken clouds.

An American voice murmured: "Look, we're turning."

Barely moving, the ship began nosing to starboard. When it pointed due north, it stopped. In Japanese funeral rites, the body is placed with the head to the north.

The priest blew a thin, reedy note on a flute. At the signal the engines went dead.

An eerie stillness settled over the ship. The silence was heavier and deeper without the throbbing engines and the swish of the wake. The *Shinyo* rocked gently in the swell. The only sound was an occasional splash against the side. She was a ghost ship, adrift in a nameless sea.

The flute squealed again. Four sailors stepped forward, and each gripped a corner of the board. Lifting the body, they walked slowly to the rail. The priest followed, murmuring prayers. The sailors set the foot of the board on the rail. Two stepped aside. The other two remained at the other end, holding the board level.

The priest prayed for another moment. Then he spoke to the sailors. Slowly they began raising the head end of the board. The body would slide into the sea, feet first.

A strange sound, a mingled sigh and murmur, came from the people watching. They stirred uneasily. In a low, urgent voice a woman said: "Get me out of here, Charles. I can't look at this."

Slowly, inch by inch, the sailors raised the board, tilting it toward the sea. The body did not move. Still higher. And still, at this steep angle, the body clung to the smooth wooden surface.

Suddenly the clouds parted. In bright moonlight the scene was like a strange, Dali-esque painting. The priest, robed in white and wearing a tall black helmet, stood facing the motionless form on the plank. No one moved or spoke. The two sailors, both short men, slowly raised the board. I had an illusion of seeing the woman's face beneath the shroud. Her sightless eyes seemed fixed on the moon.

Abruptly the clouds closed again and the moon disappeared. In that instant the body moved slightly. It slid downward with a sudden rustling sound. It seemed eager for the dark water below.

There was a splash. Then silence—infinite silence in the sky, over the sea, on the ship lying dead in mid-ocean.

The ship's engines came to life. The decks shuddered. White water boiled around the stern, like an ivory fan opening. The whistle roared once and the vastness swallowed the sound.

Chapter V

TOKYO BAY

IN THE OUTER APPROACHES of Yokohama harbor a light stabbed through the darkness. Another blinked far away, then another and another. Soon the lights twinkled all around the *Shinyo Maru* like a necklace of stars. A burst of excited laughter swept over the decks. The *Shinyo* was inching in toward land, engines at dead slow. She would dock in the morning. For hours the Japanese passengers had been milling around the decks, pacing from side to side. It was after midnight now. Their eyes strained toward shore. The "stoical" Japanese! Even the sailors, to whom this must have been an old story, occasionally leaned over the rail, peering ahead. When the lights appeared, mere pinpoints in the blackness, a woman said: "There is Japan. How lovely!"

Yokohama harbor and Tokyo Bay—every drop of water there holds something of America.

In these waters just over one hundred years ago Matthew Calbraith Perry, of the U.S. navy, anchored his warships. He came on a peaceful mission, but the gunports were open. Rows of cannon eyed the green, pine-covered coast of Japan.

The year was 1853.

Even at that late date Japan was still the "Hermit Kingdom," closed to most of the world. The government permitted a few foreigners to live and trade at one small port. No others could enter. Nor could any Japanese leave, on pain of death. For over two hundred years Japan had remained aloof.

This long isolation is one of the keys to understanding modern Japan. It explains much that came later.

In the sixteenth century, at about the time Shakespeare was in his prime, the lords of Japan began to feel uneasy about the Europeans coming into the country. The Spaniards and Dutch, warring on the sea, connived unceasingly against each other on land. Each demanded that the other be barred from trade with Japan. Both intrigued with ambitious Japanese satraps. Even in the sphere of religion there was rivalry, Jesuit pitted against Franciscan—and so on, endlessly. Europe's chief exports to the Orient in that period were her eternal quarrels.

More important, the shoguns began to fear the rapid spread of Christianity in Japan. Thousands of Japanese had adopted the foreign faith. Nobody knew how many. Did they constitute a potential "fifth column" for the European Powers? There is a story, true or not, that a Spanish sea captain openly admitted that missionaries assisted the conquests of Spain by undermining the loyalty of the people before any troops arrived. In any event, the shoguns finally ordered all foreigners to leave Japan. Not long afterward they set out to erase every vestige of the Christian religion.

People died in horrible and obscene orgies if they refused to recant. Parents saw children roasted alive over grills. Boiling mineral water ate the flesh from the limbs of the Christians. Women, stripped, were made to crawl through the streets on hands and knees, publicly raped by lepers and convicts, then thrown into vats with snakes. Japanese tortured and Japanese submitted to torture. The nation produced both the persecutor and the martyr. A Frenchman in the employ of the Dutch East India Company, one François Caron, witnessed the terrible purges. He wrote that the torments "were borne by the poor Christians with constancy to a miracle."

For all their cruel ingenuity, the shoguns never completely killed Christianity in Japan. It lived on in secret. But they did succeed in other objectives. They isolated the country from virtually all contact with foreigners. Also, they taught the people to fear and suspect all Westerners. Thus, when Portugal sent emissaries to re-establish relations, the Japanese beheaded them on the beach where they came ashore. When foreign ships approached, gunfire met them; an American ship carrying Japanese survivors of a shipwreck was driven away. Foreign seamen who succeeded in reaching shore from shipwrecks were imprisoned.

For over two hundred years the door stayed closed. Then Perry came.

He dropped anchor in the bay, defying Japanese orders to go elsewhere, and marched toward Tokyo with some three hundred sailors and marines. It was a dangerous gamble. Also, it was "an act of aggression," as we would say today. The commodore had his instructions from Washington, however, and he carried them out to the letter. A treaty was obtained at gunpoint.

What was the reason for such drastic action?

American traders had found a short cut to the Orient. In Washington they were talking about a transpacific route to China, quicker access to the tea and silk markets. By 1850 California was in American hands. Yankee merchants, studying the map, perceived that a direct route from San Francisco would save a considerable amount of time. The Committee on Naval Affairs reported to Congress:

"The establishment of a line of steamers on the Pacific would place New York within less than 60 days of Macao. The trade with China in sailing vessels, which go around the Cape, now labors under a great disadvantage in the length of time required for the voyage. It may be assumed that an average of ten months is required to make the return. . . ."

But the ships would need ports where they could put in for water and provisions. Where else but Japan? To be successful the line would have to have access to Japanese facilities. No doubt Congress made this abundantly clear to the navy. Hence Perry's firmness and daring. He coolly bluffed the Japanese, asserting that even more powerful warships were on the high seas, coming to join his squadron.

Some of the Japanese leaders urged their government to fight. Others, typically, counseled the "bamboo tactics." They said Japan should yield for the moment, learn to build ships and guns like the Westerner, and then throw him out. It seems probable that when the shoguns consented to a treaty, they had this plan in mind.

Sooner or later, beyond doubt, Japan would have been "opened" anyway. This was the Predatory Century. Europeans were rushing to stake claims in China. They moved in exactly like forty-niners in the gold fields. Force was the order of the day in the Orient. So, Japan could not have escaped indefinitely. Destiny, in the form of commercial interest, gave the opener's role to the United States.

Presently the first American consul came to take up his post in Japan. Townsend Harris, of New York, was a serious, thoughtful man, alert and curious by nature. He had had some experience in the Orient. He wanted very much to see Japan. It is difficult to imagine an American better equipped to represent his country there. His diary is a fascinating record of human experience.

First, he is conscious of the drama:

"Monday, Aug. 18, 1856. A people almost unknown to the world is to be examined and reported on in its social, moral and political state; a new and difficult language to be learned; a history, which may throw some light on that of China and Korea, to be examined; and finally, the various creeds of Japan are to be looked at."

With self-doubt he approaches his task:

"I hope I may so conduct myself that I may have honorable mention in the histories which will be written on Japan and its future destiny."

Like so many Westerners, he permits first impressions to create an extravagant picture of the Japanese:

"They are superior to any people east of the Cape of Good Hope."

Then his attitude shifts. He says the Japanese are "liars." They spy on him, deliver diseased fowl to his cook, try in a thousand ways to obstruct his work. They frustrate his efforts to obtain what he considers ordinary, nonsecret data. "The government carefully conceals all the statistics of population, agriculture, commerce, manufactures, and military." To his outraged amazement, they coolly ask him to write Washington and request his own recall. Despair grips him, and he becomes physically ill, sick with the sense of failure.

He sticks to his task and soberly examines Japanese social customs. In a note on mixed bathing he writes:

"I cannot account for so indelicate a proceeding on the part of a people so generally correct. I am assured, however, that it is not considered as dangerous to the chastity of their females; on the contrary, they urge that this very exposure lessens the desire that owes much of its power to mystery and difficulty."

At one stage he considers the Japanese social structure sadly medieval. Later he says: "In no part of the world are the laboring classes better off than at Shimoda."

He is continually conscious of the drama of his mission:

"Thursday, Sept. 4, 1856. Slept very little from excitement and mosquitoes—the latter *enormous* in size. Men on shore to put up my flag staff. Heavy job. Slow work. Spar falls; breaks crosstrees; fortunately no one hurt. At last get a reinforcement from the ship. Flag staff erected; men form a ring around it and at two and half PM of this day, I hoist the 'First Consular Flag' ever seen in this Empire. Grim reflections—ominous of change—undoubted beginning of the end. Query—if for the real good of Japan?"

What a strange flash of clairvoyance!

"Grim reflections—ominous of change—undoubted beginning of the end . . ." Townsend Harris understood that his mere presence on Japanese soil was a source of controversy. But he could hardly have known the depth of feeling stirred by the sight of a foreign flag and a foreign government official.

To the *samurai*, the warrior class, he symbolized Japan's confession of weakness, a fearful disgrace to men so proud they would readily take their own lives for much less. Moreover, to them he was a barbarian. In the good old days they would have summarily dealt with him. But the good old days were passing. The *samurai* must have sensed that their way of life, their special position would soon go. They must have shared his "grim reflections—ominous of change."

The statesmen and scholars of Japan, however, accepted the new day with varying degrees of approval. Realists recognized that Japan could no longer keep the door closed. The clock, stopped in 1630, had started again. Some were anxious to learn Western mechanical techniques if for no other reason than to make Japan militarily strong. Intellectuals looked ahead to the day when they would have access to Western learning, to a world only dimly perceived.

Between the various groups a cleavage developed. And this

is an important point to examine. For this same cleavage persisted. It lasted from 1855 up to the hour of Pearl Harbor and played its part in influencing the policies of Japan. In the 1930's the throwback type of Japanese army officer was still contemptuous of "politicians" and "intellectuals," still ignorant of the world, still prone to resolve political problems by the sword. A distinguished newspaperman, the late Hugh Byas, described this attitude in *Government by Assassination*.

An unusual man left an earlier picture of this attitude, in his autobiography. His name was Yukichi Fukuzawa. He was eighteen years old when Perry came to Japan. He became a diplomat, a linguist, a writer, a student of astronomy, bookkeeping, physics, chemistry, and modern armament. Everything interested him. If he had been sent as a consul to the United States, he no doubt would have been as effective for his country as Townsend Harris was for his.

Fukuzawa went to America in the first Japanese-built ship to cross the Pacific. American hospitality impressed him. "They did everything for us and could not have done more. To use our Japanese expression, it was as if our host had put us in the palm of his hand to see that we lacked nothing."

Again, after the ship had undergone extensive repairs in San Francisco, and the captain asked for a bill, he says: "We were met with a kindly smile and were obliged to sail away with our obligations unpaid."

Studying Western political forms, he developed an admiration for George Washington. He asked about Washington's family, thinking that he would pay his respects. To his surprise, nobody could tell him where to find any Washington—indeed, whether any descendants were living. Having the Japanese feeling for the memory of great men, Fukuzawa was deeply puzzled.

Parliamentary customs were even more surprising. He was told that two men were political enemies, and comments: "But these 'enemies' were to be seen at the same table, eating and drinking with each other. It took me a long time before I could understand these mysterious facts."

The world has changed very little in some respects since 1860. A Russian tried to bribe Fukuzawa into becoming a spy!

When he came home, he observed the cleavage between the feudal mind and that which welcomed the end of the old era. He recognized that his own position made him suspect as one of those who "were trying to mislead the people and prepare the way for Westerners to exploit Japan." He had to take precautions.

"There were, on one side, the agitating clans which clamored at the point of arms for closing the country, and on the other side was the united power of Western nations demanding the 'open door,'" he wrote. "There were almost daily assassinations. The country had become a fearful place to live in. I tried to live as discreetly as possible, for my chief concern had become how I might escape with life and limb. Militarism ran wild."

How like the 1930's in Japan!

Not even the most ignorant and chauvinistic Japanese knight could fail to read the handwriting on the wall. To survive, Japan would have to acquire power—military power—plus modern industry capable of supporting it. The Japanese determined to learn, to modernize, to become strong.

So, from Tokyo Bay, from the same waters where Perry anchored, an astonishing group of men went to discover the secrets of Western strength. There were only a handful and they were hand-picked. They studied and copied, particularly weapons. They remained abroad for years, examining machines and techniques, like shoppers in a vast department store. They chose army organization methods from France and later from Germany, naval building and tactics from Britain and the

United States, communications from one country, educational systems from another, medicine and sanitation from others. Primarily, however, they focused on the study of arms and the use of arms.

Soon Japan tested her new weapons in a war with China. It was an easy victory. A few years later, in what they considered a necessary gamble, they fought imperial Russia. The "Pearl Harbor" of that war was Port Arthur; the Japanese attacked first and declared war later. Again they won.

Out of these two wars came another lesson, the next step in the education of a people studying modern manners. They learned that power politics is as important as military power if you are to consolidate your gains.

In the war with China the Japanese occupied a peninsula on the mainland. They expected to keep it as part of the spoils of war. Other nations had their "spheres" in China, and Japan now attempted to get in the game. No luck. Three European governments forced her to withdraw from the peninsula. Needless to say, morality had nothing to do with it, for a few years later Russia calmly annexed the same territory.

But the situation changed after the war with Russia. By that time Russian maneuvers in Asia worried the other European Powers more than Japan's efforts to get in the game. Thus, when Japan checked Russian expansion by force, a great round of applause came from the chancelleries. The peace treaty was signed in Portsmouth, New Hampshire. This time Japan was allowed to keep a peninsula—Korea. There were no objections now to letting her have a foothold on the mainland, in territory adjacent to the Russian sphere in Manchuria.

All these events—Perry, the British bombardment of Kagoshima, and the maneuverings after two wars—were lessons in power.

The big nations, the big Power units, constantly aligned and realigned in ever-changing combinations. Now A and B are allies. Next time they may be enemies. Each move responded strictly to considerations of self-interest. Statesmen paid lip service to principles, the sanctity of treaties, international morality, historic bonds of friendship, blah-blah-blah. But everybody understood that this was sentimental nonsense.

It was a tough world that Japan entered. If she soon began comporting herself like a Dead End Kid, it is hardly surprising.

Tokyo Bay . . .

Some fifty years after Perry had entered Japan, American warships again anchored in these waters. They were on a trip around the world, ordered by Theodore Roosevelt. Not the least of their objectives was to give the new Power unit, Japan, some idea of America's naval might. As each American battleship dropped anchor, a Japanese battleship took station facing it.

So quickly had they learned.

Chapter VI

NATIONAL

SCHIZOPHRENIA

"THERE IS JAPAN," the woman on the ship had said. "How lovely!"

Where was the loveliness? I stood on the docks in Yokohama, looking at shipyards, steel mills, smoking factories, and a vast confusion of shops and foundries. From the city came the clank and roar of machines. The air quivered with a feeling of furious activity. Beyond the city I could see a residential district, the Bluff, and that was disappointing, too; Western-style houses covered the heights. (I did not know that they had been built primarily for Westerners.) It was like any American industrial city. Not even Lafcadio Hearn, who seldom took off his rose-colored glasses when he wrote about Japan, could have found any beauty here.

To conceal my disappointment I said to the Japanese immigration officer: "Busy place."

He beamed. "Very busy. Japan got lots big factories. Get more all time."

This, I learned, was typical. Japan is a fairyland, and the people love the mountains and forests, the silvery lakes, the beaches. If you remark on the delicate beauty of a landscape, they quietly agree. But if you express surprise over the vast industrial plant, they explode with pleasure.

"Japan," someone has said, "is a chunk of the mechanized West in the middle of the agricultural East." The Japanese take great pride in this.

On the way to Tokyo from Yokohama the train passed through a drab and melancholy district. More industry. Flimsy little houses lined both sides of the railway; they were the homes of factory workers. By any standard but that of the Orient these people were poor. The steel worker had a box of rice the size of your two fists, plus a dab of fish or pickled plum, for lunch. (The Japanese infantryman marched and fought all day on the same ration.) His principal pleasure was the public bath, "the poor man's club." It cost him a penny or two. His wife seldom had more than one dress-up kimono. His son wore a plain, dark blue school uniform every day. His daughter, in all probability, had been indentured to a textile mill for a lump sum. Or, if she was pretty and seemed to possess some talent, she might be leased to a syndicate to be trained as a geisha. Labor unions existed, but in that day they were a joke.

In such conditions you would expect to find fertile ground for Communism. We found some Communists among the university students, but apparently there were very few among the working classes. For one thing, the government fought any form of Leftism tooth and nail. The police were not above using torture in order to extract information from a Communist. Apart from that, however, Japan had barely emerged from the feudal era. The tradition of obedience came naturally to the people. Moreover, they were imbued with a certain *mystique*, an undefined but powerful sense of belonging to a nation-family, in which the image of the Emperor and one's ancestors played a part. The Japanese did not reason this; he simply felt it.

Thus, in a remarkably few years Japan had built a great industrial establishment and moved in formidably on world markets. Only the long hours and low wages made it possible. The Chinese Communists are attempting to build the same thing today, under the same forced draft. The Japanese of a generation ago worked as he did simply because it did not occur to him to demand a greater share of the goods he produced or a greater reward for his labor. Even for the bare essentials, life was an unrelenting struggle. Yet he managed to do a little better than the bare essentials.

On the outskirts of Tokyo that day the train stopped while a track crew finished some repairs. I was able to see into one of the little houses opposite the car window. The *shoji* had been thrown open and a mattress lay over the sill, airing. Inside was the main room of the house, where the family ate, slept, and received friends. Except for a low table, there was no furniture visible. (The Japanese sleep on thick mattresses on the floor and put them in closets, clearing the room, during the daytime.) Everything spoke of poverty.

Two small objects softened the picture, however. One was a vase holding a few branches of some shrub. Beside the vase stood a slab of dark wood shaped like a rough crescent and highly polished. Together they formed a design, clean and simple. The color and relationship were pleasing. They drew your eye away from the worn matting, the naked electric light bulb dangling from the ceiling, the weathered walls.

From time to time, as the train moved on, I caught glimpses of other such rooms. In each there was some small focal point of beauty. To buy even flowers or a vase must have represented a sacrifice to these people. Yet the instinct toward decoration had been obeyed by them.

No wonder the Japanese have built temples so beautiful that, as Charles Lindbergh remarked, "they should be kept under glass."

But the Hotel Hosenkaku was neither beautiful nor very Japanese. It stood on a noisy intersection in Kanda, a district in downtown Tokyo, with a motorcycle repair shop on one side and a wine merchant on the other. It was drafty and cold, shabby in appearance, a hangout for Japanese traveling salesmen. We went there because it was cheap. And it turned out to be wonderful.

The entire staff—four maids, a room boy, the owner, and his wife—rushed outside when the taxis drew up at the entrance. They bowed low, as though on cue, chanting "*Irasshai, irasshai*. Welcome, welcome." Did any of us speak Japanese? No? Never mind. The owner delivered a little speech, anyway. The room boy translated in copy-book English. "We are most perfectly honored. . . . Gentlemen are first foreign guests to honor Hotel Hosenkaku. . . . We shall try most hard to render comfortable and happiness. . . . Now please to come inside."

Well, you may go to all the Ritzes and Savoys and Waldorfs in the world, dropping names and hundred-dollar bills, and never receive such a greeting.

Inside, the owner led us directly to the telephone. It was a copy of the ancient metal types you still find today in some Paris hotels. They were very expensive, and even businessmen waited for years to get a telephone in Japan then. "Of course, the American gentlemen know how to use a telephone," said the manager. "If not, the room boy will always oblige." He was very proud of his telephone.

They led us to the bedrooms, which were small, dark, and shabby, like the rest of the hotel, and furnished foreign style with the undersized chairs and tables which fit most Japanese but very few Westerners.

The maids and the room boy stood watching like curious children while we unpacked. They pecked on the portable typewriters and oh'ed and ah'ed over our neckties, which were Joe College, for the most part, and pretty bad. A dollar bill, however, left them unimpressed; their own yen notes are larger and more decorative. A girl's photograph stopped the show completely. *"Kirei, kirei,"* they said. "Pretty, pretty." And one asked: *"Koibito?"*

"That mean sweet-u heart-u," said the room boy, covering a grin with his hand.

When they learned we were going on to China, one of the maids giggled and said something to the room boy. The others laughed.

"She say maybe you find Chinese husband for her," he said. "We call that 'hands across the sea.' "

When he translated, the little maids rocked with laughter, and the one who asked for a Chinese husband pretended to slap at him. He must have embroidered the remark somewhat.

Eroticism in painting and drama is as old as Japan itself. The goings-on of the ladies and gentlemen of the medieval courts have been portrayed in detail in words and pictures. Some of the most beautiful Japanese screens are devoted to this theme. Plays during one period became so spicy that the authorities suppressed them. One of the most interesting Japanese lessons I ever had dealt with this period and the plays themselves. I never studied more diligently.

But for some reason the Japanese consider the Chinese even more expert in erotic pursuits. They tell countless stories of Chinese ingenuity and credit the Chinese with the secret lore of love potions and philters. *Ching P'ing Mei*, a sixteenth-century Chinese novel, is a long legend of amorous acrobatics. To the Japanese all Chinese are like the characters in the novel, busily slipping into someone else's bed, just as the English often picture the French.

(When you consider it, in fact, a parallel appears between the British and the Japanese, on the one hand, and the French and the Chinese, on the other. Here are two seafaring peoples inhabiting two island nations that are highly industrialized and dependent on overseas trade. In manner both appear wooden and unemotional. Both endure hardship and pain in silence. Both respect authority at all levels. Even in the matter of food and cooking they are alike—largely uninterested. And here are the Chinese and French, both vivid, voluble, highly excitable, highly individualistic, great talkers and humorists. Politically both believe the least government is the best, and both have gone through long periods of political chaos—and, in my opinion, even the iron Communist control will not speedily change this Chinese characteristic. Both adore food and wine and, as a result, both have developed cooking to a high art and produced an uncountable number of complex and beautiful dishes. So the generalization goes on and, of course, like all generalizations, it has its flaws.)

Someone has said: "An Englishman loves France as a man loves his mistress."

The Japanese feeling about China is different. They cherish Chinese culture and admire much that has come from that ancient civilization. But in the thirties they considered the Chinese soft, luxury-loving, decadent, always susceptible to the "silver bullet." They expressed contempt for the Chinese fighting forces and, in general, considered the Chinese (and certainly other Asiatic people) inferior to themselves. Chiang Kaishek's government had just come to power. It could scarcely be said, however, that he "governed" China yet. At best he had achieved only an uneasy truce with the bigger war lords. A little later, as Chiang gained more control, his regime began to disturb the Japanese militarists. But, on the whole, at that time China looked like easy picking.

All the rooms in the Hosenkaku were Western in style except the bath, which was Japanese. Everybody used it, even the hotel staff. The room boy showed us the routine. First you used the handsome little wooden buckets to throw water over yourself. Then soap. Then more water to sluice off the soap. Finally you climbed into a vat—the one at the Hosenkaku was big enough for three persons—and sat there as long as you liked, in extremely hot water, soaking and full of euphoria. The Japanese custom is more elaborate and certainly more fun than solitary bathing. Also, at first it can be a little startling.

On my first night at the hotel I put on a *yukata*, a cotton dressing gown, went down the hall, and slid back the panel at the entrance to the bathroom. A lady was standing there, wet and shiny. Instantly she covered herself, in the classic manner of a Greek statue, and turned her back. I closed the panel, mumbling apologies. A half-hour later, having ascertained that the room was empty, I went inside. First I merely poured the water over my shoulders. But then I threw a bucketful up toward the ceiling. It felt like warm rain. Then I threw another and another, and, of course, burst into song. With all this splashing I did not hear the panel slide open. One of the chambermaids walked in. She was fully dressed. Evidently I looked like a startled fawn, for she burst into laughter and said: "*Go-yukkuri kudasai*," which means roughly "Please relax." She brought over a small wooden stool and indicated by signs that I should sit down. Then she took a small hand towel and, in a thoroughly businesslike fashion, began scrubbing my back. She was tiny, but amazingly strong. In no time my back began to sting. I indicated I had had enough. The maid looked puzzled, but handed me the towel and departed. For all the interest she displayed, she might as well have been currying a horse.

Townsend Harris was mistaken when he called mixed bathing "so indelicate a proceeding." In the Victorian view, of course, nudity could seldom be innocent, especially in the presence of the opposite sex. It is in Japan, however. On many occasions later, particularly in remote country inns, I saw mixed bathing. If anyone else was in the room, a woman would turn her back during the soaping and rinsing. Then, as she stepped into the pool, she would cover herself with the hand towel. On a memorable afternoon in Hailar, in Manchuria, I had the company of no fewer than seventeen geishas in the bath. They were more modest in the process and certainly less self-conscious than a well-stacked woman sunbathing in a bikini.

Today in the cities a different type of public bath has developed. Here the client has a private room. A pretty little girl conducts the proceedings. First she gives him a bath and then a bone-cracking massage. Sex is very much in the air, but not in the bargain. The little masseuse wears only a halter and very short shorts. But, obviously to discourage hanky-panky, the door is left unlocked and waitresses keep popping into the room. One offers beer, another has tea, a third suggests fruit, and so on. In short, privacy is a fiction and the setup is a teaser. The customer may arrive with other ideas, but all he gets is a bath and a rub.

This is plain prurience. Mixed bathing is a hot bath.

"*O-jishin*" means "Great Earthquake." It is a figure of speech, symbol of the period in the late nineteenth century when Japan stepped abruptly out of her medieval era and rushed pell-mell to modernize and foreignize. The Great Earthquake brought factories and railways. It put mailboxes on the streets and Prince Alberts on the men. It changed the externals of Japan. But the inner forms remained. Old beliefs and ways of thinking survived, though badly shaken. Out of the shock of this sudden change came tensions, doubt, and confusion.

The Japanese attempted to live in two different worlds at the same time. Here was the warrior race, divinely descended, endowed with the mysterious Japanese Spirit, superior to all other peoples, capable of anything. In 1895 a Tokyo newspaper serialized a sensational novel in which Japanese fleets engulfed most of the British empire, sailed up the Thames, and took full revenge for the British bombardment of Kagoshima.

And yet, Japan's science, her technology, and all the products of these—in fact, everything new and efficient came from foreign brains. Doubts arose. Was Japanese superiority real?

A kind of national schizophrenia developed. In the thirties what Japan needed was the psychiatrist's couch.

One day we came to a primary school in a village in the north—a long, two-story building. As we approached, the windows suddenly filled with clusters of small, solemn faces. Along the whole length of the building the children jumped up from their desks to look, and remained staring until we were out of sight. They were utterly silent, owl-eyed with curiosity.

Our host was a Japanese who had lived in New York and taken graduate courses at Columbia. He laughed now.

"Quite a show," he said, "and typical of Japan. This village is only a few hours by train from Tokyo, from modern Japan, but I doubt that those children have ever seen a white man. They dropped everything to look."

"As though they had seen the Abominable Snowman."

"Not far from it," he said. "It isn't only because you are tall and fair-skinned. It's your eyes. Japanese demons have green eyes, like yours. Blue is just as bad."

"They didn't seem frightened."

"Oh, no," he said. "At this stage they still believe all foreigners are inferior to Japanese. The trouble begins a little later." He related his own experiences. "If you study science, particularly," he said, "the time comes when you begin to wonder about our alleged superiority. You begin to doubt everything Japanese, even our culture. In studying, moreover, you have to try to think like a Westerner. It is very hard to think like a Japanese in the morning and like another person in the evening. You get pulled every which way. And then, there is the language problem to make things worse."

Japanese is not as explicit as Western languages. It tends to convey meaning by indirection, often by inference. It is written in Chinese characters, and thus, over the centuries, endless complexities of meaning and pronunciation have arisen. Americans studying Japanese used to have a joke—"This is the *'hito'* of the *'nin'* in *'jin.'*" These are pronunciations of the same character, "man," used in different circumstances in Japanese. Newspapers using a complicated Chinese character frequently set simple Japanese phonetic signs beside it to clarify it for the reader. A Japanese politician told me he once lost an election because the characters in his name are too difficult for the average voter. "I will change my name for the next election," he said.

The language is a wonderful vehicle for mood and feeling, for poetry and philosophy. It probably conveys the misty esoterics of Zen Buddhism clearly to a student. But what torture for the Japanese struggling to grasp the precisions of science in a language of indirection! The gears clash, our host said. Frustration almost drove him to suicide.

Since he had mentioned religion, I wanted to ask him how he felt about the Emperor, but hesitated for fear of offending him. He opened the way himself, however, in discussing Japanese political forms.

"The Diet," he said, "is not Parliament or the American Congress. Like so many other things in Japan, it is a foreign product which we attempt to graft on our own institutions. The people don't understand democracy. When they think of government at all, I imagine, they think of the Emperor and the Elder Statesmen."

"And the Emperor. Do you think of him as a divine being?"

He hesitated. Then he said quietly: "I think of him as a very fine gentleman and a great spiritual force."

"Is that the—well, the general feeling?"

"I couldn't say. Probably many people consider him a god. I doubt that the educated upper classes do. It isn't something we talk about. We seldom express our deepest feelings. Perhaps we would be less mixed up about many things if we did."

We found the Japanese students groping, searching. They wanted change, social and economic change, but seldom described explicitly what new forms were needed. Like the young men in many countries at the time, they were dissatisfied and hunting for answers. Some thought they had found the answers in Communism. In the daybook from which we wrote our reports there is this passage:

"At each of the universities, we have been able to get acquainted with groups. A large portion of the 100,000 students of university rating in Tokyo are studying English or German. . . . They seem much more concerned about social and political conditions than the average American collegian.

"We heard frequent talk of revolution; Marxian philosophy is being absorbed quite widely by them, handed out in simple doses for the less literate."

This was an understatement. Some of the Japanese students were talking what is today recognized as a straight Communist line. Whether there were "cells" in the schools or card-carrying students I do not know. However, that phrase "simple doses for the less literate" is standard Communist technique. Some experts must have been at work in the universities.

Very early the Japanese perceived that Communism was an instrument of Soviet foreign policy and not merely an economic and social theory. In 1922 the government outlawed the movement in Japan. Student organizations were ordered to disband. They retorted with a clandestinely issued manifesto containing two significant demands—"Hands off China" and

"Repeal the Peace Preservation Law." (The law prohibited subversive political activity.)

You can see here the workings of long-range Communist policy. The Communists already were established in China. They had marked it for their own. Hence the agitation, via Japanese student groups, for "Hands off China."

The army, of course, had other plans. The government might talk peace. Indeed, in his year-end message to the Diet the Prime Minister, Yukio Hamaguchi, said: "War among nations, and racial animosities, are things of the past." But the militarists, eying China, coolly calculated the odds in a showdown with Russia, as well. Some of the industrialists were with them; some were not.

So, the many cleavages in Japan that arose from the Great Earthquake were: a political system ill suited to the country and not understood by the masses; unrest among the students; the gathering struggle between the military and the civilians for power.

One thing alone remained relatively unchanged by *"O-jishin"* —the Japanese woman's relation to her world.

We come now to Akiko-*san.*

Chapter VII

AKIKO-*SAN*

ON THE SCREEN Greta Garbo and the hero neared the moment
of parting. Japanese women in the dark theater sighed, murmured, and silently wept, luxuriating in grief.

"And now, good-by," Garbo's creamy voice sobbed.

From beside the screen came a male voice, also aquiver with
feeling. "*Ima, sayonara.*"

The "talkies" were new in Japan then. It was before the day
of superimposed titles for the dialogue. Instead, a man stood on
stage, translating the lines of the players, women as well as
men, into Japanese. His own performance often surpassed
theirs. When the villain spoke, the translator snarled and
gnashed his teeth, like a *samurai* bent on slaughter. To convey
the words of a woman in love, he would pitch his voice to a
fluttering falsetto. The translator added a flavor to the movies.

"Good-by," Garbo said again, more slowly.

"*Sa-yo-o-na-ra,*" groaned the translator.

The camera brought the farewell kiss into a closeup.

Akiko looked at the floor. Love scenes, she said, embarrassed
her. Especially the kissing scenes.

On the ship coming over, where I had first met her, she recalled the first kiss she had ever seen. In San Francisco, she
said, she had been riding in an automobile, and the car came
up behind a couple in an open convertible. She hesitated,
blushed, and giggled in embarrassment. "Suddenly," she said,
"they kiss."

"What of it?"

"But it is afternoon! On busy street! Everyone see!"

"If it's a real kiss," I said, "you don't notice the time or place. Like to try it?"

Akiko looked at me gravely and without approval. "Kissing is not Japanese custom," she said. "And I am Japanese." She walked away.

Indeed, she was Japanese—consistently, unwaveringly Japanese.

She was short and delicately formed, with an oval face, bright brown eyes, and dark hair. Her skin was ivory. She had a silvery little voice full of unexpected cadence and color. Best of all were her hands. Essays have been written about Japanese hands, and Akiko's were a perfect example—long, supple, beautifully contoured.

She had a thoughtful expression usually—sweet, but thoughtful. When something amused her, her smile was like a sunburst, and the silver bells rang in her laughter.

Being young and unmarried, she was entitled to wear the gayest kimono. She liked blue, all shades of blue, and she combined them with an unerring instinct for harmony. In kimono, walking or dancing, Akiko seemed to float.

Essays also have been written about the exquisite qualities of Japanese women—their gentleness, their delicacy, and their fragile daintiness. The first impact of these on a Western man is apt to be shattering. Western women seldom possess these qualities in the same degree; therefore the Japanese woman seems like a creature from another world. Underneath, the difference is not as great as it appears. A Japanese woman can turn into a tigress, raging with volcanic emotions and capable of direct and effective action.

Not that Akiko ever revealed this side. Once or twice I caught a glimpse of her innermost feelings, but the instances were rare. She seemed as secret and eternally serene as Fuji, the sacred mountain.

"Akiko is my treasure," her father would say.

Unlike her, he prided himself on having acquired Western ways. He was a wealthy businessman and he had to travel constantly. "Tokyo is my home," he would say, "but New York is my second home. Or perhaps Rio. Anywhere in the world I am at ease." And he would add, somewhat aggressively: "I am not like the old-fashioned Japanese. If one of my children should wish to marry a foreigner, I would not say no."

Akiko lowered her eyes.

I took advantage of this to ask whether I might see her after we reached Japan. "Of course, certainly. Take Akiko to the movies like an American girl. You like cinema, don't you, Akiko?"

"Yes, Father," she said, still staring at the deck.

On our first date in Japan, however, we went to a park in Tokyo—Ueno Koen. The *kuruma,* taxi, stopped across the street from the gate. As we started toward it, I took Akiko's arm. She pulled it away. A Japanese woman, she said, does not need help to cross a street.

I was offended. I told her she sounded stuffy.

"What's mean 'stuffy'?"

"Never mind. I was only trying to be polite."

"Thank you. I'm sorry you anger. But our way is different."

We walked along the gravel paths, over gracefully arching bridges, watching the carp and the goldfish. Considering the Japanese genius for landscaping, Ueno is not a beautiful park. I was disappointed, but Akiko was happy. I discovered that where I looked at a whole scene, she admired a single detail— the shape of a branch, a reflection in the water. I saw surfaces. She felt something beyond them. Her shy stiffness began to ease. She smiled and talked more readily.

"Oh, park is good," she said. "Many time I walk in garden of my home and make poem. Is right word 'poem' or 'poetry'? I wish I can speak English enough to say you my poem."

"I wish I could speak Japanese, Akiko-*san.* How do you say 'I love you' in Japanese?"

Her eyes narrowed. She laughed, a hollow little laugh. "Japanese do not say that."

"What do they say?"

"They say many, many things, but not that."

"Then how do you know if somebody—"

"They know. It not necessary say."

"People just sort of get the idea after a while, is that it?"

"Yes, that is our way. It's take long time. But maybe you know first time, too."

"Now I'm confused," I said. "And I'm sorry if I offended you."

She laughed again. This time the silver bells tinkled. "I teach you Japanese saying. It is easy. Say *'Koi-wa shian-no hoka.'*"

I repeated it and asked what it meant.

She looked in her English phrase book. "It's mean, 'Love is blind,'" she said. "Yes, something like that."

"So love is not only silent but blind in Japan?"

"Yes, I think so. Now we talk other things, please."

We came to a bench on the pathway. Before we sat down, Akiko drew a handkerchief from her *obi*. She flicked it over the bench, dusting carefully—first on my side, then on hers. If there was any dust on that bench, however, it was totally invisible. "Now," said Akiko, "please to sit down."

Ascend thy throne, O Lord and Master! Thy humble servant has made it fitting.

Thus, with the subtle perfumes of deference and attention, does the Japanese woman mesmerize a man. Whatever she may think of him in her heart, she pretends he is the Lord of the World. The Japanese, of course, expects it and takes it in his stride. But to me it was completely devastating. Akiko could make you feel like a combination of Hercules, Clark Gable, and Winston Churchill.

It seems strange that the positions are reversed in the West. Whereas the Japanese woman literally serves her man and considers this her rightful role whether he is worthy or not, the American woman seems to resent her position.

As Akiko was dusting the bench, I suddenly caught a glimpse of blood on her handkerchief and more on her hand. "What is this?"

"Nothing." In a flash she wrapped the handkerchief around her fingers and put her hand behind her back. "It not hurt."

I made her show me. One nail was splintered and the flesh was torn on two fingers. I insisted on knowing how this happened.

"In *kuruma*," she said. "Door shut. I not looking."

When we left the taxi, she had refused, as usual, to let me help her to the street. She had stepped down as I was paying the fare. Without noticing her hand, I had slammed the door on it. She had given no sign whatever.

We say misery loves company, and believe that sympathy helps somehow. The Japanese idea is different. They try not to show pain. Your friend suffers, albeit vicariously, on your account, and in their view you have no right to bring even that kind of pain to anyone else. I think the logic is sound.

Years later, when Japanese troops were fighting in China, I went to tea one afternoon with a Japanese family. Everything appeared normal in the home. The wife supervised and then sat down and talked quietly with her guests. Afterward I learned that on the morning of this very day they had received word that their eldest son had been killed in battle.

Akiko's mother had died in childbirth. Akiko often spoke of her in a curious manner, as though her mother still lived. I supposed that this was because, knowing so little English, she usually spoke in the present tense. Besides, it was difficult sometimes to know whether she meant her real mother or her stepmother.

One day—it was the day before we sailed for China—she said: "Please would you like meet my mother today?"

I assumed that this was a formality, in some way connected with the departure on the following day.

On the way, however, Akiko said: "You will not like Japanese grave, I think. It is dark and . . ." She searched in the phrase book. "Lonesome. Yes, here is word—'ronesome.'"

A moment later she stopped the taxi, saying she would get some flowers.

"Let me get them."

"You do not know flowers." She pinched my wrist and made a mischievous face. "You are baby."

She was in no way sad or depressed. On the contrary, she prattled, pointed out the sights on the way, teased me some more. I had never seen her so gay. "My mother will be glad to see us," she said.

The taxi stopped in an outlying district of Tokyo, on a busy street crowded with stores and shops. There was no indication of a burial ground here, much less a parklike cemetery.

We entered a passageway that led between two buildings, then between two more gray stone structures, which may have been temples. Then we came into a square enclosure, surrounded by high walls. It was bleak and cold. The sound of traffic outside, a mere hum, seemed to deepen the chilly silence.

Each grave was marked by a headstone about four feet high and shaped somewhat like a stone lantern. They were set close together, ranged in squares, bounded by narrow avenues. Sticks of punk smoldered in front of some; fresh flowers in vases decorated others.

An attendant came forward. Akiko said a few words to him. He disappeared among the headstones. "He prepare my mother," Akiko said. "We walk a little."

She walked slowly. Her sandals shuffled and hissed over the flagstones. The bright colors in her kimono flamed amid the dreary grayness. She talked about her mother without constraint and certainly without sadness. She spoke exactly as though we were waiting to meet a living woman.

"She has never met American," Akiko said. "I hope she like you, yes, I hope so."

It was an eerie sensation.

The attendant beckoned. Akiko led the way along a path to the grave. It was like the others, the headstone somehow like a small shrine, with Chinese characters carved on one side. Thin wisps of pale, gray-blue smoke floated upward from the sticks of punk, freshly lighted, on the shelf.

Akiko took my arm and pulled me close to the headstone. "This is my mother," she said cheerfully. She began arranging the flowers, setting them in the two vases. I tried to help, but broke the stems badly and knocked some out of the vases. Akiko laughed. "I told you you are baby," she said.

When the flowers were all arranged, she stepped back a pace. She bowed once and closed her eyes. A charming little smile curved the corners of her mouth. She prayed only for a moment, although it seemed much, much longer. Then she bowed again and turned toward me. Her expression was radiant. "My mother is happy," she said. "Now we go."

The burial ground was far from her father's home, on the opposite side of the city. Darkness had fallen by the time the taxi drew up at the gate. Every other time she had said good-by here. Now she told the driver to wait. "Come," she said.

It was dark and still in the garden. A winter wind rustled the branches of the plum trees. Her arms were like steel bands. Time stopped. When I could speak again, I mimicked her voice on the ship: "Kissing is not Japanese custom, and I am Japanese."

"Please not laugh," Akiko whispered. "I say you good-by now, American way."

Chapter VIII

SOUNDS IN THE NIGHT

THERE WAS GUNFIRE the first night.

Upriver from the university, rifles crackled and spat. The sound came from somewhere near Canton. It ripped through the chilly darkness, echoing across the campus and against the walls of the room in the dormitory.

There was gunfire everywhere in China then. Across the whole vast reach of the country, Chinese were killing Chinese. They killed as soldiers, mercenaries, and bandits. They killed unarmed peasants for loot and women and children who happened to be in the way. Not infrequently they killed "foreign devils," too, in the sporadic eruptions of nationalist feeling against the white man.

Battles flared up like brush fires, sometimes involving thousands of men, sometimes only a skirmish in a single village. Powerful war lords and the Communists, who were weak at that time, both contested the authority of the central government, the new government headed by Chiang Kai-shek. And in this whirlpool of violence and chaos bandit gangs operated purely for loot, food, and the rewards of kidnapping. They struck like lightning, pillaging and killing, and disappeared before any organized force could be brought against them.

Misery and hunger gripped the peasant. His only avenue of escape, frequently, was to take arms as a mercenary or a bandit. The farmer boy gave his services to anyone who could feed him. Not that he wanted to risk his life in battle, but too often the alternative was slow death by starvation. If he was wounded, he lay where he fell. No medic rushed to him with plasma and morphine. No aid station fought off the gangrene in his torn flesh. If the government troops captured him in a brush with the Communists, they would cut off his head in public. If the Communists wanted to make an example of him, he would suffer the "Death of a Thousand Cuts," in which an artful torturer turns a man to mincemeat while keeping him alive and conscious as long as possible.

So long as he survived, however, he did what hired fighters have always done. He looted villages which were like his own village. A peasant himself, he tortured peasants to make them tell where rice or money was hidden. There was a great traffic in actual photographs of these tortures—men cutting off a woman's breasts, perpetrating more unspeakable acts. You could buy these photographs by the bale in China at that time.

This was December 1929 in a tortured land. There was no peace. The sound of guns was as common as thunder.

I jumped out of bed that first night and ran to the window of the dormitory. There was nothing to be seen, no flash of gunfire in the blackness, no sampans fleeing down the river. A rifle spoke somewhere, automatics answered in a staccato shattering. Then silence. A moment later there was another rattle of firing, followed by a longer silence.

The naked cement floor felt like a sheet of ice. I went back to bed, shivering, pulled the blanket and my overcoat around my shoulders, and wrote a note for the diary that I had just begun:

"Fighting broke out last night somewhere near Canton. Just think—a real battle on our first day here. A warlord, whose name sounds like Fat Quail, is in the vicinity and apparently his troops have clashed with the Kuomintang, the government party. They say you never can be sure who's fighting who. We

heard about the various characters raising hell here, but hardly
expected to see it so soon. We came up the river from Hong
Kong yesterday."

Coming up the river, no one spoke. The first sight of China
strikes you dumb.

China was movement and muffled thunder, animal smells,
vastness, and, above all, vitality—riotous, cascading vitality.
Japan had been all greens and grays. China was red—dragon's-
blood red—and ancient yellow. Japan had felt clean and cool.
The breath of China was hot. Not weather-hot. A raw winter
wind was sweeping the river that day. The feeling of heat
rolled out in waves, as from a furnace—the heat of so many human beings, fiercely alive and hotly spawning still more life.
China leaped out like a tiger.

Approaching Canton, the river boat maneuvered through
fleets of Chinese boats, hoarsely whistling them out of its path.
Thousands more lay massed against both banks of the river.
Great ocean-going junks with lateen sails and brightly painted
eyes looked down on sampans carrying whole families. They
were all packed solidly together, side creaking against side, a
forest of spars, a floor of gently heaving decks. You could have
walked from the middle of the Pearl River to the Canton
wharf, a thousand yards away.

These were the river people. They lived out their days on
the junks and sampans. They fished, carried cargo and passengers, and kept a sharp eye out for anything salvageable.
Garbage and excrement floated around the boats, and the water was alive with God knows how many types of killer bacteria. Yet the river people bathed in it, drank it, used it for
cooking. The river suckled them.

How many river people? A million? Two million? Who could

say? They lived on the water because there was not a square yard of land left to farm. Other millions were scratching for life on land, the number in any given area limited, inexorably, to the number that bit of land could support—and no more. Few peasants owned land. The overwhelming majority farmed for landowners. Yet they fiercely resisted competition from any newcomers. Besides, by living on their boats and constantly moving, the river people could escape the tax collector. No, the odds on the water were no worse than on the land. Starvation hovered close to both.

I had the impression of looking into a womb—the great, pulsing womb of China. Human beings swarming on the river, human beings covering the fields like ants, human beings thronging the city streets—a heaving ocean of flesh and blood stretched across the thousands of miles from Canton to the Himalayas and the Gobi Desert.

Sheer pressure of population was, and still is, a dangerous problem for any Chinese government. The pressure began mounting early in the nineteenth century. Disastrous bloodlettings from famine, flood, epidemics, and war never checked the growth for very long. The exuberant fertility of the Chinese went on, adding more and more millions to the total horde.

Eventually overpopulation began to outstrip the sources of life—food and the means of buying food. China groaned and stirred uneasily. Unrest created the climate for rebellion. Long before 1912, when the last imperial dynasty went under, waves of strife beat against the central governments of the country. Next came the Nationalists. History will never know whether they could have met the problem. War with the Communists, overlapping with the attacks of Japan, gave them small opportunity.

The Communists clearly saw opportunity in the eternal struggle for food and jobs. They began preaching their solution in the early 1920's. Today they claim a population of six hundred million, and demographers who study the Communist census figures consider them fairly accurate. The net increase probably approximates twelve million a year—like adding almost the equivalent of a new state of New York every year. The Chinese Communists glory in the staggering figures. They profess to believe that sheer numbers constitute "national strength." In an age of weapons capable of snuffing out the lives of millions in a single attack, I wonder if the men in Peiping really believe this.

In any case, the burden is now with them. And the penalties of failure will be terrible.

The river boat nosed into the pack of sampans near the wharf. They bobbed and spun like corks in the water. A storm of shouting and general pandemonium rose on all sides. Sampan men hooked onto the boat and were towed toward shore, bumping other sampans along the way. Crowds swarmed and moiled on the wharf, obviously awaiting the river boat. As her side groaned against the pilings, coolies swarmed over the rails. The river people, agile as monkeys, shinnied up the poles by which they had hooked onto the boat. It looked like an assault. Indeed, river pirates often did attack river shipping in this manner. The sampan men collided with the coolies pouring in from the wharf in a dizzy, deafening swirl. Guards and the crewmen lashed out at them with long, willowy rods. The rods smacked bare flesh, raising welts and drawing blood.

The coolies crowded around the hatch covers, elbowing each other out of the way, struggling to be in the front ranks when the baggage began coming up. From the deck of a sampan below, a river woman watched. Her face was heartbreaking to see. Portering the baggage meant money, and money meant food. Far more clearly than words, the expression in her eyes bespoke the hope and pathetic eagerness that her man would be lucky this day.

A young Chinese secretary had come up to Canton from the university to meet us. "Quite a brawl, isn't it?" he said, smiling.

"Fantastic. Is it always like this when the boat comes in?"

"More or less. I would say a little more today, knowing foreigners were on board. Foreigners always travel with lots of luggage."

"But how could they know we were coming?"

"Ah," he said, smiling more broadly, "that is one of the mysteries of China. You will discover that these people always know everything about you, sometimes before you know it yourself."

The coolies began wrestling boxes, bags, and trunks out of the hold. They hung the heaviest pieces on carrying-poles, shouldered by two men. They walked in short, springy steps, chanting "*Hay-ho, hay-ho*" to keep a rhythm. I asked the secretary how they were paid for this work.

"There are no fixed rates," he said. "A few *cash* for a trunk, a few more for a heavier piece of the cargo."

"How much is a few *cash?*"

"In your money? Less than a penny."

Less than a penny. It took a moment to sink in . . . people so poor that even a penny had to be broken into still smaller fractions before they could use it. What could you buy in America for less than a penny? Not a stick of gum, not even a handful of peanuts from the machine in the railway depot. Here it bought human labor.

"It means a bowl of rice and some vegetables," said the secretary. He was no longer smiling. "Many days they eat less."

I looked past the coolies toward Canton, along the streets lined with tamarind trees, past the foreign settlement on Shameen Island, and beyond to the hills and a white-walled monastery surrounded by terraces of ginger root.

China.

A coolie passed, bending low beneath a heavy trunk. He was barefoot and naked to the waist. Patches of sweat stained his trousers. He saw me watching him and smiled, a shy, warming smile. His features were intelligent and sensitive. Across the road another coolie set the shafts of his ricksha close beside the toe of the man who had hailed him. The same rare quality of natural refinement was in his face. He looked more cultured, in fact, than the fat man in beautiful brocaded silk robes whom he was pulling. Here were coolies, Chinese who lived and worked exactly like animals, who could neither read nor write, who knew nothing but harsh, brutalizing labor. Yet frequently they had such faces. Who can explain this mystery? Is it possible that five thousand years of distilled civilization can shape the features of a coolie on the bund in Canton?

Farther down the bund an old woman, wearing the customary black cotton pajamas, sat in the dust beside a little pyramid of tangerines, calling out for buyers. Two slits alone remained where her eyeballs had been. Syphilis or trachoma. A beggar pulled back his sleeve and waggled the hideous, pointed stump of a severed arm. "*Cumshaw*," he begged, holding out his one hand for money. Two little boys trotted beside a white man in a ricksha, whining over and over: "No mama, no papa, no whisky soda. Please give *cumshaw*." Sometimes they said: "Me very hungry." But they had learned that foreigners were more apt to laugh and loosen up when they heard the "no-whisky-soda" touch, so this was more popular.

Flies clung in black clusters to the chunks of pork and the sausage strings hanging on hooks in front of the windowless butcher shop. A man came out, holding a sausage in one hand and dragging the bloody pelt of a dog with the other. He held it by the tail. As the man walked, the dog's head, which had been left intact in the skinning, bounced over the stones, and the jaws seemed to be snapping at the man's heels.

A squat, flat-faced whore stood in a doorway, dickering with two young men who looked like students. Suddenly, screeching with laughter, she grabbed them both in the crotch and pulled them into the building. Nearby, a soldier in a faded uniform staggered against the wall in a frenzy of coughing. He spat a mouthful of blood on the pavement, almost at the feet of an elegantly dressed Chinese, who lifted his skirt and glared. Down the hill from the monastery came the deep voice of a gong.

China—monstrous, savage, glorious China.

The launch bound for Lingnan University honked the departure signal. The university is on an island about three miles downstream from Canton. The fare was twenty-five cents in Chinese money, one silver coin. The conductor stood beside the gangplank, collecting fares. As each passenger came aboard, the conductor took his coin and dropped it on an iron pommel, fixed in a plate. If it rang true, he stepped aside.

Passenger, clink. Passenger, clink. Then, plock, a dull leaden sound came from the iron pommel. Without a word the conductor handed the coin back to the man before letting him pass. Another was produced. It rang silver. Not so much as a glance passed between the two men. Evidently it was only common sense to try to pass off the counterfeit coin that someone else had succeeded in passing off on you. There were no hard feelings.

"You will find a great deal of counterfeit money," said the university secretary. "Please be careful. When they are new, the fake coins look exactly like good ones. I presume the counterfeiters have access to the genuine dies."

Occasionally, he said, the police caught a counterfeiter and put him in jail. Somehow the lead coins kept turning up, though. He left the inference unspoken but clear—official corruption.

"It is a tragedy when one of these people"—he indicated the coolies—"discovers too late that he has been given a lead coin. He will try to pass it along, of course. But the merchants and food vendors are very watchful. They test all coins, just like the counterfeiter here, before filling a rice bowl. When this happens to a coolie, he goes hungry. Poor soul, he has many such days as it is."

He told the story of a kitchen maid who worked for a foreign family on Shameen. They paid her six dollars a month, less than two American dollars. One payday she went shopping. When she paid the merchant, he discovered immediately that the dollar she gave him weighed less than it should. So did two others. Someone had sawed the coins in half, chiseled an ounce or two of silver from the inner sides, then neatly resealed them. By a slight filing of the rims, the marks of cutting had been blurred. Half the maid's wages for a month were worthless.

"She killed herself," said the secretary.

It sounded incredible. "But surely if she had taken the three coins back to her employers, they would have given her—"

"Perhaps," he said, "but I doubt it. I am sorry to say that very few employers would be so generous. Suppose they didn't believe her?"

"Why shouldn't they believe her?"

"Because it is a very old trick. You insist that someone has given you bad money and demand a good coin. Only the tourists are ever taken in by it and so they pay twice for something. Besides, the maid could not prove that these were the same coins."

I asked if counterfeiters also printed paper currency. The secretary said he believed there was very little in circulation because the engraving was difficult and expensive.

"An American firm in Shanghai, by the way, prints large amounts of Chinese currency. It is a very good business. They must be on excellent terms with the right people to retain this concession." He paused and then quietly added: "Of course, in many ways China is under the thumb of the foreigners. But things are changing."

He spoke in a "nothing-personal-mind-you" tone of voice. He had merely stated an unhappy fact of life.

Hostility toward foreigners had been rising in China for years. The foreigner by his very presence symbolized the era of China's weakness. He had forced his way into the country at gunpoint, compelled the signing of the "unequal treaties," carved out "spheres of influence," and exploited his position for all it was worth. The "concessions" in the cities were islands of foreign territory where Chinese authority stopped at the border. Foreign troops stood guard over them. The Chinese resented every bit of this, down to the smallest detail.

Moreover, the Old China Hand seldom bothered to disguise his feeling that the Chinese were an inferior people. "Amusing people, intelligent, make good servants, did great things in the past—yes, all that. But they'd gone to seed. China isn't a nation. It's just a hell of a lot of people. No government. No sense of patriotism. No idea of law and order. It's every man for himself in this country. Poor beggars, you can't blame them. Nine tenths are illiterate and one jump ahead of starvation. Too bad, but that's the way it is."

But the tide of nationalism had started to rise.

On one level it took the form of a great clamor for the revision of the "unequal treaties," with or without the consent of the West. On another it manifested itself in strikes and boycotts. On still another it flared into physical violence. The Nanking Incident in 1927, when Chinese troops killed foreigners and stripped their women and threatened to rape them, was explained away by calling it the work of "extremists" or "Leftist elements." But there were many, many other incidents, all

over China, in which the fiery new nationalism vented itself
in attacks on foreigners. It did not spare the missionaries, for
all their good works. On the contrary, since many of them lived
in remote places, far from the protection of foreign troops, they
became favorite targets of the Chinese. Schools, hospitals, and
mission compounds were attacked, and a whole new crop of
Christian martyrs was growing in China.

Few Americans at home knew about this. Not many in
China realized the hour was so late. The archives of the State
Department bulge with official reports and demands for protection during that period. But these were not a matter of common knowledge; they were not amply reported in the newspapers nor were they related to the great storm sweeping China.

The illusion that China looked on Uncle Sam as her best
friend and great champion persisted. History books described
John Hay's efforts to stop further European encroachments on
China with the Open Door notes. Chinese students were study-
ing in American colleges on scholarships created out of the
Boxer Indemnity. The United States had no concessions or
military bases on Chinese soil. For these and other reasons
Americans assumed that the Chinese put them in a quite dif-
ferent category from other foreigners. It was the kind of illusion
Americans like, to feel firmly enrolled on the side of the angels.

The time would soon come for China's revenge on history.
When it did, Americans would not be excepted from the other
"foreign devils."

The launch veered toward shore. The pilot cut back the engines.

"Here we are," said the young secretary pleasantly. "Welcome to Lingnan."

Chapter IX

MR. LEI'S CASTLE

THE UNIVERSITY BUILDINGS covered most of Honan Island, which lies in the Pearl River, opposite White Cloud Mountain. The island is low and flat, with few trees. The earth has an ashy, exhausted look. Much of the soil in China looks exhausted. Yet an acre there supports many more people than an acre on an American farm—in some places ten times as many. For centuries the farmers have been using excrement, human and animal, to make the land produce. The idea of acres lying fallow, much less the concept of a "soil bank," would be inconceivable to a Chinese farmer. This is the reason why the item for fertilizers is so large in the list of imports by the Communist government today. Even so, the swarming millions will need more and more land—human locusts eating up acreage. Who knows where they may turn next? Toward Burma and Thailand, which are relatively crowded? Or toward Siberia, which is relatively empty?

The village beside the wharf was called Sun Luck, "New Happiness." Whoever chose this name had a delicious sense of irony. The pitiful little huts were built of mud and thatch. They had no floors, no windows, seldom more than one room. The women washed clothes in the river and cooked over open fires. Life in Sun Luck was only a little less harsh, only an inch less primitive than in a village of Australian aborigines.

Nearby stood another world, an incredibly different world. What were the thoughts of the peasant squatting on the earthen floor of his hut in Sun Luck as he looked across the field at the university? What did he see?

First of all, he saw a cluster of sturdy two- and three-storied buildings for dormitories, classrooms, the mess hall, student recreation, and housing. All were solidly built of brick and stone. Lights glowed in the windows at night and shadows from the fireplaces danced on the walls. The blocky, unimaginative Western lines of the buildings were relieved somewhat by Chinese-style roofs, with graceful, upswept eaves. From a distance the campus could pass for a small Chinese city. A network of paths neatly trimmed and lined with trees cut across wide stretches of lawn. Lingnan looked something like a small Midwestern college in Chinese fancy dress.

Actually, it was anything but fancy—by Western standards. The missionaries pampered neither the students nor themselves. The equipment in the dormitories provided creature comforts but little more. The students slept on pine boards, not mattresses. (Campus joke: "Where else in the world do you have to sleep with the board of education to stay in college?") Not all the rooms had carpets and the floors were cement. A naked electric light bulb hung from the ceiling over each desk. The unsteady power supply caused the lights to flicker, and the words in a book hopped around like fleas. There was no central heating. As for bathing, I vacillated before the same dilemma every day during the winter: is the trickle of hot water in the shower worth the round trip through icy cold hallways to the communal bathroom and back?

In their homes the missionaries lived almost as simply. They had more comfortable furniture, a fireplace, books, and occasionally a piano or a pedal-pump organ. They ate plain food, usually Western, but sometimes Chinese. They decorated the rooms with objects that were beautiful and, being Chinese, beautifully cheap then—vases, figurines, sometimes a scroll painting, the exquisite lace that came from Swatow. And, of course, even on a missionary's salary they could afford servants. At best, however, the missionaries led a thin, austere life.

But to the villager in Sun Luck all this must have presented itself as the very lap of luxury, a Persian dream of palace elegance. He could see the tennis courts and the athletic grounds. What wealth to be able to use land for games instead of rice! And he could see the pretty English instructor, in her jodhpurs and white shirt, riding every afternoon along the river bank. How does it feel to have time for anything but work?

What else did he see when he looked at Lingnan? He saw security. Security in the form of armed guards patrolling the fences. Security in the sentries on duty day and night at the two gates. Security in the brick and glass to shut out the cold and rain and the sickness they brought every winter. And a more special security in the bags of rice delivered daily, the meat and provisions, and the vegetable gardens on the northeast side of the campus.

On one side of the fence a man could sleep nights, beyond the reach of the elements, protected against bandits, assured of food for tomorrow and next week and the week after that.

But on the other side all this was largely a matter of luck, blind chance, and a million devils lurking in darkness. Here indeed, across a narrow field, primitive man looked at the twentieth century in wonder and envy.

The missionaries knew the situation and worried about it. The difference in standards was not their fault. They could not change the fact or escape from it, although some tried by "going Chinese," living like the peasants and coolies. I was told they seldom succeeded. In the big cities, to be sure, the contrast was not so great. The missionary school, the hospital, and the compound stood among other modern, Western-style buildings. But in the country these buildings, symbols of the rich and powerful West that had forced itself on China, stood beside mud huts. It is doubtful that the coolie perceived any difference between the missionary and the foreign merchant. More and more he was beginning to believe that all white men were in China to exploit him and to profit from his misery.

To the east of the campus stood another and still different hallmark of the times—the "castle" of a minor war lord. It was a large, grimy confection, originally white, a maze of verandas and arcades, surrounded by gardens and spacious courtyards. Inside, a grand staircase connected the upper floors with the baronial hall and grotesque dining room on the ground floor. The whole added up to an unhappy marriage of Chinese and early MGM.

The erstwhile owner had been a man named Lei Fuk-lum, who had started his career as a small-time bandit and passed through the usual cycle—big-time bandit, minor war lord, provincial boss—then curtains. A bigger war lord did him in, appropriating his soldiers and his women.

One of the concubines, it was said, still lived in the castle, having somehow avoided becoming the property of General Lei's successor. She must have been a tough, shrewd woman to have survived the elimination tournament regularly conducted in a house full of concubines. The ladies used poison, strangulation, and intrigue to get ahead. Also, she must have had a strong stomach. For when I saw General Lei's establishment, it had been taken by another Cantonese general for use as a military hospital.

Here is an excerpt from a feature story I wrote about the hospital and sent to the home-town papers on January 17, 1930:

"The wounded lie on the stone floor, in dark, unventilated rooms, reeking in filth, their open wounds exposed to every sort of infection. By day and by night, giant rats worry them.

There are no doctors, no nurses, no attendants. There are guards who stand by the front gates with fixed bayonets to quell disturbances. And there are stretcher crews to haul off the corpses as, one by one, the men die from their wounds, exposure, malnutrition or starvation.

"At the university, we have been shivering under the lash of a raw wind for the past two weeks, even with pounds of bedding. And yet some of the rebels—about 300 of the original 1000—have survived, lying on the stone floor with only their ragged uniforms and a wisp of straw for protection."

They tried to help each other. In the garden one who seemed proficient rolled bandages and made slings out of the pieces of uniform stripped from those who had died. Some were hobbling around on sticks in lieu of crutches. A soldier gingerly rolled back a knot of bloody rags and peered curiously at the stump of his leg, amputated above the knee. He looked, for all the world, like a monkey searching for fleas. Another, hardly more than a boy, smiled a wan little smile when I snapped his picture. His gentle, sensitive features look out of the photograph today, and in the background there are the motionless bodies on the flagstones and the great streaks of blood on the marble. Outside the castle, as well as indoors, the smell of death filled the air, heavy and clinging. Days afterward I could still smell it in my clothes and on my hands, in spite of soap and scrubbing. I went into a room, a dark and terrible room. Here at least some straw had been spread around the stone floor. Coarse sacks covered some of the still figures.

It took a moment to adjust my eyes to the darkness. Then I saw a man almost at my feet. He gasped, convulsively gulping air. His chest and diaphragm heaved like a bellows. Each breath sucked his stomach down to his spine, and he looked cut in half. Then, with a last shuddering sigh, he stopped breathing.

In this man's death there was no meaning, no purpose, no glory. He was only one of many in the castle, and the castle was only one scene in the infinite number of death-house scenes all over China.

For this was civil war.

It is not to be compared, however, with the other civil wars in history, the North and the South, or Lancaster against York. No moral or constitutional or ideological issues put the armies in the field. Except in the later years, the conflict did not lie between two distinct groups of Chinese alone. It was many wars in one, instigated by bosses who sent millions of men out to die in battle and in the process killed other millions, including women and children, in their homes.

All were victims of the war lord.

A war lord was an ex-general or an ex-bandit who had acquired control over a given region, sometimes a province, sometimes a bigger area. He might have seized it by military force, inherited it, or acquired possession in some other way. In any case, he ran it as a private preserve. He collected taxes, organized a private army, appointed officials, and administered justice (if any). For revenue he squeezed the landlord. The landlord squeezed his tenant farmer. And the tax collector squeezed for all the traffic would bear, pocketing as much as possible. Caught in the middle was the poor, patient, wonderful Chinese peasant.

The war lord fought for power. He fought for power and position and the rewards they bring. He fought to advance personal ambition—nothing more. One or two at that time evidently dreamed of becoming masters of all China. Others, I have no doubt, would have settled for suzerainty over a single province.

It would be almost impossible to identify all the figures in this great tragedy and fix each in his particular setting. There were too many, literally scores, marching and countermarching their private armies. Some commanded very large armies. Feng Yu-hsiang, the so-called Christian General, had four hundred thousand troops in his gigantic fief in the northwest. Chang Hsueh-liang, the "Young Marshal," whose father had been the boss of Manchuria, could field an even larger force. And there were many smaller fry.

As I have pointed out, hunger, in the main, provided the war lords with man power, an inexhaustible supply of footsloggers. Some were conscripted and others took arms for other reasons. But the majority joined up because it was the only way to be reasonably sure of eating regularly.

The war lords paid lip service to the central governments of China when it suited their purpose. Meanwhile, they formed alliances with others of their ilk, shifting this way and that, first with one group then another, always to the end of retaining and increasing their power. Through more than a decade they played their intricate game, using human lives for chips.

By the time I reached China in 1929 the pattern had crystallized, owing to the establishment of the newest central government. This was the regime set up by the Kuomintang, "People's Party," and led by Chiang Kai-shek. After three years of bloody struggle with the war lords, Chiang Kai-shek announced the "unification" of China on July 6, 1928. Seventeen days later the United States recognized Chiang's group as the legitimate central government of China.

Thus, technically, the Chinese Revolution ended and so did the Era of the War Lord. In fact, however, the war lords still controlled huge areas of China. They did not rush to lay their swords at Chiang's feet and invite him to send government officials to administrate their domains. It was as though the true authority of the U.S. government was restricted to a perimeter, bounded by the Ohio River in the west, the Adirondacks in the north, and the Great Smokies in the south. Outside the perimeter in China the Old Hands went right on with the old game. When one of them saw an opportunity to challenge the Nationalists, fighting broke out. When Chiang moved his troops to meet the challenge in one region, the boss in another would take the field. Depending on the prospects, others might move in or remain neutral. All were opportunists and played the game accordingly.

To illustrate a single tiny segment of all this, we return to Lei Fuk-lum's castle.

In the diary note I wrote on the fighting around Canton, I mentioned "a war lord whose name sounds like Fat Quail." Actually he was only a would-be war lord, an infantry division commander, but he had bigger ambitions. His name was Chang Fa-kuei.

The details of his checkered career in politics and the army are unimportant. It is enough to say he was a shifty character who had his eye on the main chance. At one point he had been loyal to the Nationalists. Then he began dealing with a political rival of Chiang Kai-shek. Finally, at a moment when the Nationalists were involved in a major campaign against a coalition of war lords in the north, Chang seized the opportunity to set up shop for himself.

Exactly like a one-man government, the general issued proclamations on political reforms and demanded that his own man, Chiang's political rival, replace Chiang Kai-shek as head of the central government. Then he launched his troops on a southward drive to take Canton, biggest city in south China and the erstwhile Nationalist base. Nationalist forces met him near there and smashed his expedition. It was a skirmish in this fighting about which I had heard my first night at Lingnan.

One ambitious general. One shabby little adventure. For this, and no more, men died in agony in Lei Fuk-lum's castle. Multiply this episode and this scene by ten thousand and you have China at that moment in history.

The war lord is much more than a piece of historical curiosa, a mustachioed figure, booted and spurred, gathering dust in the museum of Chinese horrors. In many ways he helped deliver China into the hands of the Communists.

In the first place, he inflicted untold suffering on the Chinese masses. Year after year hordes of hired soldiers swept through the villages, looting, murdering, raping, and destroying. The war lords consumed blood and treasure like Chinese Baals. And they had a long ride. Chang Tso-lin, the "Old Marshal," controlled Fengtien province as early as 1913. Huge war-lord armies were still fighting in 1930. In short, a whole generation of Chinese grew up with little or no respite from the bloodletting and chaos caused by these men. The war lords not only sapped the country, but delayed the formation of a strong central government, which might have given China peace and law and order at long last.

Second, when that government finally did come, the war lords robbed it of time, precious years. In so doing they gave the Communists needed time. Who can say how different the story might have been if the powerful provincial bosses had joined with the Nationalists in 1928, creating a truly "unified" nation? Instead, from time to time they took the field against the government. Meanwhile, the Communists were digging in, preparing for the showdown with the Nationalists.

Third, the cruel depredations of the war lords created an ideal climate for the Communists when their turn came to move among the masses. They saw in the peasants' plight the real source of power in China and shrewdly set out to tap it. Many observers have described the iron discipline of the Communist troops in the villages and cities. There was no raping, no pillaging, no carrying off of farm animals. If they took so much as a tangerine, they paid for it. What kind of Chinese army was this? The peasants had never known such treatment. "The people are the sea," said Chu Teh, the Red commander, "and we are the fish who swim in that sea." In *Red Star Over China* Edgar Snow has described the impact of these unheard-of tactics used by the Communists in their Long March in 1934. The troops did more than merely treat the peasants well; they also took *from* the wealthy and the landlords who oppressed the peasants. Robin Hood with a red star on his cap. Thus, by the time of the great civil war, after V-J Day, the Communists were in a position to say: "We are poor people, too. We have come to liberate you from the tax collectors and oppressors. All we want is peace and bread. If you help us, these things will come sooner." To people who had suffered for such a long time, the Communists must have looked like angels. It was a shrewd job of capitalizing on misery.

Finally, and most important, the war lord was a product of the disintegration of China, a process for which the West bears a heavy share of responsibility.

The predatory white man fought the Opium War in 1839. It led straight to another clash with Britain and France a few years later. Then Japan moved into the picture. It was a century of foreign pressure on China, successive humiliations and defeats. Forces inside the country and marauders on the outside began tearing at the foundations of a proud empire.

The wars sapped the strength of the government and at the same time exposed its military weakness. Chinese revolutionists grew bolder. Western governments, exploiting the internal conditions, established spheres of influence in China and staked out concessions. In due course the British, French, Russians, Germans, Italians, and Japanese firmly installed themselves on Chinese soil. The "unequal treaties," obtained at gunpoint, began to be recorded, thus giving their actions a form of legality. The United States did not establish any "American Concessions," as such, but Americans insisted on being accorded the same treaty rights as were enjoyed by other foreigners in China.

These events also brought the Christian missionary back to China after centuries of banishment. Unwittingly he hastened the process of breakup. Like the merchant, he set foot in China as a consequence of armed aggression. He was able to remain only because foreign guns protected him. And, like the merchant, he was seldom loath to call on his government to use force, or threats of force, in disputes with local Chinese authorities. If this seems curiously un-Christian, the missionary of that day justified the means in terms of the end.

Christian teachings reached a man troubled by visions. His name was Hung Hsiu-chuan. Somehow he began to identify himself with Jesus Christ and eventually convinced himself that he was Jesus' younger brother. He began preaching against idol worship and, incorporating odd bits and pieces of doctrine from a number of sources, invented his own theology. Hung made some converts. Out of this the great Taiping rebellion exploded. Cutting a bloody arc across one thousand miles of territory between Canton and Nanking, the Taipings raged over the country for ten years.

They might have lasted longer but for the military ability of two white men. One was an American, Frederick Ward. The other was an Englishman, Major Charles Gordon, the famous "Chinese" Gordon, who later met his fate in another such adventure in the Sudan. Ward and Gordon led an army of foreign soldiers of fortune against the Taipings and helped put an end to the rebellion.

At this point the Chinese authorities found themselves squeezed between forces from within and without—rebellious Chinese elements and the voracious foreigner. Sometimes the white man assisted the government against its rebellious enemies. Sometimes by his mere presence he weakened the formal authority. Simultaneously he played a dual role—the burglar and the policeman.

The result, in part, was still another and more conclusive explosion—the Boxer rebellion of 1899-1900. It takes its name from the secret society "Order of Righteous Harmonious Bands" or "Fists." The Boxers struck, not at the government, but at the foreigners, and the doughty old Empress Dowager encouraged them. Chanting "Protect the country, destroy the foreigners," the Boxers attacked missionaries and Chinese Christians, especially in north China. Murders, horrible tortures, and destruction of foreign property took place. Then the Boxers converged on the lovely old Legation Quarter in Peking and laid siege to it.

The most exciting movie thriller is tame stuff compared to the drama of this siege. The whole diplomatic corps, plus missionaries, merchants, Chinese Christians, and hundreds of women and children, fought through the heat and dust of June and July, desperately defending themselves. An English newspaperman later described the siege for me. "Every night we could hear them howling like wolves outside the walls," he said. "They tried a few attacks, and once or twice it was a very near thing. Then they settled down, with the idea of starving us out, I suppose. At times the position seemed hopeless to me. Meanwhile, of course, we kept watching the horizon for some sign of relief. We saw a column of infantry in every dust storm. Damn discouraging when the dust settled, I can tell you."

In mid-August a composite force which included American troops reached Peking and scattered the Boxers. In true scenario tradition they arrived not a moment too soon. The besieged were near the end of the rope. A disgraceful epilogue followed. The white men, grateful for deliverance, joined the troops in looting Peking.

For all practical purposes, the Manchu dynasty ended here. The imperial court fled far inland. With that, the last semblance of central government crumbled and China rushed headlong into revolution.

From this point on for a full fifty years there would be no

peace, and blood would flow in rivers. War lords and civil wars crucified China through 1930. In the next year Japan struck. The great contest between the Kuomintang and the Communists already had begun and it continued into the second Japanese assault in 1937. Then came World War II and after it, from 1946 to 1950, the conflict that carried Mao Tse-tung to power and exiled Chiang Kai-shek to Formosa.

A half-century of chaos and the thunder of guns.

Of all the things the people wanted, their most fervent prayer was for peace. Is it any wonder that the Communists, promising peace, promising stability, promising land reform and the end to usury and taxes, promising sufficiency, promising to restore the ancient glory, but above all, promising peace —is it any wonder they succeeded in seducing so great a people?

How long now before China demands payment on these promissory notes?

Chapter X

SHAMEEN ISLAND

THE COLD PROBED with icy fingers between the chinks in the "board of education." A pale light came from the winter sky. A student waddled past the window, heavy with clothing. It was going to be another seven-*sha'am* day.

A *sha'am* is a long flannel shirt worn beneath a padded gown or even a Western suit. As the temperature dropped in winter, the Chinese put on extra *sha'ams*. They rated the weather according to the total number of *sha'ams* they wore. Four or five described an average cold day, but when they said "This is a seven-*sha'am* day," it meant a bitter cold day and a harsh wind as well. *Sha'ams* calibrated the Chinese thermometer.

Of course, only the fortunate few met the cold with so many layers of clothing. The river people, the coolies, and most of the peasants went through the winter in the only garments they owned—thin cotton pajamas, rags, or a dog's pelt. Or, rather, they tried. Not all of them made it.

On the floor beside my bed lay an English-language newspaper dated January 4, 1930. I had picked it up on Shameen a few days before. I reached out from under the covers. The cold bit through my pajamas and sweater. On the front page, buried in a column of chitchat, there was this item: "An old-timer says this is the most severe cold snap in 32 years. Many poor parents, unable to feed and clothe their children, have abandoned them in the woods and committed suicide." Very terse journalism with the always desirable economy of words.

The question arose again: would it make a feature story for the papers at home? If there were a few more facts, some actual cases, it might be a shocker. The trouble was it no longer shocked me. In China such stories became commonplace very quickly, and one's capacity for amazement diminished. I remembered the wagon in Canton.

It had rumbled down the road and stopped beside the figure of a man. He lay in the dust beside a wall. The wagon driver and his helper bent over, shook the still figure, touched its face. They exchanged a quiet remark. Then they picked up the corpse by the hands and feet, swung it—alley oop!—and tossed it into the wagon. The head banged against the wooden sideboards. A handful of people stopped to watch. An old woman, hobbling past on "lily feet" deformed by binding, murmured "*Ai-yah.*" Then life flowed on as before over the spot where a man had frozen to death.

What was today—Monday? I had an appointment in Canton with a foreign correspondent. My study project, "Journalism in China: the Influence of Periodicals on Public Opinion," was making slow progress. With each day it seemed less practical. Perhaps the foreign correspondent would have some ideas.

My first doubts about this project had stirred during the first language lesson I attended at Lingnan. The instructor began by drawing a musical scale on the blackboard. He explained that Cantonese has nine tones and Mandarin, the "official" language, four. Having located them on the scale, he said: "If you pronounce a word in the wrong tone, you may say something quite different from what you intended." The students had an endless stock of rude jokes, presumably true, in which a foreigner, attempting to express some exalted thought, used the wrong tone and described an intimate act instead.

"Also," the instructor said, "it is because of the tones that Chinese languages sound singsongy to a foreigner's ears." He illustrated in a number of different dialects. There are perhaps one hundred million people in south China who speak different Chinese dialects, communicating with difficulty among themselves and not at all with other millions elsewhere in China.

Apart from the spoken languages, the immense complexity of the written language, with its uncounted thousands of characters, lies beyond the reach of most Chinese. "To read the ordinary language in a newspaper," said the instructor, "you will need at least two thousand characters. But to read a treatise on philosophy, you will have to know at least twenty-five thousand characters." He paused, smiling cozily, while we considered the appalling prospect.

Then he illustrated the origins of some characters. They began as pictures, drawings of definite objects. The character for "horse" still looks like a horse, and the characters for "man," "woman," "moon," "mountain," and so on, are still more or less recognizable from the original pictographs. But these are all concrete objects. How do you draw a picture of an idea?

The instructor drew two outstretched hands on the blackboard and explained how the character for "friend" or "friendship" developed from this. Then he drew the composite for the word "to hinder" and pointed out, deadpan, that it contains the character for woman. (The Japanese have a word, *yakamashisa*, which roughly means noise, gossip, chatter, idle rumor, etc. It is written as a composite of four characters— three women under one roof!)

"Perhaps the best way for you to begin this work," the instructor said, "would be with the thousand-basic-characters method, developed by Doctor Y. C. Yen. After all, he has demonstrated that totally illiterate coolies can be taught to read in about four months." He smiled his cozy little smile and, dismissing the class, left that thought with us.

Well, "Jimmie" Yen was doing wonderful work in China then, but probably well over ninety per cent of the people were still illiterate. That being so, how does one go about determining the effect of periodicals on public opinion?

That morning I left the dormitory, Java Hall, and hastened
through the gate toward Sun Luck and Mr. Lew Ong's eating
house. With his assistance I had invented a breakfast.

In the college mess hall at that hour the students were lining
up around the huge vats filled with steaming white rice. Having taken some rice in their bowls, they sat down at bare
wooden tables. A plate, a porcelain spoon, a teacup, and a pair
of bone chopsticks marked each place.

The Chinese way of dining is more intimate than ours. There
are no individual servings. In the center of each table in the
mess hall were three and occasionally four dishes, one of meat
or fish, the others of stewed vegetables of some sort, usually
cabbage, kale, or chard. Another dish often contained watermelon seeds. When eating a watermelon seed, you crack the
shell between your front teeth and extract the seed with your
tongue. It is a fine art and I never mastered it. The food in the
center of the table is equally shared. Each person takes a
morsel of this and a spoonful of that, one at a time, and puts it
on his plate. At first sight it might seem that a slow eater would
be at a disadvantage. Being inexpert with the chopsticks, I
usually fell behind the others at my table. Yet they always left
some food on the dishes in the center.

The Chinese at Lingnan had exquisite manners. Mine were
less than perfect, but the students pretended not to notice. Until I learned better I ate "coolie style," putting the bits of meat
and vegetable in my rice bowl so that the juices would flavor
the rice. It is roughly equivalent to sopping up gravy with a
biscuit and, like so many sensible customs at table, not quite
correct.

The mess-hall food was plain, somewhat monotonous, but
perfectly adequate. If a student could afford it (and most of
them could) he would order the kitchen to prepare a special

dish—small, highly seasoned pork sausages, or *pih fan yu,* the white-rice fish, or *sam-li,* a Cantonese fish that tastes something like pompano. Once, I was told, a particularly well-off young man even ordered the famous *sam see chee,* which is a kind of hash made of chicken, pheasant, shark meat, bamboo shoots, and other ingredients. The cooks, however, sadly reported they didn't have all the fixin's.

In no time, two or three days at the most, I no longer thought of these dishes as Chinese "chow." They were simply lunch or dinner, and in no way exotic. Breakfast, however, became a problem. Boiled rice, stewed vegetables, and tea somehow failed as a substitute for scrambled eggs, toast, and coffee. What to do? My solution may sound a little unlikely. But it worked. The basis of my invention was *tsau mein,* which is Cantonese for "fried noodles."

A friend came along to translate on the day I consulted with Lew Ong in his eatery. "Tell him I will be coming here for breakfast frequently," I said, "and I will always want exactly the same thing—fried noodles."

Mr. Lew or Mr. Ong (I have forgotten which was his surname) looked puzzled and replied at very great length.

"He says he doesn't usually make up noodles in the morning, but for a little extra he can do it."

"How much extra?"

Now Mr. Lew talked even longer, obviously setting forth the immense difficulties involved and the heavy expense to which he must go. The "extra," when it finally came, amounted to a penny or two in American money. As a matter of principle I protested, and the proprietor finally agreed to shave it down a little.

"That's not all," I said. "This is the important part. I want the noodles fried in a special way, very tight."

"What do you mean, 'tight'?"

"Crisp," I said. "So crisp they'll stick together."

"He says he can do it," said my friend. "But he asks why you want the noodles spoiled?"

"They'll taste something like toast, I think. And tell him to put two fried eggs on top, sunny side up."

"Sunny side—? Ah, yes."

It was a delicious dish. The noodles, fried into a mat, looked something like a flattened-out bird's nest. In the first few days the Sun Luck people came to watch, commenting gravely and occasionally cackling with laughter. But in a week or so my invention ceased to interest them. I do not believe it ever became a permanent fixture on Lew Ong's menu.

When I recommended it to Tsui, he said: "Why don't you just get a loaf of bread on Shameen and let him make real toast?"

I did and was surprised to find that it tasted flat and uninteresting in comparison with the matted noodles.

From my table in Lew Ong's (there were only two) I looked out across scores of low humpbacked mounds dotting the fields. These were graves. Carved stone or crumbling brick work marked the older ones. When the missionaries chose the island as the site for Lingnan, they had to bargain long and hard to persuade the villagers to sell. The Honan people agreed only on condition that the missionaries paid a premium for each grave when they opened it and removed the bones of the Honans' ancestors. Frequently the bones were the ribs and femurs of cattle and other animals. The villagers, however, said Grandfather had been a very big man or an unusually small one, as the case happened to be, and they insisted on collecting the agreed bonus.

It was only a step from the graveyard to the wharf, where you
went aboard the river launch or took a sampan to go to Canton. The launch was much faster, of course, but my appointment with the foreign correspondent was not until late afternoon. Besides, I hoped to find *"Tu Nip"* and make the trip with
her.

She would maneuver her sampan through the mass of boats
clustered near the landing, exchanging swift and no doubt
wholly unladylike words with the other sampan people, who
clamored for the chance to earn twenty-five cents, silver. *"Djow
shun, djow shun,"* she would say. "Good morning, good morning." Then, as I stepped aboard, she would smile, and a wonderful incandescence would light the river clear to Hong Kong.
Her eyes would sparkle like polished amber, and two dimples,
two miraculous Cathayan dimples, would blossom in each
cheek. She was about seventeen or eighteen, short, slim-
waisted, and supple and strong from oaring a sampan on the
river. It had seemed important to learn the Cantonese word for
"dimple," and a student said it was *"tu nip."* He may have given
me the wrong word as a joke. Or perhaps I mispronounced it.
Anyway, one night on the down-river trip from Canton I had
touched her face and said: *"Tu nip* one, *tu nip* two." She
laughed uncontrollably. She had stopped rowing and, taking
her hands from the oar, let the boat drift sweetly with the
current.

But today the river gods were in a sour mood. No *tu nip*. The
usual storm of yells broke out as I came to the wharf. The river
people bumped boats, jockeying to get closest to the landing.
An old woman won. She was thin, leathery, and deeply wrinkled, with wispy gray hair. She looked too old and emaciated
to push the sampan against the current to Canton, although it
was only a few miles. I hesitated, and she began to whine, urg-

ing me to get into her sampan. Boy Scout deed for the day, I thought, even if it does take her twice as long to get there.

As often happens with good intentions, this one became a paving stone.

The old crone pushed out from the wharf and headed up stream with a strong, steady pull. A sampan is propelled in somewhat the same fashion as a Venetian gondola. The oarsman, standing on a deck in the stern, sweeps a long, narrow-blade oar back and forth, twisting it, just as a fish waves its tail. In no time, driving against the current, the old woman brought the sampan to the stone steps leading up to the bund in Canton. Not once had she drawn a long breath.

I gave her a shiny new twenty-five cent piece, went up to the street, and hailed a ricksha. As the coolie set the shaft close beside my foot, there was a sudden clattering and commotion behind. The old sampan woman came running across the street, yelping and holding something in her hand. She looked like one of the Furies.

A young Chinese student stopped. He spoke to her. A volcano of words spewed out, punctuated by gestures of grief and rage. The student turned to me. His expression was a picture of cold contempt. "She says you have cheated her."

"Cheated her? I gave her twenty-five cents to bring me from Lingnan. That's the regular fare."

"Yes, but you gave her this." He took the coin she was holding and laid it in the palm of his hand. It was nicked and battered, obviously a well-chewed counterfeit.

"I didn't give her that coin," I said. "Anyone can see it's a fake. I know that trick."

The student translated. The woman screamed and tore at her hair. By this time a knot of Chinese had gathered. They began talking, to the student, to the woman, to each other. An ordinary conversation on a street in China frequently sounds like a furious argument. The din now was deafening.

There was no question in my mind that the sampan woman

was pulling the old trick. But the atmosphere began to feel ominous. Then I had an idea. "Ask her why she waited until I was up here on the street," I said to the student. "Why didn't she refuse to accept that phony coin on the spot?"

The old woman waved her arms and spat out words. In the crowd a man said "*Ai-yah*" and glared at me.

"She says you got out of the sampan and threw this bad money into the boat and tried to run away," the student said.

"Well, she's lying like hell."

I sat down in the ricksha and said "Shameen" to the coolie. He picked up the shafts.

The student said something, and the ricksha boy answered impatiently. The student struck him on the shoulder with his fist. Then he turned to me. His face was working with anger. "You must give her good money," he said. "She is poor, and you must not cheat her."

"Nothing doing. I have paid her and I'm not paying twice."

A low murmur rumbled through the crowd. Another man pushed close to me. "You think because you are English—"

"I'm an American."

"It's all the same. Foreigners all think they can do anything they want in China. But you can't. Unless you pay, the ricksha will not go."

"Okay, I'll find another," I said.

I stepped down into the street. Without a word the men pressed close together, a solid wall of unsmiling faces.

At that moment the old woman spoke, chattering rapidly to the student. She handed him another coin. I did not know it, but the inevitable face-saving compromise, a very important thing in China, had begun.

"This is Shanghai money," the student said. "It is worth as much as the silver pieces, but she would rather have the local money. The money changers charge a few cents to change it, as you may know. Will you give her twenty-five cents silver for this?"

"Sure," I said, vastly relieved. "It's a deal."

It was all over in an instant. The crowd broke up. The old woman walked down toward the dock. At the bottom of the steps she said something to the other river people. They all laughed uproariously. Well, I thought, I'll find out in Shanghai whether she gypped me.

The ricksha boy started off in a steady, rhythmic jog. He could trot for hours at that pace. An instant later a stone whizzed past my head and smacked against the wall on the other side of the street. A memory stirred in me, the memory of a stone thrown long ago at a Japanese farmer by a boy on a bicycle.

The ricksha coolie made it plain, with emphatic gestures, that he could not or would not go into Shameen. He stopped on Sha Kee Street, opposite a humpbacked bridge. A narrow canal separated Canton from the island. On this side was China; across the bridge was a tiny sliver of Europe, flying the flags of Britain and France.

A short, wiry Annamite soldier stood at the island end of the bridge on guard duty. He wore a steel helmet and carried a rifle with bayonet.

The tableau made a curious impression on me. The little Annamite, his gun, the bridge, and Shameen gave meaning and reality to words that had only been words before—"foreign concessions," "unequal treaties," "the humiliation of China." On the Chinese New Year in 1930, for the first time in nearly seventy years, I was told, Chinese had been permitted to promenade on the bridge. Prior to 1930 the guard would stop any Chinese from crossing the bridge except on specific business. The gloomy old Victoria Hotel, the bank, the business offices, the shops, and the fine foreign homes and apartments lay outside Chinese authority. Legally this was British and French territory, a little plum from the "Arrow War" of 1856. It had no intrinsic value like that of Weihaiwei or the big foreign preserves up north. You could put Shameen in Jessfield Park in Shanghai. It was only a sand bar (Shameen means "Sand Face"), but nevertheless a microcosm of the whole Western position in China.

In my schoolboy French I asked the Annamite if he knew the address of the foreign correspondent. He smiled and shook his head. Next I approached a Sikh policeman. He was a giant, towering head and shoulders over me, a massive turbaned figure with a magnificent black beard and mustache. He came to attention as though on parade.

"Yes, Master?"

Master. Master, pronounced with a broad *a*, addressed to me by one of my elders and doubtless one of my betters. What a strange echo of Victoria's wars and the works of Clive and Kitchener and Tommy Atkins!

The white man in the Orient, however hard he might try, seldom could avoid developing a full-blown superiority complex, especially in China. But here I must point out a curious fact: apparently some of the Orientals in China felt superior, too. The little Annamite sentries seemed to enjoy threatening the ricksha boys when they lingered near the bridge at Shameen. And I saw the big Sikhs wade into masses of Chinese during strikes and demonstrations in Shanghai, whaling away with their long, stout *lathis*. They laughed with the sheer fun of it. The Japanese, of course, simply held the Chinese in contempt as weak, venal, disorganized people, and joined other foreigners in extracting privileges. If there was a spirit of "Asia for the Asiatics" at that time, it did not seem to embrace China.

It was late afternoon. I passed through the park, a manicured greensward on the river front. Chinese *amahs* were pushing perambulators, gossiping, and keeping a sharp eye on the swarms of fair-haired children chasing each other around the

banyan trees. Three young Englishmen, probably clerks in
the bank or in the shipping offices, were working up a sweat
dribbling and passing a football (soccer style), "keeping fit"
against the easy life on the China coast.

Spacious apartments with great French windows looked out
across the park to the Pearl River. Even a consular clerk, let
alone a *taipan,* big boss, could afford these apartments, as well
as servants to make him comfortable. The servants called his
wife "Missy," and each of them, to secure his own position,
made very certain that she need never lift a finger around her
home. They marketed, cooked, cleaned, cared for the baby,
washed, ironed, sewed, polished the silver with the palms of
their hands, kept the decanters filled, kept busy incessantly. If
necessary, they invented little chores so that "Missy" would
never catch them standing idle. They went to ingenious lengths
to be indispensable around the house. You have heard the
story, and doubtless considered it a fable, that foreign wives in
China often told the cook at noon and even later: "Oh, by the
way, there will be fourteen for dinner tonight." It was no
fable. Dinner would be on the table, beautifully prepared and
served, no matter what scurryings and magic had to be performed. To the servants "Missy" meant square meals, wages,
life itself. They knew only too well how many hungry people
would be glad to replace them.

For both "Missy" and "Master" life moved at an easy, gracious pace. "Master" would be in his office around nine thirty
or so. Shortly after noon he would go to the club for "tiffin."
But first he would have a gin and "it," and usually several,
rolling dice in the bar to see who paid—poker dice, liar dice,
golf dice, beat-it-you-bastard dice, and ordinary cameroons.
"Three sixes all day . . . four deuces never loses." After lunch
he would often take a nap in one of the deep leather chairs in
the reading room. If he remained at the office as late as six
o'clock, it was because of something unusual. Then, especially
in summer, he might go to another club for tennis or golf, fol-

lowed by some more dice and gin in the bar. But if he went straight home, he would find a bath already drawn. His dinner clothes, freshly pressed, would be laid out with studs and cuff-links in his shirt and a fresh handkerchief carefully set in the breast pocket of his jacket. From close observation, the house-boy knew the exact moment when to arrive, bringing a drink, and ready to tie "Master's" shoelaces.

As for "Missy," unless she happened to be out of the norm, the days were blissfully empty of much that was purposeful. In every foreign community only a handful of wives studied lan-guages or made a hobby of one of the arts and crafts, such as flower arrangement in Japan. The majority, however, were con-tent to shop, lunch, go to tea, play bridge and *mah*-jongg (not infrequently beginning in the morning), and wait for George to come home. This, of course, did not apply to the wives of missionaries.

No wonder foreigners adored life in the Orient, especially in the Treaty Ports. In the Shanghai Club one day I eavesdropped on six men talking about where they proposed to live after re-tirement. Only one said "Homeside." The others intended to stay in the Far East.

On their first tour of duty, however, people often "counted boats." The principle is the same as a convict checking off days from the prison calendar. Knowing the date for his home leave, a man made reservations more than two years ahead of time on a particular ship. Then, every time that ship came into port, he checked off the trip. Nine more round trips . . . eight more . . . seven. "Well, my dear, we are only two more sailings of the *Cleveland* from the start of our leave. I can hardly wait."

Then, as a rule, they could not wait to get back. The old home town was a disappointment, drab and stale against the glitter of the Orient, its color, its ease of life, its mysterious and indefinable something in the air.

The foreign correspondent turned out to be a lawyer. In his spare time he acted as a "stringer" for several London dailies and an American agency. A "stringer" is retained, or paid per specific assignment, in cities where news develops too seldom to require a full-time correspondent. The regular correspondents at that time made their headquarters in Shanghai or Peking. They traveled as much as possible, although travel was a grim ordeal except for the famous "Blue Train," or "Shanghai Express." After the Kuomintang made Nanking the national capital, the correspondents went there frequently. (*Nan-king:* "Southern Capital"; *Pe-king* or *Pei-ping:* "Northern Capital.") But it was the "stringers" who were relied upon to get the routine news in outlying cities and in the interior. Quite a number of missionaries covered fires, floods, and earthquakes along with the work of the Lord.

I asked the lawyer what he had filed recently.

"Bits and pieces," he said. "They asked for a word or two on Chang Fa-kuei and the Kuominchun. But of course there's a war lord under every rock these days, and it's all too complicated for most editors. I expected to have a stand-by message from some of them on that business in December. We were a bit windy here. . . ."

He referred to a government declaration affecting the "unequal treaties." For several years the Chinese had been agitating for a revision of these treaties. Finally they simply attempted to wipe them off the books without discussing the matter with the other parties. In 1926 they abruptly abrogated the treaty with Belgium. Two years later they tried to walk out on two treaties with Japan. The Japanese replied that they were willing to negotiate, but would not permit the Chinese to erase the treaties on their own.

J. V. A. MacMurray, the American Minister in Peking, wrote

a brilliant report in 1935 of China's maneuvers in "Developments Affecting American Policy in the Far East." Of this period he said:

"This drive for getting rid of 'extrality' was pressed throughout the summer. The Powers . . . found it impossible to take any firm unified stand, one element of their difficulty being that our government postponed its decision, and throughout the most acute stage of the controversy, gave no reply to the requests of the Peking Legation for instructions.

"The Chinese, conscious of the advantage accruing to them through the disunity of the Treaty Powers, undertook to cut the Gordian knot by simply declaring, on Dec. 29, 1929, that the extrality provisions of the treaties would be void as of Jan. 1, 1930."

"Extrality," or "extraterritoriality," exempted foreigners from the jurisdiction of Chinese courts. This provision was one of the main pillars of the "unequal treaties." The Chinese had long been working up a head of steam against them.

Shameen, for all its smallness and relative unimportance as a "concession," had special reason for uneasiness over the December 29 decree. Four years before, a massacre had taken place on Sha Kee Street, near the bridge. It grew out of a clash in Shanghai between the police and a crowd of students and demonstrators. In Canton shortly afterward the students organized a demonstration to protest the Shanghai incident.

British infantry and French marines took stations, facing Sha Kee. Massed thousands of Chinese marched past Shameen, without incident. Then shooting began. Both sides denied firing first. Then a sharp exchange took place. Evidently the Chinese military cadets were armed, but there must have been others, as well, carrying arms in the demonstration. Chinese writers fixed the Chinese casualties at fifty-two killed and one hundred and seventeen wounded, "including students, laborers, merchants, and cadets."

Chinese hatred of foreigners, therefore, focused particularly on little Shameen.

"Sooner or later we are going to have to show the Kuomintang what's what," the lawyer said. "The Chinese are feeling their oats, of course. Can't understand what's wrong with our bloody government, or any others, for that matter, to stand for this nonsense. Mark you, the Japs won't take much more of it."

I told him about the incident with the sampan woman and the student and asked whether that sort of thing happened often.

"Very seldom," he said. "More than it used to. When I first came out here, we'd have shot a Chinese for less. Now you have to be a bit more careful. They found an American, chap named O'Sullivan, floating in the bay in Hong Kong not long ago. Got in some sort of fight with a Chinese. Nobody knows just what happened."

As I was leaving, he said: "About that project of yours—I'd give it up. Talk to the students. They're the only real influence on public opinion right now."

Chapter XI

CONVERSATION
AT MIDNIGHT

"WHAT DO WE KNOW about the peasant?"

Martin Fong crossed the room and dropped another chunk of coal on the fire. Sparks rose like a swarm of fireflies. The clock on the mantle showed two fifty five. It was not the first time a bull session in Martin's room had lasted so late. Once we had talked until dawn. The sessions usually began in the mess hall at dinner, or in the recreation room. Then, at closing time, they moved to a student's room in Java Hall, preferably a room with a fireplace. The argument went on and on, always about China and the shapes of things they hoped to see in the near future.

Very serious college bull sessions.

They made a deep impression on me. I assumed they were peculiar to Lingnan. But later, at Shanghai College, St. John's, Nankai University, Yenching (with its beautiful setting), and every other school where we worked, there were the same passionate discussions, always on the same general theme—China.

In the college dormitories at home, bull sessions were going on, too, but they were seldom political. Our perennial topics had been What about Women? and Is There a God?

"What is there to know about the peasant?" said Eddie Chen, looking at Martin. "He is born. He breeds. He hopes to have

enough left to eat after the landlord and tax collector have cut
him up. Then cholera, typhus, bandits, or a flood kills him, but
seldom old age. And that is all. What else is there to know
about the peasant?"

"The peasant is the heart of the problem," said Martin.
"Everything must start with him. Therefore, we—"

"For Christ's sake, don't say 'we intellectuals.' "

"—we have to know a great deal more about him before
there can be any mass education or any social reforms in the
villages."

"At the risk of sounding a little old-fashioned," said Eddie,
"I contend that government, not the peasant, has to be the starting point. And by government I mean the élite, the scholar, the
able few, the trained official. That's the one tradition, the one
point where I believe the old Confucians were on the beam."

"You are talking about methods," said Martin, "about the
tools and the machinery. I am saying where they must be used
first. There is no basic disagreement between us."

"Hold it." Philip Li, scribbling at a desk, looked up from his
note pad. "I can't keep up with all this penetrating thought."

"No doubt this will appear in the next issue of *Crescent Moon*
all as your own idea."

"Maybe," he replied. "But so far you haven't said anything
worth poaching."

Phil wrote constantly for the student magazines. They paid
nothing, but he said frankly he wrote for the satisfaction of
seeing his name in print.

Literary publications mushroomed in every city and around
every Chinese college—*Crescent Moon, The Crier, The New
Group, The Fiction Writer, The Creatives,* and a hundred other
titles. Some of these magazines published fiction in the new
literary form launched a decade earlier by the celebrated scholar
Hu Shih. "Matter is the slave of manner," he had said, breathing a fresh new spirit into both the content of Chinese writing
and the literary language itself. Some specialized in satire, rid-

iculing the old traditional Chinese forms, family life, social customs, and the classical scholar. Some were obviously influenced
by European philosophers, notably Rousseau and Ruskin; the
Communist line bobbed up in others.

They all led a precarious existence, threatened by the police,
on the one hand, and extinction through lack of funds, on the
other. But no matter how many died, others appeared. They
reflected the enormous mental vitality of the students, the fer-
ment of ideas, and the impatience of the young Chinese to
build the new order in China.

Phil Li, for his part, denied any such motives. He laughed at
idealism and professed to find what he called "the world sav-
ers" as funny as the outworn patterns of life in China that they
wanted to change. Phil came from Malaya. His father had
moved to Kuala Lumpur as a young man, opened a little food
store, carefully nourished his small gains, and eventually become a millionaire from dealing in rubber.

Martin Fong and Eddie Chen also were the sons of rich men.
Eddie was American-born, a native of Hawaii. His parents had
sent him to Lingnan solely because they wanted him to have a
Chinese education, whether it had any practical value or not.
In this, they reversed the normal procedure of that day. Most
Chinese scrimped and saved to send their sons to the United
States or Europe for an education.

Martin's family lived in Tientsin. He intended to study engineering, not because he liked it or had any special aptitude
for it, but because, as he said, China needed more engineers
and fewer merchants, government officials, and scholars.

In the fashion of that day the students had taken Western
first names, and even when they talked Chinese they addressed
each other as "Eddie" and "Martin."

"You both weary me," Philip Li said. "What is all this about
peasants and good government in the 'New China'? I see China
as a jungle and not likely to be changed by any of you. All three
of us are lucky that our fathers happened to be tigers and not

sheep. I feel sorry for the millions of sheep, but there are too many of them for anybody to do much about and I'm not going to try. No bloody fear."

"Then why are you going into government?"

"Because I expect to find a cushy job. Preferably in Shanghai. And preferably one that will keep me informed, in advance, about foreign loans and the manipulations of currency by my future colleagues. Then, in a comfortable house—in the French Concession, I should think—I shall settle down quietly to writing, being a gentleman, and sleeping with White Russian dancers and little Chinese virgins."

Martin stared into the fire. "You like to sound blasé, Phil. I wager you will join the sheep and not the tigers when the time comes."

"Come and visit me in Shanghai in about five years, my friend. I promise not to say 'I told you so.' "

"I'm inclined to agree with Phil," said Eddie. "China *is* a jungle now. Or, rather, a mare's nest—"

"Augean stables," said Philip. "And where shall we find the Hercules to clean them by diverting the Yangtze River?"

"Certainly not Chiang Kai-shek."

"Nor his wife's family and their mates," said Philip, "the Soong dynasty."

"I think you're wrong," Martin said. "The Kuomintang is by no means perfect. But give them time. What chance have they had in these last three or four years? You must admit the war lords and Wang Ching-wei and the Communists have kept them pretty busy. Somehow I have confidence in Chiang. I think he's a sincere, dedicated man who will bring it off in time."

"Hallelujah, Brother Fong. Put a nickel on the drum and be saved."

"No doubt this government hasn't had much chance yet," said Eddie Chen. "But, seriously, Martin, do you see any indication that the Kuomintang know where they're going? Have a program? They talk about this being a period of political tutelage after which there will be democracy at all levels, national elections. Well, when? They say civil liberties will be granted. When? What have they done, in short?"

Philip Li stuck a splinter of kindling into the fire and lit his pipe.

"Now you put me in the position of being the devil's advocate," he said. "With all due respect to this silent and inscrutable Occidental, Mr. Morin here, I reluctantly applaud one thing the Kuomintang have done."

"And what is that?"

"They have taken a stand against the white peril."

"Do you mean us foreign devils?" I said.

"Precisely. We have been talking about a starting point. Very well, I say the starting point must be the present treaties with the foreign devils. They must be either torn up or rewritten. I am in favor of the Kuomintang position on that."

Martin shook his head. "It's only a smoke screen," he said, "a move to please the extreme Chinese Nationalist. Suppose the treaties are revised. Will that stop the corruption? The usury? Will it put more rice in the peasant's bowl? The treaties have nothing to do with him."

"I disagree," said Phil. "When the 'unequal treaties' are gone, when the foreign concessions and foreign courts are gone, the Chinese businessman will be able to compete on equal terms with the foreigners. Exploitation will end. In the process, all Chinese benefit."

"One billion, two hundred million dollars a year."

"Correct. The good doctor never explained how he arrived at that figure, but whatever it may be, we could use it," said Phil.

Chinese students were required to study the writings of Dr. Sun Yat-sen in the universities. At patriotic services his last will often was read publicly. In the passage to which Eddie Chen referred, Dr. Sun had said:

"Our tribute to foreign countries is 12 billions in 10 years. Such economic subjugation, such enormous tribute, was not in our wildest dreams and even now it is hard to visualize. Hence we do not feel the awful shame of it.

"If we had this tribute of $1,200,000,000 as national income what could we not do with it! What progress our society would make! But because of this economic mastery of China and the consequent yearly damages our society is not free to develop and the common people do not have the means of living. This economic control is worse than millions of soldiers ready to kill us."

Philip yawned. "It's getting late. I move we adjourn. Unless, of course, Martin can produce some of that excellent jasmine tea. Jasmine always reminds me of a little friend I visit whenever I am in Hong Kong. She passes her days in what our ancestors called 'the flower boats.' "

Martin Fong set the teakettle on the fire in the grate. We stood up and stretched. Philip wrote rapidly in his notebook. "To show you what an excellent journalist I could be," he said, "and would be if it offered the opportunities of trade or government, I have kept full notes on all wise thoughts expressed here tonight. My own, I find, are the only ones with any true perception."

"I can already see it," said Eddie. " 'Building the New China, or, The Transcendent Curve,' by Philip Li, Lingnan, 1930."

"Moreover, I have classified the various points. You will not agree with the order of importance, of course, but this is the way I have them:

" 'First—international. End the unequal treaties. Take over foreign concessions. Stop the flow of wealth from China to foreign countries.

" 'Second—military. Need for powerful modern army to back up demands. More military academies. Fan fire of nationalism among all classes of people.

" 'Third—domestic-political. Early national elections and real democratic system at all levels. Civil rights. Stop trend toward Fascism.

" 'Fourth—economic. Need for speedy industrialization. Take more people off farms. Need to develop class of trained managers. Reduction of rents. Tax reform. Land reform. Stop usury and corruption in government.' Question in brackets here— 'How?'

" 'Fifth—social.' Since do-gooders are completely beyond my comprehension, the notes in this category are sketchy. I find only a few woolly-headed propositions about universal education, as if that were possible, and replacing the Honorable Confucius with a modern society, whatever that may be."

He closed the book with a snap. "Well, there it is, gentlemen," he said. "Personally, I question whether the whole of it is as important as this cup of tea." He sipped the tea, slurping loudly.

"Quite a list," I said.

"Yes," said Martin Fong, "and it barely scratches the surface."

ɤ

The only time I ever contributed to one of these sessions was the night they discovered I came from the city where movies are made. To them the screen was a window on a strange and desirable world.

In those days, much more than today, scenes were filmed on the street. The cameraman wore his cap backward, with the visor behind, and cranked his camera by hand. Since there was no sound, the director could talk during the action. "Now you see her across the street, Ricardo. You're dumbfounded. You thought she was in Tangier. You can't understand this. Easy, now. Don't chew the scenery. That's it. Cut." Sometimes, to assist an actress in displaying grief, a violinist would play "Hearts and Flowers" just outside the camera range. I told them about these things and described some of the stars I had seen.

But I didn't know my audience. The students were only mildly interested in the way Norma Talmadge looked in person and the story of Fatty Arbuckle's troubles. What they wanted to know was whether the movies gave an accurate picture of life in America, whether they portrayed the effects of some American social customs. Taking their material from the movies, they wrote theses comparing American and Chinese forms: papers on the equality of the sexes, the differences in family life, Western attitudes toward romance and marriage. One of these theses, perceiving the potency of the screen as an instrument of propaganda, advocated using Chinese-made movies to sell the masses on the advantages of "the small family." Another, more earthy, suggested the screen as a medium for promoting the use of modern bathroom conveniences!

Always so serious. They had abandoned the old educational system of China, but the tradition of hard, earnest study and thought remained.

In the old system a student learned the classics by heart, as well as Confucian ethics and the teachings of the sages. However, in the examinations he also had to be able to explain the deep meanings in these philosophies. The civil-service examinations were important, not only for scholastic reasons, but because they opened the way to position among the élite classes of China. Success in the examinations clothed a scholar in prestige and gave him great political and social importance in his community as well. It was a system of intellectual democracy, and the scholar was regarded as anything but an egg head.

The son of the humblest peasant might rise to the élite class if his father could provide him with a tutor for the examinations. There were three types of test—national, provincial, and county. The wider the field, the more important the posts for those who qualified.

The tutor, a venerable old classicist, would charge two silver dollars a year to provide an education "in ordinary." It cost six dollars to be trained "with honors."

Imagine the fearful strain and nervous torture that must have beset a student when he came to the fateful day of the examinations. Honor, the hopes of his family, and high station rode on his answers. There is a story that the man who, in effect, touched off the Taiping rebellion, Hung Hsiu-chuan, failed in the great test for office. Shortly afterward he began seeing the visions in which he became Christ's younger brother.

Like so many other ancient institutions, the old educational system began to lose validity in Chinese eyes during the Predatory Century. The shock of defeat in war, the rapid foreign encroachment, the realization that China had ceased to be a great empire cast doubt on all the old forms. The days of glory had passed. In all truth Sun Yat-sen could recall: "When China was strongest, her political power inspired awe on all sides, and not a nation south and west of China but considered it an honor to bring her tribute."

Another morose observer wrote: "There is a Dead Sea on the western extremity of Asia and a dead nation on the eastern."

So, China, like Japan a generation earlier, began studying the institutions of the conquerors. In 1902 the government ordered a Western-style educational system to be established. Even before, the missionaries had been setting up such schools. Now they found themselves in the main stream of the trend in China.

Lingnan (meaning "South of the Ridge") was established by Presbyterians before the turn of the century. Among the first students, about a dozen in all, there were grown men. They still considered China "The Middle Kingdom," hub of the world, and believed that the King of England, not to mention minor princes, paid tribute to the Emperor so that Englishmen could live in Peking. One of the early reports from Lingnan describes these first students as "eager, intelligent, and hard-working."

By the time we reached the university, it had four colleges, a middle school, a primary school, and "feeder" schools in Hong Kong and Shanghai. At Lingnan itself some three hundred men and about sixty women were in the four colleges—arts and science, business administration, agriculture, and silk raising. An engineering school was about to be opened. In effect, there were two faculty staffs—Chinese and American. The Chinese staff was larger.

Considering that in the older tradition a scholar did not work with his hands or receive vocational training (and that women were not educated at all), these fields of study represented a very great change indeed.

The prestige of the university was such that Chinese came from all over Southeast Asia and even farther, as well as from China proper. Many of them came from wealthy families, and Lingnan was known as "a rich man's school." But, rich or poor, as I noted earlier, nobody lived in luxury there.

What impressed me most was the Chinese students' extreme seriousness. On an American campus we would have called the majority of them "greasy grinds." They went in very little for fun and games. Occasionally you could organize a rubber of bridge after dinner, but they preferred to sit and talk when they didn't have to work. Or they would go to Canton to a theater or a restaurant. Men went with men always. "Dating" was rare. Whether any heavy love affairs ever took place, off campus or on, I do not know.

If their ways seemed strange to us, ours astonished them even more.

Infrequently the Y.M.C.A. or a kind of college fraternity held a social evening. For one of these the Chinese students asked us to depict something of American college life. We rigged up a stage-set to resemble a fraternity room, with pennants, dirty corduroys lying around, and all the photographs of girls we could find. I wrote a sketch, and the others acted in it. It revolved around a poker game. The dialogue was larded with philosophizing about women and God, and talk of Saturday's

football game and the big wing-ding afterward. It may not
have been good, but it was typical. I also poached some jokes
from the Two Black Crows, revamping them to fit the situation. What exquisite torture to wait for the laugh that never
comes! Then we gave them a football yell, sang Alma Mater,
and dropped the theater curtain.

The whole thing sank in murderous silence.

Afterward a Chinese girl came to ask questions. Her face
was a picture of bewilderment. "It was most interesting," she
said, "but when do you study?"

"That's a good question," I said. "We study, of course, but
not as much as you do here."

"It must be different in America," she said a little wistfully.
"Very different."

When they thought of America, conflicting emotions pulled at
the students. They admired the United States as a successful
nation. They envied the richness and power and pre-Depression
stability. The American way, therefore, must be good and the
Chinese way, obviously, outworn and inefficient. They condemned Confucian thought for having made China "backward"
and a prey to the aggressive foreigner. According to the Confucian ideal, you strive for harmony, not to excel in competition. You "succeed" by becoming righteous and wise, thus hon-
oring your family, not by becoming rich and powerful. But in
the world as it developed after about 1840 these ideals no
longer worked.

On the other side of the coin, the students felt bitterness and
even hatred for the West. More than any other class of Chinese,
they resented humiliations and the monuments to Western privilege on Chinese soil. Listen to the words of Sun Yat-sen:

"Annam and Korea are protectorates of France and Japan

and their people are slaves. We taunt the Koreans and Annamites with the name '*wang-kuo nu*' (slaves without a country),
yet while looking at their position, we seem unaware that our
position is lower than theirs. . . . China is the colony of every
nation that has made treaties with her and the treaty-making
nations are her masters. China is not the colony of one nation
but of all, and we are not the slaves of one country but of all."

It was the student and intellectual who organized strikes and
boycotts and stirred the lower classes to action. He led the
demonstrations that resulted in the shooting in Shanghai and
the "massacre" opposite Shameen. The murder of foreigners in
Nanking and the innumerable attacks on foreign property all
over China sprang from two interacting forces—antiforeignism
and Chinese nationalism. No group felt these more keenly than
the students.

In their personal relations with foreigners they were generally friendly or at least courteous. I think the incident with the
student and the sampan woman on the bund in Canton was an
accident, an isolated case. Certainly nothing like it ever happened again. However, the students pulled no punches with
you about the actions of the United States if you invited their
opinions. America was not their favorite nation.

Some foreigners could see what was happening. I discovered
some who felt defensive about what their forefathers had
pulled off in China. Most, however, scoffed at the idea that a
Chinese could be patriotic in the ultimate sense. They con-
tended he had no idea of a "China," an abstract entity of which
he was a member. They insisted that he confined responsibility
and allegiance to his family, not the nation. In varying degrees
no doubt this was true. The illiterate peasant, the old-timer,
certainly the war lord—all fitted the old pattern. But to the students "China" existed, even though it was divided by barriers
of language, inadequate communications, and fearful economic
dislocations. They were prepared to work and fight for that
China.

The ones I knew, almost without exception, supported the new central government, the Kuomintang. They felt it offered the best promise of pulling China out of the pit. The extent of their support ranged from the enthusiastic to the hopeful to the merely watchful. They had some reservations about certain aspects. But on the whole they seemed willing to wait for the end of the "period of tutelage," after which the Kuomintang promised to set democracy in motion with elections at all levels. They resented the curtailment of civil liberties. Here again, however, most of them believed, or said they believed, such controls were necessary during the provisional period. Until a constitution could be written and a national assembly elected, they told me, the Kuomintang had no choice but to operate as an authoritarian government. After the "period of tutelage," however, they expected and would demand all the rights and liberties of citizens of a democracy. Few expressed fears of an outright dictatorship under Chiang Kai-shek.

To be sure, they sometimes referred to Mme Chiang and her relatives as "the Soong dynasty." Her maiden name was Soong Mei-ling. Her brother and one of her brothers-in-law both held top offices in the government. The sarcastic term "dynasty," however, probably was little more than a political jibe, like the jokes aimed at presidents and prime ministers everywhere.

Now, I have been relating, primarily, the opinions of the students in the missionary-founded schools, the private institutions. A very different situation unquestionably existed in the national universities, the state schools. The students there came from less well-to-do families. Tuition was much less, but even so, the struggle of these families and these young men must have been a hard one to finance a college education. For these and other reasons Leftist thought and indeed outright Communism had penetrated deeply into the state schools.

It was difficult to determine the degree of this penetration because the government (and even some of the war lords) fought Communism tooth and nail. Consequently, the professional organizer and agitator had to work in the dark. Nevertheless, he had made inroads, apparently deep ones.

Here, for example, is the text of a pamphlet put out by the students in Peking. I picked it up on the street, not far from Peking National University:

"Break capitalism; confiscate industries and banks of foreign capitalists; do away with unjust taxation; unite with the Third International; improve working conditions; overthrow the present government; unite China."

In 1928, with considerable fanfare and publicity, the Russian Boxer Indemnity Committee announced it would turn over to Peking National a fairly considerable sum of money, $4,500,-000, stretching over a two-year period. No doubt it financed this pamphlet and other operations.

In another case what started out as an innocent picnic turned into a Communist demonstration. Some students at Hsiao Chuang Agricultural School in Nanking organized the picnic. Surprisingly, the original small group grew to about two hundred students on the day of the holiday. They went in a body to the railway depot near the school. By the time they reached it, some were displaying Communist banners and placards. They boarded the train and refused, en masse, to buy tickets. "In a Socialist state students on holiday are not required to pay railway fares," they told the conductor. In effect, they commandeered the train. Some, I was told, treated it as a lark—collegeboy high jinks. But government authorities did not. Chiang Kai-shek ordered the school closed.

In the city jail in Canton—a frightening dungeon, incidentally—I talked with some students who were behind the bars on charges of Leftist activity. Later I wrote a newspaper story about it. I had remarked to the police official that the prisoners seemed cheerful, and quoted his reply in the story. "Why not? They're alive, aren't they? They know what can happen to a Communist."

Apart from the work of the professional agitator, a simple

fact explains why many Chinese students felt drawn toward Communism in that day—the problem of earning a living after graduation. There were just not enough Chinese corporations, factories, engineering firms, public utilities, railroads, mines, and so on, to provide jobs for all of them. Too much of the nation's industry and commerce was in the hands of foreigners. The opportunities for a Chinese in foreign firms were limited, both in number and prospects for advancement. He had small chance of becoming "Number Three" or "Number Two," as the idiom went, much less of moving into the front office as *taipan.*

Consequently, many of the new graduates either left China or went into government work. There they quickly became typical bureaucrats, stretching out the work, proliferating their duties, hanging desperately on to their offices. The number of government offices grew rapidly during that period, with the inevitable effect of raising taxes.

But for the ordinary graduate not even government could be the catch-all. Another factor hedged him in, the so-called returned student. A Chinese who could afford to go abroad for additional study after having finished in a Chinese school was called a "returned student." Naturally, only the sons of wealthy families, or the men who managed to get money some other way, were able to go to the United States or Europe. Many scrimped and saved for years for the chance. As China was driving hard to modernize, the "returned student," with his Western training, had the edge if he wanted to go into government work. By 1930 well over half, probably closer to two thirds of the offices were held by these men. The others, in bitterness and envy, must have reflected that nothing was possible without money, even in the "New China."

One "returned student" did very well for himself in the government, although he had to wait several decades. He finished his education in France and was a Communist before he ever left Paris. His name was Chou En-lai.

For both the Kuomintang and the Communists, the Chinese

student was a vast source of energy, a dynamo for galvanizing the Chinese masses. Neither group, curiously enough, seemed to fully realize this at the time. The Communists already were concentrating on the peasants. The Kuomintang made Dr. Sun's writings required study, and ordered many schools to observe a moment of silence in his memory every Monday morning. But something more than his image was needed to win the full loyalty and support of the student class.

Nevertheless, at that moment in China's history, 1930, it appeared to me that the balance of student opinion was tipped toward the Kuomintang, especially in the missionary-founded schools. If the government could have won over larger numbers of students and kept their allegiance, tremendous things could have been done in China.

This did not happen. Two years later more and more students began looking toward the Communists, listening to their arguments, wondering whether they, and not the Kuomintang, held the key to the salvation of China.

It was a disastrous shift.

Chapter XII

TSUI

DURING THE LONG WINTER at Lingnan a subtle change came over Tsui. At first he merely seemed preoccupied, turned in on himself, brooding. All the fun drained out of him and he stopped laughing. Then he became morose. Almost imperceptibly he began to draw away from us. More and more of the decisions respecting our project were turned over to Warren Scott, who had helped him launch it. Tsui seemed to lose interest in it. He offered no explanations and turned aside any efforts to draw him out. Even his outward appearance changed.

The Chinese robes accounted in part for this. He had put on a Chinese costume as a joke the first time. He stood in front of a mirror, posturing and making Oriental faces. "Get your cameras," he had said. "I want a record of this." Then he began to clown, impersonating an old-fashioned Mandarin. He folded his arms into the sleeves of the gown, raised his eyebrows, and stalked around the room, intoning, he said, a poem by Li Po. Next, with only a slight change of expression, he became the mysterious Dr. Fu Manchu. He finished the performance as Jade Flute, one of the maidens, more or less, in the novel *Ching P'ing Mei*. We said that not even Mei Lan-fang, the darling of the Chinese theater, could have done better. Tsui agreed.

A little later he bought robes and *sha'ams* and began wearing them frequently. I tried to needle him about "going native," but he did not laugh. He said they were warmer and added, cryptically, I thought: "It might be better if we all went a little bit native."

However, he appeared at the next group meeting in a suit and his usual sweater. We met periodically to compare notes, hear a financial report from Don Dreher, the treasurer, and plan details of the work. On that occasion the question of placements in Shanghai came up. Shanghai was the next step, and we were to split up there, using the facilities of two different schools. Tsui said he didn't care where he was assigned. He looked bored and said nothing except in answer to direct questions.

He began finding excuses for not coming when we went to Canton and Shameen to shop or merely explore the markets. As a change from the Chinese food in the mess hall, we went to the Victoria Hotel and ate through the menu from top to bottom: soup thick as mucilage; fish; roast beef and Yorkshire pudding; roast potatoes; a vegetable; trifle; savory and sulphuric coffee. The Old China Hand never dieted.

Then the markets. What has become of the markets under the Communists? Who can imagine China without the million-and-one little shops and the charming, persuasive merchants, each a one-man corporation and staunch advocate of free enterprise?

With wonderful common sense, merchants selling the same article used to cluster together in the same street. Jade Street. Silk Street. Embroidery Street. Box Street. Jewelry Street. The Edible Bird's Nest Market. It greatly simplifies shopping. If you don't find exactly what you want in one shop, the merchant next door may have it. Imagine how much time and effort a housewife would save if all the department stores in town stood cheek by jowl in the same street.

In back, and sometimes in front, you could watch an artisan carving figurines of the gods and goddesses in ivory and wood, fashioning bangles, inlaying silver with kingfisher feathers. The merchant would stand near, smiling, but making no effort to sell unless you showed interest in a particular article. On one of our first trips, Tsui had explained to the merchants that we were students, not rich American tourists. The news had an instant and magical effect on prices in every street. To us he explained something else. "The merchant wants to sell, of course," he said. "That's his first objective. But his special satisfaction comes in fitting the article to the customer, so to speak. For instance, say you are looking at a ring. He will try to sell you the ring that matches his feeling about you, about your appearance and personality. That gives him a real kick. I imagine we're the only people in the world who have that approach in selling."

We? Tsui was as American as a hot dog. Yet, without noticing, he had said "we." When had he started identifying himself with the Chinese?

As the pale winter days passed, we saw less and less of him. As he spoke Cantonese, he attended classes at Lingnan that would have been meaningless to us. His dormitory room, I discovered, had become a rendezvous for the students at night. He never joined our bull sessions any more. In the mess hall, too, he ate with them. Sometimes, when he went to the big vats to fill his rice bowl, he would pause and exchange a word and then go back to their table. It occurred to me that he might be having a love affair. The coeds often invited him to their dormitory for tea, but never *a deux*. However, if he had been seeing a girl, we would have seen them together on the campus. Instead, long periods passed when Tsui vanished entirely.

A fragment from Stanton Avery's diary says: "February 2. Tsui came back today without any of us having known he was away. This is known as 'pulling a Tsui.'"

Could he be at Teng Wu? I remembered the expression on his face that night. . . .

Teng Wu was a monastery hidden in the mountains beyond Canton. Behind its massive ramparts three hundred monks and acolytes moved quietly through the daily cycle of prayer and work. The incense, the tapers, the great Buddha, and, above all, the silence, created a sense of peace and unimaginable serenity.

Just at dusk we had heard the chanting. The chief celebrant, an aged monk, began it. His eyes were open, but unseeing. Presently another voice joined the chant. Then another and another. Gongs, cymbals, and wooden percussion instruments picked up the rhythm, locking it in cadence. More voices kept coming into the chorus. Oriental music, with its tones and half-notes that seem dissonant and even raucous, seldom conveys any meaning to me and arouses no emotion. At the monastery that night, however, the chanting conjured haunting images, shadowy images of some other world in another time.

In the middle of the rites I had glanced at Tsui. He was staring into the yellow-gold flame of the candles. He looked mesmerized. When the chanting ended, he blinked his eyes and shook his head like a man coming out of a trance.

Later, as we were going down the mountain, I said that missionary work should be a two-way street and that the Buddhists should send priests to America. "I'll bet they'd convert Americans faster than the Christians are converting Chinese," I said. "What would you call the Western equivalent of a 'rice Christian,' in that case? A 'whole-wheat Buddhist,' probably."

Tsui smiled halfheartedly. "I'd like to go back up there and stay awhile," he said. "One of these days I think I will."

He did not go back to the monastery. There was no girl, no campus romance. He had not gone anywhere those times we thought he had disappeared. He had simply been staying in his room, sometimes skipping meals. The reason for his strangeness, when it emerged, was simple, yet complicated.

Late one afternoon, while writing a newspaper story, I came

to a point where I needed some information. Tsui had been talking about the very subject some weeks before. I went to his room. He was alone there, poring over a manuscript. As I came in, he wrote a marginal note on the side of a page. (I still have it today. The note, in his precise hand, says: "What lecture could change the mind of a People?")

He gave me the information I needed, and we talked for a moment. I asked what he was writing. He pushed the type-written pages across the table. "Junk," he said. "A real mess. I can't seem to get it on paper. Probably because I don't know what I'm trying to say myself."

The sheets of manuscript looked like a rat's nest. He had scratched out whole paragraphs and rewritten between the lines. Phrases had been circled and carried over into other sentences. He had obviously reached that stage, known to writers, where words begin to wrestle with each other. His paper appeared to be a jungle stew of observations on politics, philosophy, and a new technique in lecturing. Here and there his curious sense of mysticism came to the surface.

"What is this lack of order," he had written, "these evidences of great misunderstanding?" And there were broken phrases and unfinished sentences: "the continual struggle and readjust-ment going on in the heart of China," "some phases of that mighty, unreasoning movement in China." A single passage stood untouched. "How many men in positions of importance in the world today can say of their work, 'I feel that I am in-creasing the hopes of the people, and giving them a spiritual uplift which fills them with a sense of power, a sense of po-tentiality, a sense of victory'?"

"It looks interesting," I said. "What are you trying to get at?"

"If I knew," he said impatiently, "I'd write it."

"Can't you just talk it? Sometimes you can talk an idea out of the bushes better than writing it."

Tsui hesitated. He selected one topic in his paper. This led him into a rambling explanation of the other foundations of his idea: a conversation with a bitterly antiforeign student; his personal experiences before the Chinese at Lingnan had accepted him; a lecture that came through to him even though it had been deliverd in Mandarin, a language he did not know. He had been trying to bind all this together around a central theme—the struggle in China.

As he went on talking, he began to get excited. It was like a small crevice in a dam which widened as more chunks broke away until finally the dam collapsed. Words poured out of Tsui in a flood. Suddenly he was himself again, the old Tsui.

"I want to help these people," he said. "I have to do something to help them."

"What, for instance?"

"That's just it. I don't know. I've been thinking about it for a long time, but going around in circles and getting nowhere."

He said he had talked with missionaries and the instructors at Lingnan. He had considered going up to Teng Wu and asking the monks for advice. The endless arguments among the students, he said, had impressed him deeply and given him the impulse to try to help the Chinese, but had only confused him when he began searching for the way to begin.

The dinner hour came. "Let's skip it," Tsui said. "Or get something later. I want to tell you something even more cockeyed. I've begun to feel Chinese."

"What's surprising about that? You are only one generation removed from China. I don't imagine a second generation Frenchman could go back to France without feeling the tie."

"Not exactly all Chinese," he said. "Mixed up. It's hard to explain. I seem to be looking at things through their eyes. I can feel the way they feel, but I'm an American and I think like an American, too. I've become so mixed up that there are times when—I'm not kidding—I wonder if I'm going crazy."

"You've been working too hard," I said. "Let's go to Canton tonight and see a movie or try that wine that's supposed to be an aphrodisiac."

As though he had not heard me, he said: "Do you remember the week end on the farm?"

The farm lay in a lovely little valley, two or three hours northeast of Canton by train. The owner, we were told, was the head of the twenty-sixth generation of his family. He had more than ten thousand relatives. His first act when we arrived was to introduce us, with his flashing smile, to the portraits of his ancestors. More than five hundred years of Chung patriarchs looked out from the paintings. They would have been here in the valley of Chuk Ko Uen when the Mings still ruled China. Some of them must have known the warrior Cheng Cheng-kung, whom the Portuguese called "Koxinga." There is a temptation to find a historic parallel here. When the Manchus conquered China, expelling the Mings, Cheng fled to Formosa, refusing to submit. He wrested the island from the Dutch and, like the Nationalists today, used it as a base for raids against the Manchus in south China. You can still see his castle at the southern tip of Formosa. He probably came through the same valley where the Chungs lived, raiding and plundering. Sad to say, little had changed. The twenty-sixth patriarch maintained his own private garrison for protection against the bandits in the valley. He said he could not permit us to sleep in the family monastery, which stood outside the walls of the compound, for fear of kidnappers.

Father Chung was a landlord, and a big one. On the farm were orange groves, olive orchards, litchi-nut trees, well-stocked fish ponds, and warehouses to hold the products. But this was not all. In neighboring villages he owned restaurants, pottery shops, candle-making shops, rice stores, and a brick kiln. Apparently he owned most of the land in the whole beautiful valley. He belonged to that class of men whom the Communists liquidated, usually in public executions, to impress the peasants. Thus they hoped to give evidence of their friendship for the poor and their policy of redistributing the land.

Mao Tse-tung's own father, while not as big an operator as

Father Chung, nevertheless was also a landlord, the so-called middle peasant. He employed peasants, sold rice in the cities, and seems to have acquired a modest fortune. It came, as the old-time economist used to say, from "unearned increment." And a modern psychiatrist, no doubt, would find special meaning in the fact that Mao hated his father and quarreled frequently with him before leaving home to become a Communist.

"What about the farm?" I said to Tsui.

"I kept watching the people who work on it," he said. "I thought how little hope they have of ever owning a tiny strip of land themselves. He owns practically the whole valley."

"He provides jobs, too. A lot of the peasants wouldn't be eating if it weren't for him."

"I know. That's what I keep telling myself. But the peasants want land, too. I could feel, like a pain, how hard they want land."

"But the system is essentially the same as our system," I said. "What else built America if not private capital and the incentive and personal initiative to acquire it?"

"There is no parallel whatever," he said. "The Chinese peasant has no place to go, no undeveloped West to settle, no education to take him off the land, no means of borrowing a little capital to get a start. He is hopelessly trapped."

"So, something has to be changed."

"Some way must be found to give the peasants a chance," he said.

"And do you think the Socialists or Communists have the answer to this?"

"Not in a million years," he said. "The peasant is a capitalist at heart, a free enterpriser. The reason he wants to own land is not only to have a better chance of eating, but because he believes in personal property."

It was after midnight. Tsui leaned over the desk, pillowing his head on his arm. For several minutes he said nothing. I thought he had gone to sleep.

"What are you going to do?"

He looked up. "I don't know yet. I've been trying to think what I can do. Maybe get a job with the government. Maybe see if there is a place for me in rural education. I'm thinking of the possibilities."

"Do you know the written language well enough to get into the rural-education movement?"

"No," he said. "In fact, right now I am sure I don't know anything about anything. But I expect to come to some conclusions when we get to Shanghai."

Chapter XIII

THE SHANGHAI STORY

EVERY MORNING shortly after six o'clock I went through the front gate of Shanghai College, far out on the Whangpoo River, and rode the bus to work. It jolted down Yangtzepoo Road, through the factory district of Yangtzepoo, past frowning walls, through a sea of laborers and others seeking work. As it emerged from the smoke, a marvelous sight came into view— the skyline of Shanghai, fronting the bund.

These were the ramparts of a city-state—rich, independent, and proud. Yangtzepoo and the handsome buildings along the bund were separate but related faces of Shanghai. A considerable number of the silver ingots in the bank vaults over there came from the poverty over here. Hunger and ugliness looked across the mud flats at beauty and great wealth. Other industrial districts in the Orient exceeded Yangtzepoo in size, but none in grinding injustice.

It must have looked very much like the factory districts in England at the time of Charles Dickens, or Chicago before the Haymarket bomb. Textile mills, chemical plants, and factories making shoes, hats, and cigarettes, and the go-downs bulging with silk and tea and foodstuffs were jammed together in a great arc formed by a bend in the Whangpoo. Most of the buildings were like fortresses, with massive brick walls, weathered and sooty. Jagged shards of glass bristled on top of the high outer walls to discourage thieves and rioters, and the iron gates were heavy enough to stop a mob. Windows were few, and those so dirty little light came through. In this great labyrinth more than two hundred and fifty thousand men, women, and children stood at the machines and tended the spindles. Another million in and around Shanghai waited for work. And in the Ningpo interior even more millions would have gladly gone into the factories to escape the land.

Everybody knew this—the workers, the employers, the labor unions. They understood very well that for every job there were scores of willing hands.

One morning in the heart of Yangtzepoo a torrent of men came pouring out of an alley directly in the path of the bus. The driver, a White Russian, hit the brakes, but not soon enough to avoid knocking one man to the street. Another crashed into the side of the bus and there was a metallic clang as his head hit the hood. Both men rose, shook their heads like prize fighters, and sprinted after the others. Now, some Shanghailanders used to say: "They do it on purpose. They step in front of your car just enough so you will hit 'em, but not really hurt 'em. The idea is to get a few dollars out of you." In this case, however, the men were racing toward a factory gate. The driver, in slow, careful English, said simply: "There must be a job there."

Another time an overhead trolley wire broke. It fell into the street, lashing around like a steel serpent, spitting and crackling. Wholly oblivious and probably ignorant that a touch meant sudden death, people surged over it, thronging toward a factory gate. I could not see whether any were killed.

Still another time, I was watching eight coolies manhandling a steel safe that must have weighed a ton or more. They had crisscrossed their carrying-poles to distribute the load. Each had a deep indentation in his shoulder where, in years of lifting heavy weights, the pole had bitten into the bare flesh. They would lift the safe, grunting, and carry it a few yards, chanting *"Hay-ho, hay-ho"* to keep step in rhythm, then set it down again, panting and sweating. A sudden surge of people collided with them in the alley. The safe tipped over, and a man lay there with crushed legs, screaming.

Squeezed between the big factories were scores of little shops, scarcely more than cottage industries. In a dark, cramped hole there would be a press, two or three buffing machines, and some Rube Goldberg machines turning out cheap forks and spoons, tin ware, and other light metal products. Of the usual six or eight operators the majority would be children, boys about twelve years old. They worked from six o'clock in the morning until nine at night on the average.

Many of the women who worked in textile mills brought their babies with them and cradled them in piles of yarn, where they slept, breathing in lint and dust. They nursed the babies when they themselves stopped to eat a bowl of rice and a bit of fish. How they must have envied the woman who had no child to nurse and the girl too young to have borne any.

Various commissions and investigations of both the factories and the small shops indicated that wages ranged from 43¢ to $1.58 a day for men, 20¢ to 82¢ for women, and 17¢ to 40¢ for children. These were Shanghai dollars, of course—silver "Mex" equal to about 45¢ in American money. But if the average seems low, it nevertheless was higher than the pay in some trades. The bookbinders, for example, complained that they worked ten hours a day, six days a week, for $10 a month.

Labor unions existed—more than three hundred of them at that time. They did what they could. So did the Shanghai Municipal Council, the missionaries, and some unofficial organizations. Even in the twenties serious efforts were made to improve the conditions in Yangtzepoo. However, in the chaos of that period, when China had no real central government— certainly none that cared about coolie labor—little could be done. Later the students came into the picture and spurred the unions into calling strikes. The tragic incident of May 30, 1925, when the Shanghai police fired into a crowd of students and demonstrators, grew out of a strike in a Japanese textile mill. One day as we were going through the district, a stone shattered the windshield of the bus. The streetcar employees' union in Shanghai had gone out on strike, and the White Russian bus drivers refused to support it. In fact, other White Russians, timid and inexperienced, stepped into the streetcars, and you saw their tense, anxious faces as the cars went along.

Slowly, even in the hearts of illiterate, almost destitute Chinese workmen, some concepts were dawning. The concept of a "China" exploited by foreigners. The concept that to work a man twelve hours a day even though the massive oversupply of labor made this possible might not be just.

But the foreign mill owner held no copyright on the sweating and squeezing. Chinese employers played the same game. In fact, they paid their people even less. There was no sentiment, no uplift-the-masses patriotism among the Chinese *taipans*, either.

Would not all this, plus a note on the "dog boy," perhaps, interest the readers of the Shanghai *Evening Post?*

The child was white, not Chinese, a result of who knows what forgotten encounter in a city of so many nationalities. He looked about ten years old. Rags covered his skinny little body. He continually scratched at his scabrous, close-cropped head. The first time I saw him, he was sitting in an alley, playing with a length of rope. Curious to know what a white child would be doing in Yangtzepoo, I walked toward him. He looked up. His eyes were empty—pale blue and utterly vacant. He hugged the rope to his chest. Then his lips drew back in a snarl and animal sounds came from his throat. I walked away. Something made me stop and turn around. The boy was close behind, bent low. His teeth were bared. Evidently he was about to bite my hand. When I turned, he shrank back against the wall, growling like a *wonk*, one of the dangerous wild dogs that prowled Shanghai. When I moved, he moved. If I took a step toward him, he slunk back. He disappeared only when I came out into the main road, where there was a Sikh policeman, a havildar major, directing traffic. The boy always stopped there. He waited in the alleys, and every time he saw me in Yangtzepoo he followed, snarling.

Yes, surely the dark district, with the "dog boy" and some other oddities I had picked up, would make a story for the paper.

The bus came into the bund. There were the big buildings, some of them very beautiful in the old Victorian manner. The Palace Hotel. Sassoon House. Jardine-Matheson's. The North China *Daily News*. The Shanghai Club. The Hongkong & Shanghai Bank. The Central Bank of China. The Yokohama Specie Bank. Shanghai had nearly two hundred banks, foreign and Chinese.

In the river, ships from every corner of the world rode at anchor: a gleaming white *Empress* liner of the Canadian Pacific; a *Conte* of the Italian line; a clean-looking North German Lloyd freighter; tankers, huge ocean-going junks staring at the bund with painted eyes; and the symbols of "gunboat diplomacy"—sleek cruisers, military transports, the Yangtze River warships. Guns had established Shanghai and guns would defend its independence if necessary.

I came into the office and told Al Meyer, the managing editor, about my idea to write a series of articles on Yangtzepoo.

"Nothing new in that, pal," he said. "It's new to you, of course, but not to people here. Don't want to discourage you, pal, but it's been like that for years. In fact, conditions used to be much worse. The Old Hands could tell you things that would curl your hair. Only they don't like to talk about that." He handed me a sheaf of clippings from the morning papers. "Here's some rewrite, pal," he said. "And *maskee* the fancy language."

Maskee was Shanghai slang for "never mind." Al had to cau-
tion me every morning because I was a slow writer. I would
slave over the rewrite, polishing and rephrasing, straining for
bright, minted words. The deadline would come closer, and
each tick of the clock would make me more nervous until, as
newspapermen say, I would "freeze" over the typewriter.

For this was my first real job on a newspaper. The sports-
writing I had done at home and my columns and features for
the college papers didn't count. That was amateur play. This
was a real newsroom, with real deadlines, and "straight" news.
Now I thought of myself as a professional reporter (intoxicating thought) and took to wearing my hat in the office.

It had come about in this manner. When we reached Shanghai, the others continued their respective studies very much as
they had done at Lingnan. We quickly discovered, however,
that Shanghai was a treasure trove of people, government officials, judges, editors, writers, bankers, businessmen, educators,
and social workers, each with a different experience and a different knowledge of China. So, interviewing, rather than class-
room and library study, became the emphasis of the work. We
had several long sessions with Hu Shih, one of the greatest
minds in China, and with George Sokolsky, the brilliant and influential editor of the *Far Eastern Review*. In the course of our
interviewing we also met the editor of the Shanghai *Evening
Post*, Carl Crow, a prolific writer of books on China. I told him
about my field of study and asked for a job on the paper, explaining that this would be a form of "field work." Actually, all
I wanted was a job on a newspaper. When he asked about my
experience, I exaggerated shamelessly. He probably suspected
it, but smiled and said it could be arranged. There was no
mention of salary—*maskee* that!

The day began with rewrites of items from the morning

papers. . . . The provisional court sentenced eight armed robbers to death, and extra police had to be rushed to the court-
room when their women tried to attack the judge and bailiffs.
. . . An American sailor was killed in a brawl in the Dragon
Café, 1637 Szechuen Road ("60 gorgeous dancing partners").
. . . A school for poor Russian children would be opened at
56 Route Ghisi in the French Concession. . . . The St. An-
drews Society announced a meeting, and the Shanghai Paper
Hunt Club a ride to hounds. . . . In Chapei, the Chinese suburb to the north, three army deserters were executed.

At noon the Chinese office boy brought in lunch from
Jimmy's Kitchen, an American restaurant around the corner
from the *Evening Post.* Jimmy specialized in "homeside chow,"
a sturdy pork-and-beans bill of fare. Americans kept his cooks
busy day and night. Shanghai had magnificent restaurants and
the dishes of virtually every country in the world. The French
cooking there equalled the greatest in Paris. You could find
Javanese *nasi goring,* Syrian lamb wrapped in grape leaves, a
gorgeous, saffron-colored rice dish with almonds, raisins, and
butter from India, overpowering smörgasbord, and the braised
beef à la Japonaise known as "Mongolian dog." Chinese cooking varies greatly according to region, and Shanghai could produce it all—Cantonese (most Chinese restaurants in America
are Cantonese), Hunanese, which is all pepper, and the wheat-
and-fat doughnuts, big as bicycle tires, from north China. In
food, as in other things, you could have anything you wanted
in Shanghai.

The last deadline on the paper came in the early afternoon.
Then the fate of the paper was in the hands of Ivan Mrantz
and the oddest crew of linotypers and make-up men ever seen
in a newspaper composing room. Ivan himself was a sad-faced
Russian. He supervised Russians, Chinese, stateless fugitives,
and Eurasians, who looked typically Portuguese at one moment and wholly Oriental at the next. Some of Ivan's crew
knew English, but most did not. They could only copy what

they saw. Thus, if you misspelled a word in a story, they would faithfully reproduce the error. Understandably, Ivan never smiled until the last edition of the *Evening Post* was on the street.

At that point, like a Chinese houseboy, I looked for chores and invented work in order to seem useful in the newsroom. Gradually, as no one else wanted the title, I became drama critic. In every city in the Far East with an Anglo-American colony of more than ten, there would surely be an amateur dramatic club. The Orient was too distant to attract stock companies, so the Old China Hand created his own theater. He loved it and called it "good fun," but worked hard on the plays and waited impatiently for the reviews in the paper after an opening night.

He knew what to expect, of course. No amateur dramatic-club show ever got a bad review, not because of tolerance for amateur actors, but because Shanghai was a small town in one sense. The "Number Ones" and "Number Twos" in the big commercial firms all knew each other. Their wives entertained each other frantically. They all belonged to the same clubs. Their political interests coincided, namely to preserve the peculiar international status of Shanghai. As in any small town, big feuds grew from little disagreements. So, it was simply not politic to report that Mrs. DeCourcey-Ketchup had been a disaster in *Journey's End* and should be barred by law from setting foot on a stage.

For all its notorious wickedness and sophistication, the city could be prudish in matters of good taste. A fine dispute, with hurt feelings and letters to the editor, broke out when the Americans produced *The Front Page*. The play was a raucous newspaper melodrama and the dialogue startled audiences. It was like the storm in London a century earlier when Geraldine Jewsbury's novel *Zoe* shocked the city's blue-blood roués and titled trollops. Shanghailanders might indulge in what they called "fun and games," but they did not talk about it.

Lines from the play:

FIRST REPORTER (dictating from pressroom): "The condemned man was visited today by Dr. Petrovsky, noted psychologist and author of *The Personality Gland*—"

SECOND REPORTER (at poker table): "And where to put it."

The Englishman in front of me began to chuckle. "Oh, I say, old girl, that's very good. Personality gland. Never thought of it that way. Ho, ho."

His wife, frozen-faced, whispered loudly: "After this act, we are leaving."

Very few Shanghailanders ever saw any Chinese theater which, the Chinese told me, was of high quality. To be sure, there was the language barrier. Not one white man in a thousand learned enough Chinese to understand a play. Apart from that, they would say: "When you've seen one, you've seen 'em all. They're all stylized. Damn noisy and dirty, too. People eat and talk and spit on the floor and throw orange peel all over the place, you know."

Nor did the symphony on Sunday, or the chamber-music concerts, or the soloists interest the Old China Hand very much. Good music abounded in China for a tragic reason. The refugee and stateless person needed no passport to enter the Treaty Ports and stay there. In Shanghai there were about twenty thousand Russians, probably the largest single foreign group. They had fled from the Bolsheviks. Later another wave of refugees, escaping from Adolf Hitler, made their way to Shanghai. Many of them were gifted musicians. They would perform for anything, for a meal in the kitchen. A hostess could hire an orchestra for less than the cost of the liquor at her dinner party.

The typical Shanghailander, untroubled by culture, devoted his leisure to riding tough little Mongolian ponies in the Beef Stakes at the race course, playing tennis at the Cercle Sportif in "Frenchtown," leaning over the longest bar in the world at the Shanghai Club. He was healthier, more light-hearted, and far more relaxed than his opposite in London and New York. He played more and worried less than the man at home. *Maskee* everything!

Jim Bentley, who worked next to me in the office, was a floating reporter. The floater worked his way across the Pacific, using the English-language newspapers in Honolulu, Manila, Tokyo, and Kobe. He stayed on the job only long enough to acquire money for the next step, or as long as the city interested him. From the Philippines and Japan, he would inevitably arrive in one of the Treaty Ports in China. He could be reasonably sure of his chances there because so many other reporters, also floating, were continually moving on. From China, he could try Singapore and Bangkok. Then, depending on the state of his liver and digestion, he might make the long jump to India before starting the return trip. The floater seldom came back to America. He was rootless, unencumbered, and he liked it that way. Besides, life in the Far East was more pleasant than at home, and editors in the Treaty Ports were much less demanding. The tramp reporters I knew in China no doubt would still be there today but for the Communists.

Jim had a hobby and he found Shanghai the ideal place in which to pursue it. He "collected nationalities," as he put it. That is, he studied the women of different countries and the differences, if any, between them. What interested Jim about a woman was, not her looks or personality, but where she came from. He could be very attentive to some frightening creature, lavishing money and time on her, if he had never known a woman of the same nationality.

He professed to be wholly serious in his studies and kept records in a file of cards, with a few terse details. . . . "Erika.

22. Icelandic. Over six feet tall. Very strong. Bites" . . . or . . .
"Maria. 19. Eurasian. Dutch and Javanese. Beautiful but serious inferiority complex."

There were thirty-seven cards in his file, but not one for a Japanese girl, although he had worked in Tokyo. I asked why.

"Because that was different," he said. "She was the only one I ever really cared about. She worked in a bar in Yokohama, and that's where I met her. It was almost a month before a spot opened up on the paper in Tokyo, and the money began running low. I didn't want to touch my reserves, the dough I always keep for passage, because that's a bad thing to do. You can really wind up on the beach if you can't get out of a place. Anyway, I mentioned it to Fumiko one time in the bar. She didn't say anything for a minute or two. Then she said I could come and live at her place. She had a little one-room house out near Omori. No parents or relatives. She didn't want a damn thing from me except companionship. I stayed with her all the time I was in Japan and I've never been so spoiled in my life. I guess I got pretty serious about her." He paused, remembering, and shook his head slightly. "I used to watch her wake up in the morning," he said. "She looked like a rosebud blooming when she opened her eyes and smiled."

"It sounds like a nice setup," I said. "Why did you leave?"

"I don't know," he said. "Just wanted to see this town, I guess. Anyway, I don't need a card to remember her."

Jim stayed in his apartment, nursing a hangover, on the morning of the murders; otherwise, of course, he would have been assigned to cover the story. The report came from the police early in the morning. "Take a cab and skip out to this address on the rue de Montigny," said Al Meyer. "Somebody wiped out a whole family, they say."

An ambulance and two police cars stood in front of the house, and a crowd of Chinese and foreigners stood chattering across the street. It was a big house, surrounded by the usual high wall covered with broken glass, obviously the home of wealthy Chinese.

The French Concession had its own police force, separate from that of the International Settlement. The officers were native French, and the patrolmen were drawn from the colonies of France—tough little Annamites or hulking Negroes from Madagascar. I walked up to an officer and showed him my police card.

"It is ver' bad," he said. "Even for Shanghai. *Hier soir* the assassin come here *avec un merlin.*" He made a gesture of chopping with both hands.

"A sword? A knife?"

"*Non, pas un couteau.* Heavier. Bigger. *Un merlin* is for cut meat."

"A meat cleaver!"

"*C'est ça.* And he was go through the house, from this room to this room to this room, and zoop!" He drew his forefinger across his throat.

"Cut some throats?"

"More than that. He has take off heads, *comme la guillotine.*"

"Holy smoke! How many?"

"Ten of them. Seven of the family and three *domestiques.*"

"Can I go in?"

"*Peut-être. Je vais demander.* But it is not pretty, *monsieur.*"

"This is old stuff to me," I said. "You know, reporters see a lot of—"

At that moment two Annamites came out carrying a stretcher. They apparently had wrapped the body in the bed clothing in which the victim had died. As they passed, the bloody sheets fell open part way. The body was headless. The victim, man or woman, had been very fat. The headless corpse was somehow more grotesque by reason of the corpulence— all that flesh with nothing now to hold it together. I lit a cigarette, a Three Castles, to help me keep down my nausea.

The officer beckoned from the doorway. I felt my knees

trembling when I entered the house. He led me to another officer. "This is *le capitaine*," he said.

The captain spoke flawless English. He quickly related the known details. Shortly after daybreak a loitering ricksha boy heard screams in the house. Suddenly a little boy, a child of six or seven, ran out, hysterical with fright. The ricksha man found a policeman, who went inside, saw room after room of horror, and calmly telephoned headquarters from a bedroom where two headless bodies lay. The killer had entered through a large French window leading to the garden.

"It was someone who knew the house very well," said the captain. "He knew where to find the cleaver in the kitchen. The little boy could not tell us much, but he said he heard nothing and saw no lights in any of the rooms when he wakened. The poor child, he must have run from one room to another, and each place he found—I will show you."

"A couple more questions first, Captain. Did nobody try to put up a fight?"

"Apparently only one of the servants. There are signs of a struggle there. The others, however, could not have heard a sound. He must have been a very strong man with a very sharp cleaver."

"I am told he killed ten people."

"That is correct—the man and his wife, his parents, two boys and a little girl, the cook, and two houseboys."

"Any idea who did it and why?"

"Perhaps," he said. "We know something about the gentleman who owns this house. He had connections with some not entirely legitimate businesses and also some political enemies. He had reason for needing the protection of the concession. However, it doesn't look like the work of a gang. If it were opium or smuggling or one of the rackets, the gang would not go to so much trouble and incur so much risk to remove a whole family, including the children. They would handle it much more neatly and safely with a bullet."

"Besides, there is the little boy. Why was he spared?"

"Exactly. Why? We have learned that the man discharged the cook's helper last week and refused to pay him whatever wages were due him. There was quite a row. The other servants threw him bodily out of the house. We also know that the little boy was his favorite in the family. He used to play with the child frequently. Picture him standing over the sleeping child last night with the cleaver raised, ready to strike. Suppose, at the last instant, he emerges from his insanity and remembers. A bizarre thought, is it not? Worthy of your Edgar Allan Poe. Now I will show you the rooms. Be careful. The floors are slippery."

When I came into the office, Al Meyer looked at me curiously. "You're a little pale around the gills, pal," he said. "How was it, pretty juicy?"

I gave him a summary of the facts. He asked me to describe the house. The memory of it was only too vivid.

"You'll get used to this sort of thing," he said. "When they get started, the Chinese are rough customers. There are probably a dozen cases every night like this one over in the Chinese city. Only we never hear about them." He glanced at the clock. "You've got plenty of time, pal. Now, let me give you a piece of advice about writing this story."

"Yes, sir?"

"Don't write it."

"What do you mean?"

"Don't write it. Let it tell itself. Describe it just as you described it to me a minute ago. For instance, you said a cop slipped in the blood and fell. What did he say?"

"He said 'merde'."

"Good. Put that in the story. Take the customers inside that house and let 'em walk through blood and smell it on the walls. But play it low. This is the kind of story that tells itself."

In the afternoon, when the paper was on the street, he went out to the business office and came back with an envelope.

"Here's a month's salary, pal," he said. "You're on the payroll now."

There were twelve bills in the envelope, two $100 notes, the rest in tens—$300 in Shanghai dollars, equal to about $125 in American money. In the morning it was all gone.

Chapter XIV

METROPOLIS
ON THE MUD FLATS

SHANGHAI was a world in itself—two distinct cultures in one, many nations in one, a political exoticism, a hippogriff. That Shanghai has vanished, gone with the wind. No other city quite like it ever rose on the earth before or is likely to appear again. So, let us pin down the picture of Shanghai as it was— the beauty, the wealth, the wickedness, the peculiar functions it served for good and evil, and the rare creatures who moved through the streets.

It was a Western city, remember, standing on Chinese soil, but not subject to Chinese authority. A political island. White men built it out of nothing and made it the fifth busiest seaport in the world, one of the richest. It governed itself under its own rules and regulations efficiently and honestly. Its own courts administered justice, based on Western legal principles and procedures. Foreign troops protected it, and a private army, the Shanghai Volunteers, went into uniform and took stations in moments of danger. At one time Chinese were not even permitted to live inside the boundaries of the foreign settlements. Later they flocked in, grateful for the security.

This was the proud city-state on the banks of the Whangpoo.

In physical appearance Shanghai borrowed the features of many capitals. At one corner it was London. A handsome wide boulevard reminded you of Paris. The skyline and some of the bank buildings were New York. The northern suburb, Hong-kew, was as Japanese as Tokyo. There was dragon's blood in the city's veins as well, and this overlay of China gave it a completely unique quality.

The mud huts in the Chinese city around Shanghai looked at steel- and-glass skyscrapers, fine hotels and apartment houses in the International Settlement and beautiful homes in the French Concession. In his office, high above the bund, a busi-nessman talked with Detroit. Through the window he could see the Walled City, eight centuries old, and hear the temple gong, struck by a monk. It was only a step from the elegant *parfumerie* and the *pâtisserie* smelling of napoleons in the French Concession to the stench of Soochow Creek, where the sampan people lived. At night a million lights put a great golden arch in the sky above Bubbling Well Road, the Avenue Joffre, the bund, and Kiukiang Road. Outside, surrounding the island of light on all sides, lay China—dark, silent, waiting.

One way in which to picture this is to imagine a Chinese city in, let us say, Maryland. It would be on a bend in the Patapsco River (the Whangpoo), twelve miles from Chesa-peake Bay (the Yangtze River) and fifty-four miles from the Atlantic (the East China Sea). In area it would cover between ten and eleven square miles. The rivers, railroads, and coastal shipping lines would bring the products of the Middle West, the Mississippi Valley, and most of the Atlantic Seaboard through this port. Half the foreign trade of the United States would flow over its docks. From outside the borders of this Oriental metropolis three million native Americans, squatting in the doorways of their log cabins, would gaze enviously at soaring pagodas, exquisite marble bridges, gates of red lacquer, and buildings with glazed tile roofs and curling eaves blazing like blue-green fire in the sunshine.

Who knows? It may happen to us when China extracts her pound of flesh from history.

During the Opium War in 1841 an angry Chinese wrote—prophetically, but a century too early—a manifesto:

"There is that English nation, whose ruler is as often a woman as a man, and which devours Southern peoples, first peeling the fat off their estates. Their island is a petty one. They trust entirely to wooden dragons [ships]. Could we but reach them, we should hurl them over as the blast does the thin bamboo. If we let them settle on the river, it will be like opening the door and bowing in Mr. Wolf! In the hour of our patriotism, even our wives and daughters, finical and delicate as jewels, have learned to discourse of arms. The high gods clearly behold. Fight till the golden pool is fully restored to honorable peace" (quoted by J. S. Thomson in *The Chinese,* published by Bobbs-Merrill in 1909).

He singled out the British because, of course, that was their war. But France soon joined Britain in other wars. And the Chinese patriot could legitimately have said a few words about the United States. Americans had organized a thriving trade in opium, bringing it from Turkey to China in defiance of China's prohibition of the drug.

In any event, the "wooden dragons" prevailed with an ease and celerity that surprised the world. The "high gods" veiled their faces from China. The carving-up process began.

In 1842 the Chinese gave Britain a morsel of mud between Soochow Creek and the Walled City. It was low, marshy, often threatened by the Whangpoo. Perhaps they scorned it as a sop to the barbarians, a cheap price for a lost war. Perhaps they thought malaria, typhoid, and dysentery would soon rid them of these pushy people. Or it may be that they thought nothing of permanent importance could be build on a mud bank. They did not know their Empire Builder. For the British have a sixth sense, a divining rod behind their foreheads that quivers when they set foot on land where, however unlikely it may seem, a great commercial port will grow.

Soon after the British settled in, the American consul planted the Stars and Stripes on the north side of Soochow Creek. The French followed. Then, in 1854, the three consuls—French, American, and British—sat down together and organized a merger. They put the French and British concessions into one, the International Settlement. The Americans had hopped into the game early. Shortly after the Opium War, they had obtained the "most-favored-nation" status in China by treaty. Then in 1858 in the Treaty of Tientsin they solidified their position, present and future. Article 30 said the two governments "hereby agree that should at any time the Ta Tsing Empire grant to any nation, or the merchants or citizens of any nation, any right, privilege or favor, connected either with navigation, political or other intercourse, which is not conferred by this Treaty, such right, privilege and favor shall at once freely inure to the benefit of the United States, its public officers, merchants and citizens."

Or, in a word, if anybody succeeded in extracting another plum from China, by force of arms or other means, Americans automatically were to receive the same plum. An American in the International Settlement thus, in effect, lived in an American Concession, protected from the Chinese government and immune to Chinese law.

A little later the French withdrew from the arrangement (always difficult, the French), returning to the previous status of a French Concession with its own government and courts.

Finally the Japanese arrived. They settled in Hongkew in large numbers and quickly began to agitate for representation on the Municipal Council, the governing organ of the International Settlement. They got it, too, even before the Chinese.

In its final form, therefore, "Shanghai" consisted of the two foreign entities—the International Settlement and the French Concession—plus four big Chinese communities composing "Greater Shanghai."

Population statistics are slippery. People came and went according to business considerations, peace or civil war in the hinterland, or because they were "floaters." In its heyday, however, before the 1937 war between Japan and China, the city probably had about 20,000 Japanese (the figure came closer to 30,000 by 1939), 13,000 White Russians, 12,000 British, 4,000 Americans, 3,000 French, 2,000 Germans, and 15,000 other foreign nationals. More than 1,000,000 Chinese lived in the International Settlement, probably closer to 2,000,000 lived in the French Concession, and around 3,000,000 lived in the suburbs.

The flags of thirteen nations flew over Shanghai. After the rise of the Nazis in Germany, the city undoubtedly contained more separate nationalities than are represented today in the United Nations.

And the Chinese resented every flag and every inch of Shanghai. Many of them benefited by the city's existence, as will be explained, but many more resented it. They resented it as a symbol of China's humiliations and as a fact of foreign privilege. They resented the soldiers, sailors, and marines in the streets and the warships off the bund. They resented having no Chinese members on the Municipal Council. Most of all, they resented "extrality," the treaty provisions that set up special courts for foreigners with foreign judges interpreting a case under foreign codes of law.

The spirit reflected in that Opium War manifesto never died out. Indeed, as the years passed and the students and intellectuals began to fight for China, the flames of national feeling rose high in Shanghai.

Campaigns for representation in the governments of the Settlement and the French Concession began before World War I. The Chinese argument had a familiar ring to British

and American ears—"taxation without representation." At first
the white men made token concessions. They admitted Chinese
as "advisors." But in 1926 the Chinese breached the dike. Three
took seats as voting members. The Municipal Council then consisted of five British members, three Americans, three Chinese,
and two Japanese. The action was a safety-valve move, taken
under pressure of the increasingly strong spirit of nationalism.

On the matter of the courts, however, the foreigner remained
obdurate, and his home government backed him up. The
Shanghailander held that Chinese codes and legal procedures
needed a thorough overhauling before they would be suited
to modern life. But what he feared most of all were the Chinese
judges. He asserted that a Chinese judge could be bribed, that
he would be subject to governmental pressure, that he would
be biased in cases involving foreigners. Or, at the least, that a
Chinese judge too often invoked some rule-of-thumb reasoning
of his own, some personal idiosyncrasy, in his decision. No, the
Shanghailander, however deep his roots, would not have stayed
in the city under jurisdiction of Chinese courts. He couldn't
have.

In Washington at that time, a man who was less sentimental
about the Chinese and more clearheaded in his judgment of
them than many Americans was deliberating the problem of
"extrality." He was William R. Castle, Undersecretary of State.
His diary for July 23, 1929, says:

"The Department is inclining more and more to the belief
that we had better give up these rights. I am not sure yet where
I stand. If we give up the rights before the Chinese even attempt to reform their judicial system, all Americans might as
well get out. Obviously, we should not do it unless other nations do it also.

"The Secretary's [Henry L. Stimson] idea that we should
thereby gain great credit with the Chinese is bunk. The Chinese will do us in the eye whenever they can, and will certainly
not have any great sense of gratitude which will make them

do unto us what they would not do unto others. On the other hand, if they announce to the world that extraterritorial rights are abolished, I wonder what we are going to do about it? We could not go to war, even without the Kellogg Pact."

The Chinese, as we have seen, did unilaterally proclaim the end of the "unequal treaties" as of December 31, 1929. However, they were unable to make it stick, and the Japanese attack in 1931 induced them to put aside the problem for the time being.

Apart from nationalist feeling, the Chinese attacked "extrality" on two other grounds. They claimed it gave the foreign businessman a distinct competitive advantage over the Chinese merchant. In litigation arising out of a business dispute between a foreigner and a Chinese, they insisted the foreign judge always favored the foreigner. Furthermore, they argued that "extrality" and the special political status of Shanghai made the city a sanctuary for criminals, political enemies of the Kuomintang, and other persons "wanted" by the central government.

This certainly was a fact. If a Chinese fled to the Settlement for political reasons—to evade taxes, or because he was having trouble with the government over the thousand-and-one rackets —a Chinese policeman could not arrest him there, nor could a tax collector serve him with a summons. The Chinese had to request the Settlement police to make the arrest. Even then, however, the Municipal Council did not automatically extradite the wanted man. The usual procedure was to give him a preliminary hearing in court, with a member of the Council in attendance.

Yes, Shanghai was a refuge. But not for the evildoer alone. As far back as the Taiping rebellion it had become the haven for Chinese, coolies and peasants as well as the rich, in times of danger in the country. It was during this period that they first received permission to enter the Settlement. Thereafter, whenever trouble threatened in the neighborhood, the Chinese flocked toward Shanghai for protection under foreign guns.

Moreover, a rich Chinese had a very good reason for electing to build a beautiful house in the French Concession, even though living there might mean commuting frequently to the capital in Nanking. In Shanghai he felt much safer with foreign policemen patrolling the streets than he could feel in a Chinese city. Not that they could protect him completely from assassins and robbers. But at least it was more difficult for kidnappers to operate in the relatively small Settlement.

In the wild-West conditions in China during that time, kidnapping was big business. A gang even halted the famous "Blue Train" midway between Pukow and Tientsin on one occasion. They scooped up all the passengers, including foreigners. (The incident resulted in a wonderful *affaire diplomatique,* incidentally. Traveling with an ambassador in his compartment on the overnight journey was a lady other than his wife.) The bandits immediately released the captives. It was dangerous to try to collect ransom on a foreigner. But they held the Chinese until their families paid up. In Mongolia one day a young Chinese and I hid for hours behind a sand dune, waiting for a troop of mounted bandits to move off. He came from a rich family in Tientsin. "They probably would let you go," he said, "but they would keep me. In a few days my family would get the letter."

The kidnappers had developed an efficient psychological technique for extracting the ransom money from a family. The first letter fixed the amount and the date when it must be paid. This letter said the prisoner was in good health and would remain so, provided the terms were met. If they were not, a follow-up letter arrived. Sometimes it contained the little finger or perhaps the ear of the victim. If his relatives still refused to comply, other letters with more vital parts of his body would be sent. People learned from experience that the gangs meant business. I was told that a foreign commercial firm in Hankow ignored the messages when a gang kidnapped its *comprador,* or go-between, and called in the police instead. One day a package was found at the office door. It contained the *comprador's* head.

❦

Three other groups, all victims of the world's between-wars malaise, also found Shanghai a haven.

The White Russians came in the early 1920's, fleeing the Bolsheviks. Many were well-born, but few knew a trade. How they survived was a miracle. Obviously, they could not compete with the coolies for the unskilled trades. They certainly could not pull rickshas or work on the docks with a carrying-pole. A few, being linguists, found employment as translators. All the best-sellers in the world were copied in Shanghai and sold in cheap editions—needless to say, without royalties to the authors. The majority of Russians, however, became servants, policemen, night watchmen, waiters, bodyguards. The doorman at your apartment looked like a grand duke in his winter greatcoat, and quite possibly he was. The women went into dance halls. They were famous throughout the Far East for their beauty. "Going to the Far East? Lucky boy. Stop in at the Palais de Danse, 50 Bubbling Well Road, and give my regards to Olga and Sonya." For her work a girl somehow acquired an evening gown. She mended it and tenderly nursed it and held it together as long as possible. Every night from nine till dawn she danced and talked with the customers; she was pawed over by slobbering old roués, insulted by perverts, clutched close by the scum from every ship in the Seven Seas. She collected part of the fee for each dance, even more for your drink. Her own drink would be tea, colored to look like whisky, which she frankly admitted if you asked her. She had to be tough and shrewd to stand the life, and she was. But if you showed her the smallest courtesy, the least shred of respect, it transformed her. She became sweet, gentle, understanding. Each had her own little story, a variation on a basic theme. . . . "In Russia I was a princess (faraway, remembering expression). . . . The Bolsheviks killed my parents and my younger brother (slight pause for effect). . . . My older brother and I managed to get to Harbin. He worked there until he was crippled in an accident. Now, of course, I support him (shrug of beautiful, bare shoulders). . . . It is very hard, but we live (expression of fleeting sadness followed by brave smile). . . . *Nichevo*—or, *maskee*, as they say here."

Only the details of the story varied. Naturally, no one believed them except the occasional sailor and the crying drunk. Don't be a sucker. And yet . . .

Dossia Tcherbina looked enough like Clara Bow, the movie star, to be her double. She always wore red, perhaps because because the red gown was the only one she owned, and fixed her black hair the way the actress fixed hers. It delighted her when the customers called her "Clara." On Russian New Year she invited me to the celebration at her apartment. There in a wheel chair, legs covered with a robe, sat a handsome young man. And there on the wall was a family photograph—a tall, bearded man in uniform, a queenly woman in a long white dress, holding a baby with long curls, and two boys standing beside her in a beautiful room.

We drank the pathetic, hopeless toast to the day when "those murderers" would be hanging, head down, from the walls of the Kremlin, and we would all meet again in Moscow.

Then, a decade after the Russians, came the people from Germany, Poland, Czechoslovakia, and Austria. All they asked was peace and a place to live, but they discovered this was asking a great deal, indeed, in Shanghai. For by the time they arrived, the Russians had a firm grip on the type of work open to white men. Not even minor clerical jobs in the business offices remained; they went to the bilingual Chinese. So, you saw these people—sensitive, intelligent, gently bred—coming across the Garden Bridge in the morning, searching for work. They always clutched a brief case, as they had done in Prague or Vienna. What could be in those brief cases now? Nothing but habit. They would go from office to office, walking, climbing stairs, until they dropped. To see their stricken faces made you want to cry.

Lastly, there was a third group, composed of all nationalities. Shanghai was the last port of call for the derelict, the floater, the brokenhearted, the defeated and despairing.

Oh, yes, there was a Beat Generation in the 1930's. It existed before World War II and before the Great Depression. Probably it has always existed. But you were more aware of it in Shanghai then elsewhere because of the high saturation there. For years Shanghai had been the world capital of the Beat Generation.

See that gray-haired man with the monocle? Looks aristocratic, doesn't he? He is. Comes from one of the finest families in France. Graduate of St. Cyr. Great cavalry officer. Wonderful war record. Rode in one of the first tank attacks. Family pays him to stay out of France now. He's on opium. Eats one meal a day, one bowl of rice and vegetables, and doesn't drink or smoke. How come that diet? Don't you know that opium is delicate stuff? You only get the full wallop on an empty stomach. (This, I discovered in two attempts, was quite true. All I got was a great thirst and some bad dreams.)

See that woman strolling in front of the China United apartments with the Chinese girl? The tall, rather severe-looking type? She was a teacher of Romance languages in an expensive finishing school for girls somewhere in the States. Seems she took to seducing the young ladies, right and left, and the word got around. Now she's the *amah* for her Chinese girl-friend, who is a prostitute. Quaint old Chinese custom. In this town you don't make the deal directly. You negotiate with the *amah* who walks the streets with her. Pretty fancy floozie, wot? An *amah* who speaks five languages to make the arrangements for her.

There was the tall, grave-faced Englishman, almost a ringer for Cordell Hull, who had been a great lawyer until he stole an estate. There was the ex-clergyman, now a professor of religion, who drank himself silly every night. His wife had run away with his best friend. There was the man who called himself "General" Cohen, but was better known along the length of the China Coast as "Two Gun" Cohen. He was a real gun fighter, a killer, feared and respected in a city that crawled with killers. "Two Gun" had been Sun Yat-sen's bodyguard during the dangerous early days of the Revolution. After Sun's death, he worked for the doctor's widow. His friends would say affectionately of him: "That bastard would take your eye and peel it for a grape." There was the American who shaved his head and showed up at the tea dances in the Astor Hotel, wearing the robes of a Buddhist monk.

The Beat Generation in plenary session.

What do you want?

A husband? The town's full of single men—cultured, intelligent men. They will marry you just for a passport.

A mistress? You can have a genuine countess, or the daughter of an ex-millionaire from Bucharest, or any number of Chinese girls, all guaranteed virgins, who can be bought outright. Name your color and specifications.

Forgetfulness? Liquor is cheap, but if you want something stronger, the whole pharmacopoeia of narcotics is available in Shanghai—hashish, opium, Heroin.

Wisdom? Philosophy? Learning in Sinology? Go over to the Walled City and talk to the monks.

Excitement? Tonight we tour "Blood Alley," where you will see the most frightening stews in the world, whores so rotten that not even a lascar stoker would touch 'em, killers, hatchet men who can split your skull like a coconut, pickpockets, lepers. There will be at least one glorious brawl in "Blood Alley" between the U.S. marines and the Seaforth Highlanders in a bar. When it's over, they will be picking broken glass and splinters out of the heads of at least sixteen guys on both sides, and not a stick of furniture will be left in the place. The Scotties are not tall, but, brother, they're tough. I saw a stubby little runt knock the heavyweight champion of the Asiatic fleet clean over a table the other night. Then they'll all feel fine and go to another bar and pick a fight with the Italians or the French.

Gambling? Anything you want for any amount. Roulette, baccarat, *vingt et un,* poker, dice, fan-tan. Beautiful houses, too, with good food and the best champagne. The Syrian on the rue Cardinal Mercier also provides opium and girls in case your feet give out, standing around the tables.

How about a nice substantial racket? Shanghai is the front office of all the rackets ever invented, and you can make a lot of money in a hurry. There is gunrunning, counterfeiting, forging passports and identification papers, smuggling, and, of course, opium and other dope. You know what your houseboy does with your empty liquor bottle? He sells it to an outfit that fills it with cheap wine, or maybe just colored water, recaps and reseals it, and sells it as the real thing. Even the farmers have a little dodge. They blow water and sand down a chicken's gullet to make it weigh more at sale. Those are the standard rackets. They've always been here. But now that the war has started in Europe, some new ones have sprung up. For instance, materials and machinery addressed to firms in Shanghai somehow get up to Vladivostok and go across the Trans-Siberian to Russia and Germany. Another racket has to do with the new "wonder drugs," the sulfanilamides. Here's how it works. Inflation has set in. Money is losing its value; therefore people are looking for things to buy that won't lose their value. Some are putting everything they have into bottles of the sulfa drugs. What's wrong with that? Nothing. Except that you don't sell them genuine sulfa. You either "cut" it, as a bootlegger cuts whisky, or you mix up a solution of chalk and water that looks like sulfa. People can't tell the difference, even if they open the bottles and smell the stuff. These poor refugees from Europe are really being conned, simply because some of them have a little money left.

Escape? You escaped when you got off the ship here, mister. Now the problem is to escape Shanghai. A lot of people never make it. They've got Shanghai in their blood.

It was a wicked city—cynical, cruel, dangerous. It was a wonderful city, filled with kind, generous, good people, men and women who organized benefits for the Russians and the refugees, worked hard for the charities, saw to it that poor children had a real Christmas. The contrasts in Shanghai were incredibly wide in matters of money, morals, and position. And it was a truly gay place. Good and bad, the people were all gay, laughing at themselves and the world around them. The cynicism and world-weariness took the form of lighthearted raillery. They were dancing in the dark, and they knew it, and said "*Maskee.*" The good days of Shanghai were just about finished. Either Japan or China would soon put an end to them. The Japanese could take Shanghai any time they felt like it, and after 1939 the British couldn't stop them and the United States probably wouldn't. As for the Chinese, they were closing in. Where they could get away with it, they simply canceled the "unequal treaties," on which the Treaty Port system had been built, and negotiated for revisions where they could not. Either

way, the days of privilege and big profits were numbered.
Maskee!

At this point I must jump ahead of the story a few years. During the Korean War I met an Englishman who had just come from China. When the Communists took Shanghai, some foreign business houses attempted to stay open and go on as before. They quickly discovered the impossibility of it. However, it was no simple matter to liquidate and get out. The Communists refused to let a man leave until his firm had agreed to pay heavy severance wages to its Chinese employees. The English said the Communists demanded the equivalent of $2000, gold, for a janitor. They argued that this was more than the janitor could hope to earn in his whole lifetime. The Communist official's reply is a key motif in the China of today:

"You people have had a very good thing out of China for years. Now the time has come to pay it back to us."

Chapter XV

JUKONG ROAD

THE HOUSE on Jukong Road seemed unusually dark and silent, considering that a party was supposed to be going on there. It was a big, two-story house, set back from the street by a garden. Shutters covered the windows. Not a sound nor a ray of light came from the inside as we stepped out of the rickshas and passed through the gate. There a darker shadow caught my eye. Standing in the garden, a few feet from the path, a man watched us go to the front door. I could not see his face in the dim light. He said nothing. George Ssu ignored him, although he too must have seen the man.

George was a translator on the *Evening Post*. He came from Loyang, a city in the interior, five hundred miles west of Shanghai. He had learned English at Nankai University in Tientsin. He spoke only vaguely of his work there, of his family, of most things in his life. He was a dour, humorless man, short-tempered, easily offended. We were on speaking terms in the newsroom, but not friendly. I judged that he disliked all foreigners and, after a small collision, me in particular. As a translator he combed the Chinese newspapers for possibly useful stories to the *Evening Post*. His own news interests ran to political and economic material, editorials and so on, which seldom had any value for the paper. On this occasion Al Meyer had told him to translate a crime story and give it to me to rewrite. As usual, I was watching the clock, tensing as the deadline drew near. George worked slowly, typing out a few words at a time. The clock ticked louder and louder. Finally, I asked him to let me have as much of the story as he had translated so that I could start. He refused. We had a brief argument. George looked at me coldly and said: "I have my limitations, Mr. Morin." Then, after a slight pause: "And you have yours."

So I was surprised when he invited me to the party. "Just a few people who meet from time to time and talk," he said. "A kind of a discussion group. Sometimes it's interesting, sometimes not."

"Friends of yours?"

"Well, yes and no," he said. "I don't always know everybody who comes."

Riding in the ricksha through the rivers of traffic in front of the Wing On and Sincere department stores, I asked George if the group met regularly.

"Very irregularly," he said. "There is nothing formal or organized about it."

"And do you always meet in the house where we are going now?"

"Oh, no," he said. "Different places, depending on who is the host. My place is too small. I can't afford anything better, though, on my salary and the insulting allowance my father gives me."

He did not name the host for the meeting that night.

"You're nice to ask me," I said.

George did not answer.

In the house, he led the way through the foyer into a large, beautifully decorated room. Paintings, Chinese and Western, covered the walls. The furniture was a perfect blend of French and Chinese. A heavy rug of the type made in Peking, lion-colored and with an intricate design, lay on the floor. A magnificent teakwood table stood in one corner, holding a jade cat and a tall bronze wine vessel. Both looked old and genuine. If they were, they belonged in a museum. Whoever the owner was, he had money and taste. I did not hear his name. George

casually presented me to a few persons, hardly a formal intro-
duction, for he did not say who they were.

About twenty people, Chinese and foreigners, were standing
around the room. A gaunt, bony woman with stringy hair and
bad teeth was speaking German with a lean, tanned man who
could have been almost any nationality. Two others, apparently man and wife, were examining a brass astrolabe, discussing it in French. In another group a Chinese girl was talking
English with two foreign men, one stubby and wearing thick-
lensed glasses, the other bearded and tall. A lumpy woman in
tweeds sat reading a Leftist American magazine, oblivious to
everyone. It was an odd assortment of people to be gathered
for a "party."

A few moments later the gaunt woman rapped for attention
and said: "Now we shall begin." The accent sounded Swiss-
German. "Dr. Ho is ready if everyone will please to take seats."

Dr. Ho was short, fat, and well groomed. He wore an air of
elegance. His black hair, streaked with gray, had been carefully
brushed. Polish glittered on the nails of his graceful little hands.
He wore a black suit with a gray vest. He reminded me of a
cultured, worldly priest.

He moved over beside the teakwood table and picked up a
sheaf of papers. The gaunt woman was saying: "Doctor Ho is
going to discuss the social policies of Wang An-shih" (I took a
mental note: look up Wang An-shih tomorrow. The trouble
with Sinology is that every point you look up suggests ten thousand others that need looking up) "as there is a close similarity
between conditions then and now. Perhaps his planning could
be applicable in China today. We shall discuss that when Doctor Ho has told us about them."

In the policies of Wang An-shih the Chinese can legitimately
claim to have invented a Socialist system nine centuries before
Karl Marx. To the Chinese who knew his history, Communism
brought few new ideas. Something similar to it had been in
practice in the eleventh century. Wang, an odd mixture of

politician and philosopher, held a high office in the government during the Sung dynasty. His accomplishments were many: he wrote legislation designed to break up the estates of the big landlords; sought to stabilize the prices of farm products by setting up state-owned granaries; changed the tax structure so that a farmer with more fertile land paid higher taxes than his neighbor with poor land; abolished forced labor and tried to do away with tenant farmers; took measures to prevent speculation in basic commodities; fought the money lenders by loaning State funds at lower rates than they did; instituted a minimum wage law, old-age pensions, and health insurance.

In a word, China had Socialism before there was a Russia; in fact, she had it at about the time Sviatopolk "the Damned" was liquidating his brothers in the fight for power in the first Russian dynasty.

"Imagine," said Dr. Ho, smiling. "Nearly a thousand years ago." He paused to let the point sink in.

"It is remarkable," said Dr. Ho. "But what I have long regarded as even more remarkable is that an important official of the Sungs should have cared in the slightest about the masses, had any sense of responsibility for their welfare at all. This, it seems to me, is even more astonishing than his policies."

"Very different from the present 'Soong dynasty,'" said the man with thick spectacles. Everyone laughed, even George Ssu. A hum of conversation ran around the room.

The lumpy woman in the tweed suit spoke. She had a strong English accent, but did not appear to be British. "Then there is a tradition in China for Socialist economic policies?"

"Hardly a tradition," said Dr. Ho, bowing slightly, "but at least a precedent, if I may be permitted to put it that way."

"And then did others carry them on after him?"

"Unfortunately," he said, "much of what he proposed never came into practice during his own lifetime. The State-owned granaries functioned for a time. And of course we know that the State did loan money at interest rates of less than half what the usurers charged the farmers. As for the rest, the landlords, the merchants, and the wealthy aligned themselves against Wang and succeeded in blocking the reforms he proposed."

"History repeats itself," said a middle-aged Chinese man. This time no one laughed.

Across the room from me a pretty Chinese girl, tall and rounded, shifted in her chair, crossing her legs. The slit in her tight-fitting sheath gown exposed a generous length of silk calf. She caught me examining it and grinned impishly.

Her name was Lola Liang, and it was largely because of her that I came to the subsequent meetings. Why had she chosen that name? "Because I wish to be like Lola Montez—naughty." I asked her if the people who attended the meetings were Communists. She thought a few were, but the others were only "candidates," as she put it. She doubted that George Ssu was a Communist. "He is only a grouch, sore at the world." Lola was no Communist, either, or anything else. She held somewhat the same view as Philip Li, the student at Lingnan, namely that nothing could be done for the millions of poor people in China and that one was lucky not to be among them. Then why did she attend the meetings? "Excitement. Perhaps some night the police will raid one. Also, to meet rather stupid Americans who will take me to the Little Club. Now, stop asking questions and drink that wine—unless, of course, you are afraid of Chinese wine."

I went to two more meetings. They came at irregular intervals and were held in different places, as George Ssu had said. Only a few of the same people appeared regularly—the gaunt woman, the man with thick glasses, some of the same Chinese. Lola said the thin, tanned man was a naturalized Frenchman, a journalist.

In Shanghai it was not always easy to identify a man's nationality. However, I do not believe any Russians came to the meetings. (Dr. Richard Sorge, the great Red spy, must have been in the city then, organizing his first espionage network. I did not meet him until several years later in Tokyo. Soviet intelligence agents steered clear of ordinary Party members in China and Japan.) Neither the Soviet Union nor any of its works ever came into the discussions as topics. The words "Communist" or "Communism" never were uttered by any of the regulars. Superficially the sessions appeared to be pleasant little discussions of economic and social problems, not always even contemporary problems. If the police had raided a meeting, they would have heard little that could be called dangerous. The man in the garden at Jukong Road evidently was a lookout, however, and there may have been lookouts each time. The Chinese police, remember, could not make arrests in the foreign-concession areas of Shanghai, but they could request foreign police to pick up people. Someone obviously considered the lookout a desirable precaution.

The format varied only in detail: a speaker, sometimes two, was followed by questions and answers and general discussion. The subjects seemed eminently innocent. Once a Chinese woman described current educational movements in China— vocational, rural, citizenship training, and so on. She even described projects organized by the Nationalist government, the missionaries, and others! I thought I detected a note of anxiety in one of the questions put to her. "Are these likely to succeed?" The woman thought not. A man reported on the famine in Suiyuan province in the northwest. Quietly, with studied understatement, he noted that landlords and speculators were taking advantage of the tragedy to buy up land from the peasants.

The regulars made no obvious moves to use any of this material for propaganda. They circuitously planted suggestions. In the discussion of Wang An-shih, for example, Dr. Ho asked how many in the room were familiar with the man and his story. Three Chinese and one foreigner raised their hands. With mock dismay he asked: "What is happening in our universities? What do they teach our young men and women about the history of China?"

The French journalist wondered, casually, whether means could not be found to bring that type of information to the attention of the professors and students. "Through a series of pamphlets, perhaps?"

Taken separately, none of the reports and not much of the ensuing discussion could be called subversive. There was no frantic arise-ye-masses atmosphere. From the total effect, however, a picture of China emerged, a picture of conditions growing steadily worse, a picture of a central government that refused to do anything about them. It is what we call today "the soft sell."

The third meeting contrasted greatly with the first two that I attended. An undercurrent of excitement crackled in the room. This time a foreigner I had not seen before acted as chairman. He hurried the guests into seats and then introduced the speaker. "Mister Ling brings information of an important event in the south," he said.

Mr. Ling looked tough and weather-beaten, as though he had spent a good many days out of doors. He said he had just come from Kiangsi, a mountainous province in South China. He lost no time in delivering an announcement. "A people's government has been established in Kiangsi," he said.

It meant little to me. War lords, dissident elements in the Kuomintang, rivals of Chiang Kai-shek and their supporters regularly announced the formation of another "government" somewhere in China. One by one, as he could get around to them, Chiang either persuaded them to disband, or destroyed them. But he never succeeded in destroying the one that began in Kiangsi. It became the seed of the regime now ruling China.

❦

Long afterward a terrifying echo came from the meetings in Shanghai.

When the Japanese attacked Pearl Harbor, I was in Indochina. It was then a French colony, but the Vichy government had agreed to permit Japan to station an army in the country. Ostensibly, the reason for the presence of Japanese troops in Indochina was to prevent arms from reaching China via Haiphong and Hanoi. Actually, the colony was the springboard for the attack on Malaya and Singapore. On Pearl Harbor day the Japanese interned all British and Americans. I was among them.

Not long afterward they put me through a long examination. They had compiled a very complete dossier on me. To my amazement, I found that they believed I had been a spy!

The dossier contained a note about the Shanghai meetings. "I went to two or three of them," I said, "but I am neither a Communist nor a spy."

Who asked me the first time? I couldn't remember. What were the names of some others at the meetings? Here I could truthfully say I did not know, and that anyway they probably used false names. The *Kempei-tai*, secret police, officers agreed. Had I ever seen any of the same people anywhere else? Never. None had come to Japan? I had not seen or heard of them there.

"I was a completely unimportant reporter at the time," I said. "Why would the Communists be interested in me?"

The officers looked at me as if I were an idiot. "They were interested in all journalists," one said. "You were just one of many."

Chapter XVI

THE RED TRAIL

Milestones on the Red Trail:

1919: Russia dazzles China with a glittering offer to cancel all concessions.

1921: Chinese Communist party formed in Shanghai.

1922: Dr. Sun Yat-sen, "father of the Chinese Revolution," meets an amiable Russian salesman.

1923: Sun sends Chiang Kai-shek to Russia.

1924: Russia renounces all territory, privileges, and concessions seized by Tsarist Russia. The Sino-Soviet "honeymoon" begins.

1925: Sun Yat-sen dies. Chiang Kai-shek comes to power.

1926: Chiang launches the Northern Expedition, leading to the "unification" of China.

1927: Chinese troops, under Leftist commanders, murder foreigners in Nanking; Chiang splits with the Communists in a bloody purge; first local "soviet" is set up in Hunan; the "honeymoon" ends.

1928: United States recognizes the Kuomintang as the legal central government of China.

1929: The war lords again take the field against Chiang.

1930: Communists establish first "provisional government" in Kiangsi. Chiang launches first "extermination campaign" to crush the Red regime.

1931: "Extermination campaign" fails. Communists set up first "Central Soviet Government of the Soviet Republic of

China." Japan attacks Manchuria; Chiang elects not to fight.

1932: Communists win immense propaganda victory by "declaring war" on Japan—although fifteen hundred miles from the combat area.

1934: Fifth "extermination campaign" forces Communists to leave Kiangsi. Famous Long March begins.

1935: Communists, after six-thousand mile Long March, reach northern Shensi and establish new base of operations against Chiang.

1936: A war lord kidnaps Chiang Kai-shek. His government and the Communists join forces again in a "united front" against Japan.

1937: Japan attacks north China, and the "undeclared war" begins.

1939: World War II starts in Europe.

1940: Japan joins Germany and Italy in the Axis alliance.

1941: Pearl Harbor.

1945: The United States and Britain hand over invaluable territory to Russia in the Far East, concealing the agreement from China. Russia enters Manchuria in the "five days'" war against Japan.

1946: Russians withdraw from Manchuria and it becomes the main base of Communist operations against the Nationalist government.

1947: Communists gain time, talking, while American envoys keep urging Chiang to bring the Reds into his central government.

1949: Communists complete conquest of China.

❦

The foregoing information is intended as a sketch map of the tortuous journey that began in Moscow in 1919 and ended thirty years later when the Communists raised the Red flag in Peiping in 1949.

Between these two dates lies a vast, tangled forest of history. The light of incontrovertible fact has not yet penetrated to all the twists and turns in the wilderness, and probably never will. Contradictory testimony, like a low cloud, fogs over much of it. Much remains to be explained. The footprints of many principals—Chinese, Americans, Russians, and Japanese—disappear in the underbrush. The main road, however, is visible. Along it are some tall peaks, like cardinal points, which remain always in view. They are:

1. *Russia's long-view policy on China.* Even before 1919 Soviet leaders perceived the importance of the Chinese Revolution in the blueprint of world revolution.

2. *Misery in China.* The Nationalists inherited it. The Communists, not having power or responsibility, were able to capitalize on the sufferings of the Chinese people. They needed only to promise.

3. *Chiang Kai-shek's enemies.* They gave him no peace. His government fought the war lords, Communists, and Japanese continually, sometimes in overlapping struggles. There were no long intervals of peace during which measures could be taken to alleviate conditions in China.

4. *Communist public relations.* They were good. The Reds succeeded, through various means, in bamboozling the peasants into considering them "the poor man's army," and in winning the support of students and intellectuals.

5. *The role of the United States.* Here the undergrowth is almost impenetrable. Volumes have been written on the Yalta Conference and the concessions to Russia which put Soviet ar-

mies in Manchuria, the importance of Manchuria in the civil
war that began almost immediately, General George C. Marshall's assignment to bring the Communists into the National
government, and Washington's alleged blackmailing of the Nationalists. Where, in all the pros and cons, in the conflicting
statements of principles and the furiously diverse judgments,
lies the truth?

Now to examine some of the milestones.

On July 15, 1919, the new Communist government of Russia
issued a dramatic announcement: "The Soviet government returns to the Chinese people, without demanding any kind of
compensation, the Chinese Eastern railway, as well as all the
mining concessions, forestry, gold mines, and all the other
things which were seized from them by the government of the
Tsars" and other Russians.

The effect of this dazzling offer on Chinese public opinion
can easily be imagined. Mark the date. Two months earlier the
terms of the Versailles Treaty, which ended World War I, had
been announced. Chinese delegates to the Peace Conference,
outraged on several counts, refused to sign. In China, student
demonstrations exploded. Fury against the "imperialists" and
the "unequal treaties" made China a tinderbox. Now, more than
ever, hatred for the West became a consuming passion.

At this strategic moment, and apparently for no other motive
than to render justice, one Western government restored to
China the "things which were seized from them."

To be sure, five years would elapse before the Soviets made
good on the promise. Even then they did not implement all of
it. They retained their interest in the Chinese Eastern railway,
as we have seen. From the start, it seems, welching on agreements has been standard Communist practice. Nevertheless, as

a stroke of public relations the offer was a gem. The Russians asked nothing in return except Chinese recognition of the Bolshevik government.

In his early struggle for recognition and assistance from the powers, Dr. Sun Yat-sen had appealed to the United States (twice), Britain, Germany, Canada, and Tsarist Russia. They all turned him away. Now, at last, one government extended a helping hand. Not specifically to Dr. Sun (there is some indication that the Russians may have preferred one of the war lords), but to the Chinese people.

The effect on Dr. Sun appears in his own words, in his lectures and his will. "We no longer look toward the West. Our faces are turned toward Russia.

"My experiences during these forty years have firmly convinced me that . . . we must ally ourselves in a common struggle with those people of the world who treat us on a basis of equality." (Only the Russians had done so.)

In a deathbed letter to the Soviets he wrote: "In taking leave of you, dear comrades, I express the hope that the day is approaching when the Soviet Union will greet, in a free and strong China, its friend and ally, and that the two states will proceed hand in hand as allies in the great fight for the emancipation of the oppressed of the whole world."

So the ground was prepared for the meeting in Shanghai in 1921, when the Chinese Communist party formally came into existence. Among those present was an eager, vivid, moon-faced student and erstwhile farm boy—Mao Tse-tung.

The honeymoon between the Communists and the Kuomintang party began.

A number of Russian envoys visited Dr. Sun. In December 1922 Sun held detailed talks with the smoothest of them all, a dark, thick-set little man of immense charm and persuasiveness —Adolf Joffe. A month later the two men issued a joint statement, setting the terms of collaboration. The first paragraph is especially significant:

"Dr. Sun holds that the Communistic order, or even the Soviet system, cannot actually be introduced into China because there do not exist here the conditions for the successful establishment of either Communism or Sovietism. *This view is entirely shared by Mr. Joffe* [italics mine] who is further of the opinion that China's paramount and most pressing problem is to achieve national unification and to attain full national independence, and regarding this task, he has assured Dr. Sun that China has the warmest sympathy of the Russian people and can count on the support of Russia."

In that day few people understood that a Communist seldom looks where he is really aiming. Here, perhaps, appears the basis of the fiction that the Chinese Communists were not Russian-type Communists, but merely "agrarian reformers."

Soon afterward Dr. Sun sent his chief of staff, Chiang Kai-shek, to Moscow. Chiang remained three months. He traveled, listened to Soviet leaders, observed and came home impressed by the Russians, but disenchanted about their motives respecting China. In his book *Soviet Russia in China* (published by Farrar, Straus and Cudahy in 1957) Chiang reproduces a letter he says he circularized to the Standing Committee of the Kuomintang. It reads in part:

"According to my observation, the Russian Communist Party is not to be trusted. I told you before that only thirty percent of what the Russians say may be believed. That was really an understatement . . . The Russian Communist Party, in its dealings with China, has only one aim, namely to make the Chinese Communist Party its chosen instrument."

Meanwhile, Russian military officers had been arriving in China to act as instructors in a newly founded military academy. (Chiang himself and a number of other top Chinese commanders received their military education in Japanese academies.) The famous commander, General Galen, or Blucher, headed a team of thirty instructors. A political advisor, Mikhail Mikhailovitch Borodin, also appeared. Borodin had studied in

Chicago and lived in Scotland, Mexico, and other countries. Like most Communists he used different names—Berg, Grusenberg, Borodin, etc. It was Borodin who persuaded Dr. Sun to bring the Communists into the Kuomintang party. Thereafter, training centers in Moscow sent scores of indoctrinated Chinese back to China to infiltrate the army, establish "cells" in the universities, move into the labor unions, and find means of reaching the masses of peasants.

The honeymoon lasted until 1927.

To anyone who wishes to see this period, with all its complex maneuverings, as the Communists saw it, I would recommend a Columbia University publication of 1956—*Documents on Communism, Nationalism and Soviet Advisors in China, 1918-1927*. These documents are part of a collection of papers seized by the Chinese in a raid on the office of the Soviet military attaché in Peking in 1927. They have been edited by C. Martin Wilbur and Julie Lien-ying How, who added excellent background and explanatory material. They are extraordinarily interesting because the men who wrote them were eyewitnesses, living and working in the midst of the events of those turbulent years.

In these documents, and from Chiang Kai-shek's diaries, you discover that Chiang's opinions of the Russians which he acquired on his trip to Moscow were not changed by working with them. Vice versa, they saw him as potentially useful, but dangerous.

"I treat them with sincerity but they reciprocate with deceit," his diary says at one point. "It is impossible to work with them." And again: "My Russian associates are suspicious and envious of me. They deceive me. In the circumstances, the only course for me is to be guided by sincerity."

And here, contained in a military report, the Russian advisor to Chiang's First Army, reveals his estimate of Chiang:

"We consider Chiang Kai-shek a peculiar person with peculiar characteristics, most prominent of these being his lust for glory and craving to be the hero of China. He claims that he stands not only for the Chinese National Revolution but for World Revolution. Needless to say, the degree of his actual understanding is quite another matter.

"To achieve his goal, power and money are required. He does not, however, use the money to enrich his own pocket. He never hesitates to spend huge sums of money for grants and rewards. He is extremely fond of subsidizing newspapers in order to enlist support for his programs. His analysis of Chinese and world problems is extremely good."

In another report the same advisor writes:

"Chiang possesses much determination and endurance. Compared with the average Chinese, he is unusually forthright . . . he is not free from suspicion and jealousy . . . a man of intelligence and ambition."

As though coming from an agent operating in enemy territory, another document stresses the need for complete secrecy in communications between the Soviet embassy in Peking and the advisors to Chiang:

"Send us the military code, without which communication with your office is handicapped because (1) there is only one secret code at Borodin's place. Those of us who are scattered at various places have to wait our chance to send telegrams through Borodin, thus causing great delays; (2) the present procedure does not ensure secrecy as the secret code is known to many people; (3) Borodin's decoding clerk often piles up telegrams without transmitting them."

The documents contain page after brain-numbing page of thorough, detailed instructions on the means of reaching the people with the Communist Word, the importance of the "cell," how to organize study groups (perhaps the Shanghai discussion group came from this), the need for hard study and frequent self-examination. If the Americans are to compete with the Communists, they are going to have to work as they do!

Prophetically—for the Communist-Kuomintang honeymoon was nearing its end—a Russian officer wrote his superior:

"It would naturally be unfortunate both for the Revolution and for himself if Chiang actually wants further to attack the Left. Yet Chiang can never destroy the Left for, warmly received everywhere, the Left has substantial force."

Chiang broke with the Communists abruptly, and in a sea of blood, in the summer of 1927.

The Northern Expedition, Chiang's military campaign that opened the way for the establishment of the Kuomintang as the National government, had swept north from Canton, past Shanghai, and into the Yangtze Valley in a series of swift victories. On March 24 the army entered Nanking.

An evil spirit must hang over Nanking. It is the scene of two terrible incidents. In the first, Chinese troops entering the city suddenly began attacking foreigners. They killed some and threatened others. Women were stripped of their clothing. The soldiers systematically looted foreign property and destroyed a considerable amount. Foreign gunboats in the Yangtze River opened fire, laying down a barrage under which the missionaries and other foreigners escaped. Otherwise the dimensions of the incident might have been much worse. It was bad enough, but not to be compared with the savagery of the Japanese troops when they captured Nanking in 1937 and were permitted to run wild in an orgy of rape, torture, and murder.

Dr. Hu Shih believes Russia deliberately planned the Nanking Incident of 1927. Her purpose, he believes, was to provoke military intervention in China by the United States and other Western governments so that an "imperialist war" would hasten the Communist take-over in China. In his article in *Foreign Affairs*, October 1950, shortly after the start of the Korean War, Dr. Hu said:

"The Nanking Incident seems to be the last of a series of deliberate anti-foreign moves designed to force the foreign

powers to resort to armed intervention and thereby create a
situation of a real 'imperialist war'—which, we must remember,
Stalin and the Comintern regards as the necessary 'objective
condition' for the victory of the Revolution. The commanding
general of the offending army in the Nanking Incident was
General Ch'en Ch'ien, who is now with the Chinese Communist regime. And . . . Mr. Lin Tsu-han, the chief political
commissar of the Army, is one of the most prominent Communist leaders today."

A month later Chiang Kai-shek split with the Communists.
Borodin and the other advisors hastily fled. Heads rolled.

From that moment forward, including the period when the
two parties ostensibly united in a common front against Japan,
it would be war to the knife between the Communists and the
Kuomintang.

The Communists, gathering in mountainous regions of south
China, soon began setting up local soviets, and finally in 1931
they established the "Central Soviet Government" of China.
Chiang Kai-shek organized four major "extermination campaigns," but failed to dislodge them. The fifth, in 1934, succeeded.

Had he been let alone in the 1930's, Chiang probably would
have destroyed the Communist "government" and crushed its
army. No doubt the Communists would have continued to
foment revolution, but they would have been underground and
dispersed. Instead, the Red regime was able to remain secure
in a fixed base of operations, guarded by organized armed
forces.

Chiang was not to be left free to concentrate on the Communists. In 1929 and 1930 a coalition of war lords forced him
to fight a major campaign. Then, in 1931, Japan struck. Japanese troops quickly overran Manchuria.

Chiang did not oppose them. Why? Hollington Tong, in his
biography *Chiang Kai-shek*, says the Generalissimo had two
alternatives—armed action, or an appeal to the Powers to force

the Japanese to withdraw from Manchuria. "The second alternative had worked in the Shantung impasse of 1921," Tong writes. "It held out promise in the present instance in view of the fact that the Manchuria move had been made on the initiative of the Army, obviously without consultation with the civil authorities in Tokyo." Tong quotes Chiang himself as saying: "Politically, the National Government . . . was compelled to make compromises and to swallow criticism; in short, it had to do its best to tide over the difficult internal situation."

Hu Shih (in *Foreign Affairs,* October 1950) says: "The Generalissimo was determined to exterminate the military power of Chinese Communists before he had to face the greater war of resistance against Japan."

In any case, a wave of indignation against Chiang's decision swept China. Demonstrations broke out and mass meetings called for war with Japan. Some of these were Communist-organized, but not all. A number of my personal friends went to jail for participating in the demonstrations. They say, even today, their sole purpose was to force the National government to fight.

All this was a juicy dish for the Communists. What better way to take the military pressure off their strongholds in south China? The Communists do not believe in heaven, but perhaps there is a special Red heaven that brought the Japanese attack at this critical moment in their struggle against the Nationalist armies. They milked the situation for all it was worth. They offered to co-operate against the Japanese with any "white" army, under certain conditions. They organized student demonstrations and "Resistance-to-Japan" societies, and posed as the only true reliquaries of patriotism in China. Although their forces were more than a thousand miles distant from combat theater in Manchuria, they "declared war" on Japan.

It reminds you of that old joke in which the manager says to his battered and groggy prize fighter: "Tear right in there, kid. He can't hurt us."

For the Communists were not only a great distance away
from Manchuria, but they could be pretty sure the terms they
laid down for sending their forces into battle would not be accepted. Remember, they had not offered to co-operate with the
National government as such, but only with any of its armies.
Even if their terms were accepted, they stood to gain more than
they would lose, as we shall see.

The man on the street, however, outraged and shouting for
action against Japan, saw only the surface fact—the Communists had made an offer, and Chiang, instead of accepting, permitted Japanese troops to overrun Manchuria. At this point,
without question, great numbers of students and intellectuals
who had been loyal to Chiang Kai-shek began to withdraw
support from him and the government. This is not to say that
they switched immediately to the Communists. It was not a
straight either/or case. My friends told me they were simply
confused, disheartened, badly disappointed in the Generalissimo and his associates. The wedge had been driven.

It added up to a major propaganda victory, almost a triumph,
for the Communist directors of public relations.

Militarily, however, the Communist position in Kiangsi soon
became critical. In the fifth and last of the "extermination campaigns" the Nationalists achieved a degree of success. A plan
devised by the German generals advising the government cast
a net around the Communist strongholds. Gradually, it began
to tighten. Nearly a million Nationalist troops engaged in the
operation. The Communists, faced with annihilation, laid plans
to escape and find another haven in a more remote part of
China.

On the night of October 16, 1934, having concentrated most
of their forces at one point of the Nationalist ring, they attacked
and broke out of the net. Then began one of the most spectacular achievements in human history. An army of men, women,
and children, fighting much of the way, through wilderness

and over mountains, walked six thousand miles to new positions. This was the famous Long March, a truly great feat.

The best account I know of it is in Edgar Snow's remarkable book *Red Star Over China* (published by Random House in 1938). Snow, a meticulous reporter and a suction pump for information, tells in detail what the Communists told him of the Long March soon after it ended.

In October 1935, only a year after they began their march, the Communists came into northern Shensi in the remote northwest. They had walked a distance nearly twice the width of the United States, in a giant arc, and settled down at a point about as far from Nanking, the Nationalist capital, as Kansas City is from Washington.

They escaped the net and the pursuing Nationalist troops. They survived as an organized group. They preserved the Red army. And they accomplished another result of priceless value. Again, it is in the field of public relations.

In their long retreat they passed through villages and towns, through uncounted millions of people. Remember that in the years of civil war the arrival of a Chinese army always signaled one thing to the civilians—rape, looting, and killing. The Communists maintained iron discipline, treated the people kindly. Shrewdly gauging the effect, they paid for everything and let the women alone. On the other hand, they seized food supplies and money from the landlords and gentry along the route and distributed these among the peasants, Edgar Snow reported. Even before the Long March, he says, they had formulated eight rules of conduct in their meetings with civilians:

"1. Replace all doors and windows when you leave a house.

"2. Return and roll up the straw matting on which you sleep.

"3. Be courteous and polite to the people and help them when you can.

"4. Return all borrowed articles.

"5. Replace all damaged articles.

"6. Be honest in transactions with the peasants.

"7. Pay for all articles purchased.

"8. Be sanitary, and especially establish latrines a safe distance from people's houses."

The most powerful of all advertising influences is what theater managers call "the word of mouth," the chain-reaction effect of one person telling others, who tell others. Imagine, then, the impact on millions of Chinese when the peasants told each other of this strange new army. Verily it was an army of liberators—"the poor man's army." They could not know what lay behind this strategy or the tyranny that would spring from it.

The next great turning point appeared a year later on December 7, 1936. It is curious to see how frequently this date, December 7, comes into the star-crossed story of the Far East. It is the date of Pearl Harbor, of course, and of another event involving the United States, China, and Japan—the mysterious Sian Incident.

Sian-fu is a city in south central Shensi, not far from the region where the Communists had established their new base.

The full story of what happened has never been told. There are several versions, different interpretations. The surface facts, however, are these: Chiang Kai-shek flew to Sian, ostensibly to plan a sixth great campaign against the Reds. Chang Hsueh-liang, erstwhile boss of Manchuria, now deposed, arrested him after killing some thirty of his bodyguards. Chou En-lai, one of the three top Red leaders, then turned up in Sian and talked face to face with the Nationalist leader. On December 25 Chiang was released amid a flurry of apologies and breast-beating quotes from the principals. And finally, soon afterward, it was announced that the Communists and Nationalists had agreed to rejoin, forming a "united front" against Japan.

Nobody "lost face." Chang Hsueh-liang went unpunished; in fact, he was publicly forgiven. The proposed sixth campaign against the Communists was called off. Strange goings on.

Who induced Chang Hsueh-liang to kidnap Chiang Kai-

shek? How was it that Chou En-lai could freely come to Sian
for the talks? Did the Nationalists have to make concessions to
save Chiang from being killed? If they did make a deal, what
were the terms? And who, in fact, arranged for Chiang's re-
lease? The answers are not yet fully known.

In "United States Relations with China," dated July 30, 1949,
the State Department says:

"The Chinese Communist Party . . . at first favored the exe-
cution of the Generalissimo, but apparently on orders from
Moscow shifted to a policy of saving his life. The Chinese Communist concept, inspired from Moscow, became one of promoting a 'united front' with the Generalissimo and the National
Government against the Japanese; this concept seems to have
played a considerable role in saving the Generalissimo's life."

In *Chiang Kai-shek*, however, Hollington Tong says that
Chiang himself formulated the idea of calling the Communist
into a common front against Japan:

"Chiang's attitude toward the Communists had not altered
after his experience at Sian. However, in the uncertainty of the
Northwest situation, he saw little gain to the government in ex-
hausting its resources in further military action against them
. . . He began to explore in his mind the advantages of reaching an agreement with Mao Tse-tung's forces, and assuring
their cooperation in the inevitable showdown with Japan."

Whatever the truth, something happened at Sian that induced Chiang Kai-shek to abandon plans for another major
operation against the Communists. Once before they had escaped by flight, that time through some labyrinthine conspir-
acy.

Sian marks a vital point along the road. For, as many special-
ists believe, it probably accelerated Japan's second attack on
China in 1937. As long as the Nationalists and Communists
kept busy killing each other and expending national resources,
the Japanese militarists could procede leisurely with whatever
timetable they had drawn for further operations in China. A

united China, however, would be a much more formidable problem. Seven months after the Sian Incident, the "undeclared war" began in north China.

If the State Department is correct in its assertion that Moscow ordered Chiang to be spared at Sian, the question arises: why? What was Stalin's motive in the paper coalition between the Nationalists and the Communists?

The conjecture is that he foresaw another Japanese attack on China. When it came, the Nationalist armies would bear the brunt of the fighting and take the heavier casualties. The lightly armed Reds, operating guerrilla fashion behind the lines, would suffer much less. Whatever the final outcome, the Nationalists would be weaker and the Communists stronger in the end. This is the theory. If it is accurate, Stalin was a very shrewd forecaster, indeed, for it is precisely what did happen. In the depths of World War II, with the Japanese occupying cities and control points in a wide area of China, the Communists, like will-o'-the-wisps, operated in the same territory under their very noses.

Japan need never have worried about the "united front." It was little more than a myth. The two Chinese groups always watched each other more closely than they watched the Japanese, seldom stopped skirmishing, and were several times near an open break. This is part of the reason for the heartbreaking struggle between the late Lieutenant General Joseph Stilwell and Chiang Kai-shek. "Joe" Stilwell was a warm, wonderful personality, an inspired leader, a great soldier. We all loved him in Burma. He wanted to use Chinese divisions, trained and equipped by Americans, to drive the Japanese out of Burma. The plan never came into actual practice, however, because as Stilwell saw it, Chiang preferred to hold those divisions for eventual use against the Communists.

The Nationalists seriously damaged their cause in the eyes of the Americans in Burma at that time, not only because of that strategic matter, but because of the peculations and thievery that already had begun. It could not help but affect your view of the government, even though the regime, far away in Chungking, was virtually powerless to stop it. Even the ordinary GI was affected.

One day a blond youngster from Oklahoma, barely nineteen years old, but already with battlefield decorations, came into the press billet, cussing a blue streak. He said he had been heating some rations near a stream when a Chinese soldier came and squatted down beside him. "He sat there for a few minutes," the boy said, "holding up his thumb and saying ' 'Melicans ding how,' 'Melicans ding how.' Seemed to want a cigarette, so I gave him a handful. He said 'ding how' a couple more times and walked away. And the sonofabitch took my musette bag with him."

One of my colleagues arranged, through a hush-hush American unit, to join a Nationalist commando unit operating in Japanese-held territory in the CBI. He came back soon afterward. I asked him what they were doing against the Japanese.

"Not much against the Japs," he said. "Occasionally, they pick up a prisoner or knock off an outpost. Mostly, though, they keep busy raising hell with the Communists in the neighborhood. I suppose that's why they wouldn't let me stay."

On February 8, 1941, a message came to Chiang Kai-shek from President Roosevelt. It said:

"It appears at ten thousand miles away that the Chinese Communists are what in our country we call Socialists. We like their attitude toward the peasants, towards women, and towards Japan. It seems to me that these so-called Communists and the National Government have more in common than they have differences. We hope they can work out their differences and work more closely together in the interest of our common objective of fighting Japan."

The message is important on two counts.

First, the date. It was ten months minus one day before Pearl Harbor. Was Roosevelt already at war? Only four months before this message, he had made the "again-and-again" speech assuring the voters their sons would not be sent into foreign wars. Did his message mean fighting Japan with economic measures, "measures short of war?" Or did it mean exactly what it said? Watching Roosevelt's policies, from various points in the Orient during the last fateful years, it seemed to me there could be no other answer than that he had decided on a shooting war.

Second, the phrase: "Communists are what in our country we call Socialists."

To be sure, in 1941 very few persons had seen the true face of Communism and could appreciate its deadly purpose.

But more than three years later, on June 21, 1944, Vice-President Henry Wallace, on an official mission, held a conversation with Chiang Kai-shek. In the notes summarizing the discussion appears a somewhat similar note:

"Mr. Wallace said that President Roosevelt had talked about the Communists in China. President Roosevelt had assumed that inasmuch as the Communists and the members of the Kuomintang were all Chinese *they were basically friends* [italics mine] and that 'nothing should be final between friends.' "

The message is published in Hollington Tong's biography of Chiang Kai-shek. Tong held a number of high posts in the Chinese government at the time and later became ambassador to the United States. He says the President's special envoy, Lauchlin Currie, delivered this message to Chiang. The Wallace conversation summary appears in the American White Paper on China.

Over and over, Americans ask how we could have misjudged

the Communists so completely, failed to see their true purpose in China, called them "agrarian reformers," and propounded the belief that they could be induced to put aside their differences and join the Nationalists. Controversy still swirls around the point and recriminations are still flying. To some Americans it smells of treachery somewhere. Others more charitably regard it as an error in judgment—terribly fateful, but still an honest error.

Roosevelt prided himself on his knowledge of China. He liked to describe how his ancestors had traded with the Chinese and what he had learned. Stilwell relates in his memoirs how the President filibustered on this subject while Stilwell waited for an answer to a key question on wartime China. Perhaps in 1941 Roosevelt thought, as did others, that the culture, the psychology, and the traditions of China made it stony ground for the growth of Communism. Perhaps in 1944 he thought that the important thing was to get the Nationalists and Communists together so that China would fight more effectively against the Japanese.

In any case, it was a fatal misconception that the so-called Communists were "basically friends" with the Nationalists.

The President's view of the situation could not help but affect the views of Americans generally. . . . "After all, he has sources of up-to-date information on conditions in China and the background of knowledge and experience on which to formulate his judgments. In short, the Boss must know what he's talking about."

Moreover, the effect of this attitude on the State Department and Foreign Service officers all along the line must be taken into account. Among the functions of an embassy are to gather facts, to analyze and evaluate them, and to report to Washington. If you know "the line" Washington is taking, and especially if it is "the line" of the President himself, there is a great temptation to go along with it in your reports and evaluations. The ambassador who likes his job, the counselor of embassy who wants to be an ambassador, and the officers farther down the ladder do not like to disagree with Washington's view of a given situation. At best they may be ignored, at worse they may be transferred to a less important post. I dare say that not even the Soviet embassy in Washington often challenges Mr. Khrushchev's evaluations of the situation in the United States on a given point.

In any case, the United States apparently had adopted this as a policy toward the Chinese Communists. Hollington Tong describes it as "the American inclination towards appeasement of the Chinese Communists." Thereafter, he continues: ". . . a procession of well-meaning American envoys came and went in China, from 1941 to 1949, in an effort to bring the National Government and the Communists together."

Then Yalta. In February 1945 the Big Three met. The United States and Russia wrote the terms of the deal by which Russia would come into the war against Japan after V-E Day. Not all the top American military commanders wanted the Soviets in, and it has been suggested many times that Stalin would have rushed into Manchuria anyway to seize the fruits of victory.

In addition, the terms of the agreement affected Manchuria and the ports of Dairen and Port Arthur, to all of which China could lay legitimate claim. No Chinese delegates attended the conference, however.

The agreement stipulated that Russia's "former interests" in the Far East should be restored, promised to safeguard her "pre-eminent interests" in the railways and Dairen, and gave Russia the Kurile Islands and other Pacific territory. The "pre-eminent interests" were not defined.

"It was unfortunate," said the White Paper, "that China was not previously consulted." It further says: "The primary motivation of the Yalta Agreement was military."

Britain joined the agreement, but Winston Churchill says in *Triumph and Tragedy* that neither he nor Anthony Eden played any part in shaping it. He adds: "We were not consulted but only asked to approve. This we did. In the United States there have been many reproaches about the concessions made to Soviet Russia. The responsibility rests with their own representatives."

China not only was not consulted about the terms, but was not even advised for some months. Churchill says he notified the dominion prime ministers "in the most rigid secrecy." The White Paper's explanation of the fact that China was not advised is that Roosevelt and Stalin "based this reticence (sic) on the already well-known and growing danger of 'leaks' to the Japanese from Chinese sources." One may ask: suppose they had "leaked?" Would this have moved Japan to greater efforts, or convinced her that the cause was utterly hopeless? In any case, that is the official explanation.

Finally, Chiang Kai-shek was to be presented with a *fait accompli* and asked to concur without having been consulted. "The President will take measures in order to obtain this concurrence on advice from Marshal Stalin," said the agreement. Roosevelt had been maneuvered into a position where, in Chinese eyes, the United States would bear the major responsibility for Yalta.

"At no point did President Roosevelt consider that he was compromising vital Chinese interests," says the White Paper.

Roosevelt was a tired, sick man. He had only two more months to live.

Thus the ground was prepared for Russian troops to come into Manchuria, the cockpit of the Far East, which would quickly be converted into the main base for the Chinese Communists.

The war ended. Swiftly four Chinese Red armies moved into the four northern provinces—Jehol, Kirin, Chahar, and Liaoning. As the Russian divisions disarmed the Japanese, they moved out, leaving arms and ammunitions to the Chinese.

American ships brought the Nationalists to the area, but by the time they arrived, the Communists were astride the main lines of communications. It became clear that a showdown must come in Manchuria unless, of course, Chiang Kai-shek elected to avoid it.

Lieutenant General Albert C. Wedemeyer, an exceedingly competent officer, genuinely trying to help China, reported in November:

"He [Chiang Kai-shek] will be unable to occupy Manchuria for many years unless satisfactory agreements are reached with Russia and the Chinese Communists.

"It appears remote that a satisfactory understanding will be reached between the Chinese Communists and the National Government."

Nevertheless, when President Truman sent General George C. Marshall to China, the instructions read in part: "Specifically, I desire that you endeavor to persuade the Chinese Government to call a national conference of representatives of the major political elements to bring about a unification of China, and concurrently, to effect a cessation of hostilities, particularly in North China." Truman noted that Communist representatives were among those holding discussions in Chungking at the time, and said this should provide Marshall with a "convenient opportunity."

In other words, although the Pacific War had ended and military considerations of China's contribution no longer applied, the American policy of "unification" still was to prevail.

Dreary, hopeless discussions continued. Time passed. The position of the Communists in Manchuria grew stronger daily. It served their purpose, therefore, to continue the fiction of honest bargaining. They were gaining precious time.

Mao Tse-tung, however, had a different view:

"To sit on the fence is impossible. A third road does not exist. We oppose the Chiang Kai-shek reactionary clique . . . We also oppose the illusion of a third road. Not only in China but also in the world, without exception, one either leans to the side of imperialism or to the side of socialism."

Finally, the moment came. In the summer of 1947 Mao was able to say that the Communists no longer were on the defensive in Manchuria. "Our armies have turned to offensive attacks on a nation-wide scale," he announced.

By 1949 it was all over.

Could China have been saved? In the wisdom of hindsight, probably. Amid the misconceptions of the middle 1940's, no. Consider the picture:

1. After V-J Day China was in a desperate condition. Physical destruction had been enormous. Inflation was running wild. Starvation confronted an estimated seven to ten million people. The people's morale was at the nadir. They were shambling and dispirited. China, like a man suffering from shock, needed quick transfusions.

2. To make matters worse, corruption, nepotism, and inefficiency were clogging the wheels.

In August 1947 Wedemeyer stood before the State Council and all the top officials in government and spoke bluntly. He described draft dodging by the rich, touched on economics and the military position, and said that the Nationalist armies—by contrast to the Communist forces—had incurred in the Chinese a "feeling of hatred and distrust," owing to their looting and thievery. Their attitude toward the people, he said, was "that of conquerors instead of deliverers," both in China and on Formosa. He added these prophetic words:

"The Central Government cannot defeat the Chinese Communists by the use of force, but can only win the loyal, enthusiastic and realistic support of the masses of people by improving the political and economic situation immediately. The effectiveness and timeliness of these improvements will determine, in my opinion, whether or not the Central Government will stand or fall before the Communist onslaught."

It was reported that one of the ministers wept openly. The others were outraged.

Was this an American view alone? A Chinese newspaper in Nanking published an editorial entitled "Lose No Time in Winning the People's Confidence." It said:

"At this moment when the nation's fate is flickering, and when the people are suffering terribly, what hope is there for them? The special privileged classes still enjoy their privileges and the people can do nothing to them. Even now nothing can be done to these public enemies of the people who are able accomplices of the Communists. Nepotism rides on . . . and the people have no right to say anything. What are we going to do with national affairs like that?"

The list of evils in this category is long—profiteering, speculation, manipulations in currency etc. Almost every American report for the period contains a phrase or more to the effect that "conditions are deteriorating."

But, in the bewilderment and dismay over the disaster in China, Americans have tended to oversimplify, to ascribe the Communist triumph almost exclusively to these evils. It is not often noted that even with complete peace the Nationalists would have had great difficulty remedying conditions quickly. For one thing, they lacked trained administrators—the immense corps required to take charge in such a vast territory. Communications were badly chewed up by the war, and it was in the Communists' interest to see that they remained so. Where repairs were made by the government, the Communists speedily disrupted them again.

3. A "pox-on-both-your-houses" sentiment welled up all over China.

Many Chinese felt that anything would be better than the Nationalists. Many did not want the Communists. They wanted

something new, but what? From Manchuria it was reported
that the people would welcome the return of the war lord
Chang Hsueh-liang, deposed by Japan in 1931. After all, under
him and his father there had been relative peace and prosperity in Manchuria as opposed to the ceaseless fighting in
metropolitan China. Again, however, the Communists capital-
ized on the popular desire for peace and security, maintaining
discipline and holding to the tactics they had used during the
Long March. The opposite picture of the Nationalist troops was
described by Wedemeyer—"hatred and distrust."

4. American military observers reported Nationalist troops
fighting halfheartedly, when at all.

They had superiority in numbers, approximately a million
and a half to a million, and did not lack equipment. But the
Communists, imbued with an idea, disciplined and organized,
had something to fight for. American observers cited instances
where Nationalist units abandoned positions without a fight or
even joined the Communists.

5. Underlying everything lay the basic difference between
the Americans and Chiang.

In effect, they said to him: "You are fighting an idea, not
merely armed forces. To fight that idea you must correct conditions, grant the people civil liberties, institute true democracy,
and broaden the base of government by bringing the Communists into it." As late as 1948 the American ambassador reported
to Washington: "He [Chiang] seems unable to think of Communism as an extreme force of social unrest which cannot be
extirpated by the combination of military force and gracious
compassion . . ."

Chiang's retort was that he was fighting an armed rebellion
—moreover, one directed from Moscow. If the Communists
were prepared to acknowledge the authority of the central government and lay down their arms, he was prepared to make
concessions. Naturally, the Communists would not do so. Why
should they?

He also could and did reply to the Americans that even in the eleventh hour they still failed to comprehend the Communists' objective and their tactics. He could hardly be expected to agree that they were "what we . . . call Socialists" and that merely because they were Chinese they were "basically friendly" with the Nationalist Chinese. He did not expect them to take what Mao Tse-tung called the "third road," any more than they did.

6. Finally, almost the last vestige of good will eroded away.

Hollington Tong wrote that the Nationalists considered that President Truman used American assistance as a club over them. He says: "Should China reject the American proposals, the inference in the Truman statement was unmistakable: China would receive neither military nor economic aid from the United States.

"Many Chinese thought and said that this looked like a choice between modes of suicide."

The Nationalists would have been less than human, too, if by that time they were not a little disenchanted with the United States. There was Yalta. There was the suspicion that "appeasement of the Chinese Communists" had been American policy. There was the constant American pressure, during and after the war, to have them bring the Communists into the central government. There was the "unmistakable inference" in Truman's statement on economic aid.

No, given all these conditions—economic, military, physical, and psychological—China could not have been saved from the Communists. History was against it—history and the careful planning and hard work of men who knew what they wanted and how to get it.

"The road to Paris and London," said the old Bolshevik, "leads through Peking."

Chapter XVII

THE BLUE TRAIN

THE "BLUE EXPRESS" rolled out of North Station in Shanghai, rounded a bend, and smoothly gathered speed heading northward. A few moments later it came into a large village and slowed again. Swarms of women and children walked beside the cars, hands extended, whining for food, for *cumshaw*, for anything. Fortunately the "Blue Express" no longer carried a dining car. It is a blighting experience to sit in a diner, confronting gleaming linen and plates of food, while outside there are hungry children watching and begging. What do you do? Pull down the shade? Ignore them? Either way the food suddenly turns to cardboard. The train picked up speed again. They ran until it was moving too fast. No one gave them so much as a grape.

It was a bright May morning. May 1930. A spring breeze brushed across the wheat fields and etched delicate, fan-shaped ripples on the pools in the rice paddies. Peasants with carrying-poles toiled up the sides of terraced hills bending under the weight of the water for paddies higher up. In the villages merchants already had removed shutters from the shop fronts. Chunks of raw pork and beef, entrails, and pressed chickens, glazed and shiny, hung in the open air. Farmers squatted beside baskets of vegetables brought in before dawn from fields miles away. A ricksha coolie slept in his ricksha, undisturbed amid the noise and the movement and the bright sunshine in his face. Two women stood gossiping, one of them nursing a child. She handed it to the other woman, who bared her breast, and they went on talking. Immemorial China.

All too soon the "Blue Express" came into open country. All too soon Shanghai fell behind. Our time there had ended. The schedule called for the next move, northward to universities in Tientsin and Peking. Now the moment had come. Already I missed Shanghai and longed for the cramped, murky little newsroom on the *Evening Post*. They would be on the rewrite by this time. Carroll Alcott, the city editor, would have found a funny item and would be refurbishing it, silently chuckling as he wrote. In the composing room Ivan Mrantz would be examining the pots of molten lead, his face a picture of Slavic gloom. I opened my notebook, which was filled with page after page of vignettes on Shanghai:

"A ricksha coolie followed a foreigner into the lobby of the China United, whining for more money, as they always do. The man knocked him down. . . . The coolies are often cheated because strangers don't know the difference between 'big' money and 'small' money. . . . The bitter, acrid smell in the opium dens in the Walled City is like no other smell. People look thoughtful but not exactly transported when they are smoking. . . . In the storm the other day the water backed up and sewage gushed out of the drains like fountains. An Englishman stalled his car in it. He got out and sloshed through the goo. Today he died of some infection. . . . Alcott showed me how to drink vodka. You eat a little something between each sip. . . . At the Birthday Ball in the Majestic I sat next to the Japanese ambassador's wife. She is charming, and I wanted to ask her to dance but didn't have the nerve. . . . The real foreign correspondents, like Reginald Sweetland, of the Chicago *Daily News*, work hard building up contacts and sources of information. . . . When ricksha coolies crowd around you, the man and the ricksha somehow look like a big, dirty bird. If you seem undecided, they think you want a woman and they start yelling:

'I gotta Korean girl, I gotta a Belgium girl, I gotta nice 'Melican girl.' "

Some of this had been published with my name on the stories. "Frankly, it's old stuff," Al Meyer would say, "but I'm going to run it because it will remind the customers of the way they saw this town when they first came. Nothing is ever old if you get a fresh slant, pal."

But March merged into April, and the days fled toward that date in May when we would leave. In the spring of 1930, however, a new coalition of war lords, both in the north and the south, challenged the authority of the Nationalist government. Two powerful chiefs in the north, Yen Hsi-shan and Feng Yu-hsiang, called on Chiang Kai-shek to resign. Some fifty other generals and local bosses signed a public condemnation of him and the government. In the south other war lords wheeled out their forces. Fighting began in Shantung province, between Tientsin and the capital at Nanking.

A comic-opera flavor often tinged the operations of the war lords. They took the field, then decided to stop fighting, and the government forgave them. An item from the *Evening Post* says: "Gen. Shih Yu-shen, who recently reaffirmed his allegiance to the Nationalist Government, is releasing all the rolling stock which he previously commandeered. Shih received $800,000 to transport his troops to take part in the campaign against the Ironsides (a rebel force) but as he did not go, this sum will be deducted from the government's future allowance to his forces." And however big and bloody the war zone, life tended to move through it as usual. In this case, word reached us that it was possible to travel overland to Peking in spite of the fighting in Shantung. Trains, although interrupted by a no man's land between the armies, were still running.

In its heyday the "Blue Express" was a famous luxury train, beautifully appointed and celebrated for its food and service. It owed its existence to the presence of foreigners in China, to the wealth they created, and to the rich Chinese, who could afford it. It was a bright strand amid the universal poverty.

The reputation of the "Blue Express," however, was not based on its speed. It made the seven hundred and fifty-mile run between Shanghai and Peking in twenty-eight hours and fifteen minutes, an average of less than thirty miles an hour. The roadbed, built by European engineers, permitted much higher speeds, but there were other determining factors, peculiar to China. Bandits had learned how to loosen the fish plates on the tracks, along with other less sophisticated means of stopping the train. Once, as I mentioned earlier, they boarded it in wild-West fashion and kidnapped all the passengers. Because of the bandits the express became the most brilliantly lighted train in the world. As it rumbled through the night, batteries of powerful searchlights swept the track ahead and the countryside around. Guards rode in the engineer's cabin and drowsed at both ends of the coaches.

In the compartments, glowing with damask and thick Peking rugs, rode the whole range of characters on the China coast: that is to say, war lords and their harem favorites, spies, intriguers, gangsters, Chinese millionaires, foreign *taipans,* diplomats, card sharps, and the silken ladies who made the trip so often they could have taken over from the engineer. Thieves prowled the corridors. Fortunes, and not infrequently careers, were lost in the bridge and poker games. If a passenger disappeared along the route, it was prudent to know nothing of the circumstances.

As time passed, the blight creeping over China touched the "Blue Express." War lords took locomotives and rolling stock for their operations. With increasing frequency, civil wars disrupted service. Bandits grew bolder. The line fell into disrepute, and the uncertainties sent more and more passengers to coastwise ships. On the May morning when we left Shanghai, only three of the original coaches remained. We had one of them to ourselves.

❦

Tsui settled into the seat beside me. I closed my Shanghai notebook. "Haven't seen much of you lately," he said. "Learn anything in Shanghai?"

"Plenty," I said, "but not the sort of thing we can put in the day book or the reports. What about you?"

He said they had made short trips to Nanking, Hangchow, and Soochow. There was a Chinese saying then—"Canton for cooking, Swatow for lace, and Soochow for pretty girls." I asked about the girls in Soochow. Tsui said it had been a dark, rainy day with poor visibility.

He described an orphanage on a hilltop above Nanking. Near the entrance, he said, the automobiles passed between rows of boy scouts standing at attention. A guard at the gate had presented arms, and two officials in frock coats rushed out of the buildings. "They were expecting some general," Tsui said. "By accident, I and my companions arrived first. They were dumbfounded, but they invited us to see the place." He described a roomful of sad little boys and girls in dull gray uniforms, each standing beside a steel bed. This in itself depressed him, he said, but what bothered him even more was to hear that all the orphans were children of Nationalist army officers killed in the civil wars. "Only top rankers," he said. "Nothing below a major. Everything in this country seems to be based on privilege, and to hell with the poor man."

In Nanking they had interviewed several Ministers of State

and other men of lower rank. I asked him what he thought of them. He took a moment to answer. "I don't know," he said. "Some of them seem competent enough. But the answer isn't easy. There is a . . . well, a phony atmosphere around the government buildings. You can tell from looking at the men in those offices that they all come from upper-bracket families, all from a particular class. It's a clique. They aren't killing themselves with work. I wonder if they have any feeling for the country or whether it's just a job."

"Maybe both," I said. "Are you still planning to get a job in government?"

"No more. The air in Nanking doesn't smell right to me."

"How are the blackbirds?"

He grinned. " 'By, 'by, blackbirds. That was just an emotional binge in Lingnan. The first impact of the country, I suppose. But I still want to do something." He pointed through the window. "Look—there's the Purple Mountain."

The mountain rises on the outskirts of Nanking. Sun Yat-sen's sepulcher looks out from the slope across the Valley of the Ming Tombs. It is near the tomb of the first Ming emperor. The Nationalists built it as a symbol of the Revolution, a national shrine. With its Chinese roof and glazed tile, it was meant to resemble the old tombs. But they used concrete and made it larger, more consciously imposing than those of the Mings. In a curious way it seemed out of place there, out of harmony.

Sunset turned the Yangtze into a river of fire. The plain of Anwhei blurred in the twilight. A full moon rose, melon-yellow at first, then burnished silver. The train slowed, barely creeping. From time to time we stepped out of the coach and walked beside it. The air smelled of spring and the Yangtze and the excrement fertilizing the fields. The coach was dark except for the moonlight. It was not a wagon lit with beds, but the seats were soft. I fell asleep and dreamed a panicky dream of the clock in the newsroom. . . .

In the morning the express seemed to be sailing across a sea of yellow dust. It had entered Shantung during the night, and now, stretching away on all sides, there was the plain, covered with dust so fine that even the train's crawling pace stirred swirling little whirlpools. Yellow, yellow, yellow. In the expanse of China, in the mountains, the river valleys, the plains, the deserts, and along the coasts you can find every color and every shade of color. Yet somehow the retinal image of a yellow country persists. The Yellow River. The Yellow Race. The "Yellow Peril." Shantung, yellowest of all, is the very epitome of China. In this terrain lies a good part of the story of China. Confucius and Mencius were born in Shantung. The Boxer rebellion began here. It is the region of one of the first foreign concessions, and the scene of a clash between the United States and Japan that made Americans conscious of the name "Shantung" in the 1920's. Taishan, the sacred mountain, "The Gateway to Heaven," looks out across the plain of Shantung. For two thousand years, from the time this region was known as the Kingdom of Lu, pilgrims have come to climb Taishan.

Actually, they ascend a stairway. Cut in the granite flank of the mountain and following its contours are 6,717 steps. They are worn smooth now from the passage of so many pilgrims walking and crawling. To climb a stairway is much more muscle-wearing than to walk along a ramp-like mountain path, however steep. The stone steps hurt your feet and set your ankles aching. The avenue to The Gateway of Heaven is not an easy one. It is a place of pain and sacrifice. Even this, however, was not sufficient penance for the pilgrims on Taishan that day.

Not far from the foot of the stairway, perhaps two hundred steps above, an old woman sat, apparently admiring the scenery below. She faced away from the summit. After a moment she put her hands in back of her, gripping the next step up, and hoisted herself. She rested a moment and did it again, step after step, using her hands. The old woman had "lily feet," grotesque stumps caused by binding in infancy. I assumed that she was ascending the stairway in this slow, painful manner because she could not walk. This was not the explanation. A little farther we passed a man and woman. They were not walking, either. They crawled on their hands and knees, stopping every few steps to pray. All along the stairway other pilgrims (more women than men) were crawling and lifting. At one point, where a straight stretch permitted a longer view, I saw a dozen or more people struggling upward in this manner. They looked like sluggish gray reptiles creeping over the stones. At this pace it must have taken them nearly a month to climb the 6,717 steps, and it is painful to imagine the condition of their hands and knees.

Very devout people, I thought, struggling upward from earth to heaven, from fleshly sin through suffering to The Kingdom of the Spirit. St. Paul himself would have smiled on them.

At the summit of Taishan, however, a shock awaited them. The walls of the Temple of Confucius were crumbling. Dry rot had eaten into the wooden doors. Ropes and temple cords were old and ragged. The Temple of the Jade Emperor was in the same state. Moreover, both buildings needed lashings of soap and water. Scattered over the mountain top and clinging to the slope of the mountain opposite Taishan were other monasteries and temples. All showed the effects of neglect. The monks and acolytes, shambling across the stones, wore dirty robes and smelled of grease and sweat. The expression in their faces was dull and loutish. No sense of grace or spirituality invested The Gateway to Heaven. How do you reconcile their attitude with the devotion of the pilgrims, who found walking too easy?

"When all is well and you wish it to stay well," says the Chinese maxim, "be an ethical Confucian. When in trouble, seek the Taoists. When you are dying, let the Buddhists be called in."

The Chinese (fortunately for Mao Tse-tung and his party) are not a religious people. They have no deep, excluding faith of their own. The peasants and coolies—the great majority of Chinese—are very superstitious. They believe in witches and demons and have devised many ingenious means of frustrating or appeasing evil spirits. But they do not believe in the divine nature of man, in a forgiving God, or in an ultimate purpose in life.

The Chinese absorbed foreign religions as they absorbed foreign invaders. Meanwhile they continued to be essentially an unreligious people. Very few of my student friends, for example, were more than nominally Christian, although they studied in mission schools. Probably there were more "rice Christians" than true converts. A small scene in Canton on a Christmas Eve remains indelibly in my memory. Crowds of Chinese gathered outside the lovely old cathedral, listening to the music and the birdlike voices of the Chinese choirboys. As the Mass progressed, men urinated on the cathedral walls, not as a gesture of disrespect, but just because they happened to be near.

No, the poor pilgrims, scourging themselves up the stone stairway of Taishan, represented no great spiritual force. Even if they could be regarded as "religious" in the Christian or Buddhist meaning, they represented only a minority of the Chinese. It is strange that two great Eastern nations, India and China, each with an ancient civilization, each with majestic cultural achievements, rubbing elbows, and with so many points in common, should have diverged so widely in the matter of faith. Why did India produce a Buddha and develop a deep religious sense? Why, on the contrary, did no endemic Chinese religion develop?

The Communists overcame many obstacles in the conquest of China, but a belief in God and the divine nature of man was not among them. The story would have been very different if Mao Tse-tung and his followers had collided with this stubborn road block. For this reason the Communist drive in India will be more difficult. Perhaps Communism will become the religion of China now. If so, I think it certain that there will be more "rice Communists" than true converts.

꙳

A private train with a single coach carried us to the end of the railroad line. We were the only passengers. In Tsinan-fu, a city north of Taishan, the station manager hooked the only available car, a creaking matchbox, to an equally tired locomotive. The train, he said, would leave at our pleasure. It would go as far as Yucheng-hsien, some twenty miles ahead, on the southern boundary of the combat zone. A bus would take us across some sixty miles of no man's land to the rebel lines. From there another train would complete the trip. War or no war, our tickets said "Shanghai to Peking," and the station manager was determined to fulfill the contract. He was one of those individuals rarely met in public service anywhere, a man dedicated to his duty. To him, obviously, the war was only an operational detail, an irritating but not critical accident on the line.

Except for the upcurling Chinese eaves, Yucheng-hsien could have been Oxbow Gulch in a Western movie. The main street, unpaved and deep in yellow dust, led through town to the railway depot. Horse-drawn carts and wagons were passing between the rows of one-story shops. Dust, fine as talcum, covered the whole town, fogged the windows in the depot, and put pancake makeup on the people. Every cart moved in a yellow cloud. When the train wheezed into the station, crowds rushed to the depot in a miniature dust storm. They gawked, murmuring "*Ai-yaw, ai-yaw*" at the sight of nine white men and one Chinese disembarking. The news spread and others came running. They probably suspected the war had taken a new turn, drawing in foreigners. Some men tried to talk to Tsui, but he did not speak the Shantung dialect. He brushed past them. "I'll find the bus," he shouted. "You guys bring the luggage." Another man pantomimed aiming a rifle, grinning happily. We shook our heads and made signs to show we carried no arms. Up to that point we had seen no Nationalist field positions and only a few soldiers strolling in Tsinan-fu. Yet the no man's land extended for sixty miles between the two armies. In this sector, at least, they appeared to be avoiding each other. It looked like a leisurely war.

Beside the depot stood the bus. The right front wheel canted over at a dangerous angle. There was no door, no windshield, no bonnet over the hood, no radiator cap, and only one seat, that for the driver. The motor bore a Ford insignia, but spare parts from many other models had been grafted on it. The chassis squawked when we climbed aboard. Before that, however, the driver duly examined the tickets. It is doubtful that he could read, but we waited, knowing he was gaining "face" in his home town. Then, gasping and clattering, the bus staggered through the crowds and headed into open country on a faint trace of a road. Within a few miles, steam rose from the radiator. The driver found water in an irrigation ditch. Next, sand choked the carburetor. We cleaned the screen for him. From time to time patches of deep sand and drifted dust stalled the bus. We all got out and pushed. Still, mile after mile fell behind.

The signs of war were invisible rather than visible. As the bus approached a village, people scurried into the little mud huts and slammed the doors. Not a single horse or ox was plowing the fields. Not one pig or chicken explored for food. And not one woman, except a withered crone or two, showed herself. If the bus meant soldiers, rebel or Nationalist, the villagers knew what to expect.

Toward dusk, on the outskirts of a village, soldiers sprinted into the road from a clump of trees. A machine-gun position lay concealed in the trees. In terrain as flat as this they must have seen the pillar of dust and watched the bus long before it reached their position. One man, apparently an officer, pulled a pistol from his holster and signaled the driver to stop. Then he said something. The driver stepped down, motioning us to follow him. When the officer saw Tsui's face, he took a step toward him and chattered rapidly. Tsui replied in Cantonese, the only Chinese language he knew. These were Shansi troops, speaking a local version of Mandarin. The officer and Tsui might as well have been an Arab and a Choctaw trying to communicate.

"I think he wants to know who we are and what we are doing here," Tsui said, "but I don't know how to tell him."

"Show him your clippings about the time you won the oratorical contest."

"Draw him a picture."

"Wise guys," said Tsui. "Wait a minute. You just gave me an idea. Our stationery has Chinese characters showing we are a student group. He probably can't read, but he won't admit it. Dig out a letterhead, someone."

The officer studied the paper. The soldiers looked over his shoulder. One of them said something. The officer glared and roughly pushed him away. Finally he spoke to the bus driver. We could procede.

Then we came to the rebels' main positions, defenses in depth. In a layer cake of three major sectors they had dug trenches, raised earthworks, mounted machine guns, and stationed some artillery. The equipment looked reasonably new. I remembered a short dispatch from Manila reporting that a Czechoslovakian ship, carrying arms consigned to a war lord, had sailed for Tientsin. Perhaps this was part of the cargo. Considering the cost of a machine gun, not to mention artillery, this single sector indicated the wealth of the war lords. How many taxes from how many sweating, half-starved farmers went into the purchase of one gun and one clip of ammunition?

And here, wearing ragged, motley uniforms and rubber-soled sneakers, were more peasant boys like those I had seen in the "hospital" near Canton—hungry, disspirited, apprehensive. "Tired of livin' and skeered of dyin.' " The rifle was a meal ticket.

The war-lord armies gave foreigners a totally mistaken picture of the Chinese as a fighting man. He stopped fighting when it rained. Sometimes he fired over the head of the enemy and expected the courtesy to be reciprocated. Rather than attack, he preferred, when possible, to frighten the foe with firecrackers and bloodcurdling yells. He raised great clouds of dust to simulate superior numbers and discourage attacks from the other side. The Old China Hand said determined opposition would send him packing. The Japanese had learned that bribery worked like magic on a Chinese army. Foreigners considered the ordinary soldier a reluctant dragon, dangerous only in overwhelming numbers.

What few people realized was that until the Communists entered the picture, the Chinese soldier seldom fought for something he believed in—a principle or an overmastering vision of a better life. There is a critical difference between a mercenary, interested in loot and food, and a soldier defending an ideal. The Chinese infantryman is unbelievably brave, quick to learn, durable as the Japanese, cunning as a serpent. The "human-wave" tactic, which overwhelms a position through sheer numbers and regardless of casualties, is possible only because Chinese troops die so recklessly. But the mercenary, naturally, avoids risk and tries to stay alive. (Even so, in that civil war of 1930 government figures showed 150,000 rebels killed and wounded, and put Nationalist casualties at 30,000 killed, 60,000 wounded.)

It was a much different Chinese soldier who faced the Japanese in the famous defense of Woosung in 1931 and in the "undeclared war" of 1937. I remember a Japanese officer saying after the Battle of Tai'erchwang: "They have a good army now. We must expect some defeats." The Chinese Communist soldier, imbued with an ideal, mistaken or not, met the Nationalist "extermination campaigns" with a firmness and efficiency that foreshadowed the development of a new pattern in China. On those battlefields in the pivotal 1930's a formidable new Power unit was forged.

Chapter XVIII

FAMINE

IN THE DESERT

SCOURGING ANOTHER PART of China that year were two more of
the Four Horsemen of the Apocalypse. Let me go back a little
way. . . .

Spring 1927. Suiyuan, a province in Inner Mongolia in the
northeast, at the edge of the Gobi Desert.

Warm weather has come earlier than usual. The farmer begins to watch for the first green shoots of wheat to come up in
one corner of the field, and for tendrils that will blossom with
white poppies (for opium) in another. This is all he asks of
the land—food, a cash crop of poppy bulbs, and forgetfulness
in the opium. Observing the sky and noting the color of the
desert and the metallic glint of the Sumakhada mountains, the
farmer knows a scorching summer is on the way. It will be
dry. However, there is no cause for anxiety. Heavy summer
rains are still to come.

June passes. No rain. In July great storms usually thunder
from the southeast and splinter against the mountains, drench-
ing the land. The whole region, especially in the loop formed
by the Yellow River, becomes a sheet of water. Still no rain in
July. Now the farmer feels anxiety gnawing. He dreams of
water. A merciless sun tortures the land, burning all life. It
blights the green shoots at a stroke. Parched top soil turns to

dust and sand. The mountains, gun-metal blue, are like polished reflectors focusing heat rays on the plain below. The Gobi creeps closer. Even the bull-shouldered river, the Huang Ho, "China's Sorrow," seems to shrivel, receding from its banks. The clay bakes to brick hardness.

Autumn. The farmer harvests some *kao-liang*, a native corn, hardy enough to live through the drought. The ears are stunted and the kernels juiceless and tough. A wordless message flashes between the farmer and his wife. Hunger this winter. They have known hunger before. There have been other droughts. But none so fierce as this one. He has no reserves, no store of wheat, barley, or corn, and no animals. Some of his neighbors will slaughter an ox or a horse before the long northern winter ends. The wise farmer will spare his strongest and swiftest horse, no matter how hungry he gets.

One morning a chilling wind sweeps out of the north through the snows of the Great Khingan Mountains. Snow makes a Greek frieze of the Sumakhada peaks. The sun, so fierce a few months months before, grows pale now behind cold gray clouds. This is the signal to scour the land for fuel. In a few days not a stick of wood, a leaf, a wisp of straw remains on the ground in any part of Suiyuan or the whole of Inner Mongolia. The first blizzard rides a howling wind. Between storms and the moaning of the wind, white silence settles over the land. The farmer and his wife and children hole in to wait.

They live on paste made from ground *kao-liang*, a few kernels at a time, mixed with water. The corn is soon gone. There is fire only to heat the gruel and make tea. The little pile of sticks and leaves begins to shrink. Huddled in quilted coats, strips of straw matting to cover the crops they never harvested, and every possible rag, they stay in the hut, waiting.

The farmer's wife has found a strip of rotten gunny sack. It has lain in dirt and darkness all summer. She wraps it around her neck to keep warm. The warmth of her body wakens a flea from winter stupor. It burrows through the sacking toward warm flesh. She does not feel it when the flea bites her. Five or six days later a small pain begins in her back. She feels hot and dizzy, so dizzy that the slightest movement is an effort. The farmer heats some tea. She swallows a cup and instantly retches. The next day she falls into a coma, and the day after that she is dead. Typhus.

The farmer drags her body outdoors and covers it with snow. In the spring, when the iron-hard ground thaws, he will dig a proper grave. Spring never comes for the farmer or his children. The fleas bite them, too. . . .

Famine and Pestilence gallop through Suiyuan, through Jehol, through Shensi, Shansi, and Kansu.

A third Horseman joins them.

Long winter shadows stretch freezing fingers across the desert and the plain. All is silent. The little village looks dead and deserted. Then suddenly in the distance comes the swishing thud of horses running across hard-packed snow. Faint at first, the sound grows until it is a beating thunder. If the villagers hear it in time, they summon their last small ounce of energy and throw themselves against the doors. The hoofbeats are close by now. Shots crackle and spit, and there is shrieking. It is all over in a few minutes. Doors are beaten down. Where there is resistance, a knife or a clubbed rifle silences it. The horsemen ride off, carrying whatever they found to eat or sell. Some of the marauders are farmers who had the foresight to spare their strongest horses. Gaunt, hunger-maddened wolves, they have joined bandit gangs to prey on people as poor as themselves. Dog eat dog.

This was the winter of 1927-8.

Drought still clutched the land in 1929. It held on into 1930. Through three consecutive years the harvests failed. It is these fierce weather cycles, endlessly recurring over thousands of years, that have burned a hole in that corner of China. They created the Gobi and Ordos deserts and stripped the mountains, leaving savage spires of naked rock. Rains may fail in any year, but the Great Drought lasted three harvests.

With famine came pestilence. Typhus is a perennial problem in that part of the world. The lice lurk in rags and straw, waiting for a "host." They carry the deadly bacteria, and it enters the blood stream when they bite. A healthy man can throw off the disease with a little luck and care. (How well I know!) But even a tough peasant is doomed if it strikes him when he is already half dead from starvation.

So, piles of corpses stacked up like frozen logs outside every town and village. Living skeletons stared with dazed, unseeing eyes. Some were so emaciated that their ribs stuck out like a washboard. Children walked around with stomachs bloated from eating bark, weeds, apricot pits, and clay. How many died? In Suiyuan they estimated two million. In the whole region it may have been six million. Who can say?

You may ask: "Why was so great a catastrophe unknown to the rest of the world? Surely food and medical supplies could have been rushed in." Yes, they could have been, but weren't, for reasons you will see.

We came to this scene in the summer of 1930.

On a July morning shortly before noon the screen door flung open and the major burst into the room. Outside, the temperature was well over a hundred. Blinding sunlight poured into the compound, and puffs of hot, dry air came through the screen door. I was lying in the wooden bunk in shorts, alternately reading and fanning myself with a copy of the Peking & Tientsin *Times.*

"I don't see much road building going on today," said the major.

"It's Sunday, Major," I said. "I thought—"

"Famine doesn't know about Sunday," he snapped. The door slammed as he went outside.

Major O. J. Todd was an engineer, formerly of the U.S. marine corps. He was short and wiry, with a wintry face, thinning hair, and gray eyes that bored a hole through you. There was a parade-ground snap in his voice, even when he spoke Chinese, and obedience became a reflex. He drove himself and everyone around him like a man possessed. He was on his feet early and late, skipped meals, and often forgot to put on hat or helmet when he went out into the fierce Mongolian sun. He looked tough and he was, physically and in every way. We called him "Todd Almighty" and loved him. He was a dedicated man.

Todd was dedicated to an irrigation ditch. He had come to Suiyuan to dig a canal that would carry water from the Yellow River to the Black River. In the triangular area thus formed, a system of subsidiary ditches and laterals would irrigate some three hundred and fifty thousand acres in the heart of the region most susceptible to drought. The China International Famine Relief Commission, an organization financed largely with American money, had authorized the project. Todd had taken command in 1929 during the worst days of the famine.

He lived only for his ditch. He went racing around the countryside, a human sandstorm in an old Dodge pickup truck, spurring on the coolie foremen, talking with the engineers, supervising grain payments, recruiting labor, auditing the books, riding the rock-carrying barges, occasionally taking a shovel himself, raging over every delay and setback. He was a one-man construction gang. I never could decide what drove him so hard—pity for the stricken millions, or his marine training.

We had barely unpacked in Peking when we met Todd at a reception in the university. He had been describing conditions in the disaster area. Something about the man—the controlled energy, perhaps—had been so contagious that we asked if we could go to Suiyuan. Bluntly he had replied that he would expect hard work and there would be no wages. Then, doubtless gauging the lure, he had said: "It's a little dangerous up there."

Two days later George Gambell, a student of foreign trade, and I boarded the train with Todd. The others were to follow. The train passed through the Great Wall of China at the city of Shanhaikwan, "The Gate between Mountain and Sea." Todd recalled the battles fought there during the Boxer rebellion and the time when Manchu bannermen surged through the Great Wall to establish the last dynasty in China. Next came Kalgan, a Mongol city. This name also means "gateway."

Outer Mongolia is a pure Mongol nation (and Russia and China have some unsettled accounts with each other there), but through the years the Chinese came to dominate Inner Mongolia.

Dark-faced, stubby little men with flat noses and watchful brown eyes were riding ponies through the streets of Kalgan. A Mongol never walks if he can ride. A man came out of a shop carrying a package, unhitched the shaggy little pony, mounted, and rode across the street to another shop. A moment later he rode four doors to a third shop. They wore round blue hats, long robes of the same color, and high-heeled boots. These were the descendants of Genghis Khan and the Golden Horde, fierce horsemen who swept out of central Asia, stormed through China, burning and killing, and engulfed the ancient Kingdom of Korea. Near modern Pusan, at the southern tip, they assembled a fleet and sailed out to add Japan to the Khan's domain. Fortune spared the Japanese. *Kami Kaze*, "Heavenly Wind," scattered the Mongol armada as another storm centuries later scattered the Spanish armada. Another point in the parallel between Japan and Britain.

From Kalgan the train turned southward in Suiyuan, panting through the hot night. Todd talked and talked about his big ditch. I took notes and later wrote a report on the project, sitting in a hut beside the Yellow River. Here is a fragment:

"The Suiyuan Canal and its subsidiaries constitute a large-scale plan to irrigate 2,000,000 *mau* (350,000 acres) of plain. The main canal is being cut from the Yellow River to the Black River, a distance of 40 miles through the heart of the heat-absorbing danger area. It will run at a 45-degree angle with relation to the Yellow River, forming a triangle. Thirteen subsidiary ditches, spaced at intervals of three miles, and fourteen laterals will carry water to every corner of the plain. At the fourteenth lateral, which is a part of the Black River, the water will have dropped approximately 30 feet from the point where it left the Yellow River. The cost will run to about $1,000,000, silver, most of it for labor. It is all pick-and-shovel work by an average force of 4,000 coolies. There are no steam-shovels or earth-moving machinery."

Late the following afternoon the train came to the end of the line at a town called Seratsi. Even before it stopped, two Chinese swung aboard and quickly found the major. Their eyes were rolling and they spewed out words, talking at the same time. Todd listened impassively. He broke in to say something, apparently a question. It brought another long outburst. The train stopped. Todd turned to us and said quietly: "Bad news. They killed the *pai-tou* last night." A *pai-tou* was a foreman or labor contractor. For a lump sum he hired labor crews in the villages.

A truck took us through Seratsi to a large walled compound on the edge of open country. A guard with a rifle stood at the gate. Sandbags covered the walls and the watch towers set on each corner. Todd strode through a courtyard, flung his bag beside a door without stopping, and went to another enclosure, flanked with stables.

In a niche cut in the mud wall lay the body of the *pai-tou*. He had been shot in the face several times. Only a black mask remained. One of the two Chinese who had boarded the train suddenly flung himself against the wall and burst into frantic, tortured sobbing. His fingers scratched and dug convulsively. The murdered man, Todd said, was his brother. Todd's face was bleak as he knelt down beside the sobbing man. He put his arm around him and spoke softly and gently led him away.

"Four men came into the house last night," he said. "Nobody recognized them. Anyway, that's what they say. They had blackened their faces for a disguise. The *pai-tou* was asleep. He never knew what hit him."

"What was it about?"

"Labor dispute probably," he said. "They're happening more often now. It shows things are getting better. Last year they'd work for anything. Now we're beginning to have trouble."

Rifle shots crackled somewhere nearby. We sat up in the bunks, listening. Gray dawn light glowed in the window. A door slammed. We ran out into the courtyard. A Chinese was grinding the starter on the truck, and Todd, who had never learned to drive, sat beside him gabbling rapid Chinese and rocking with impatience. We jumped in just as the motor turned over and the truck raced through the gate in a swirl of dust.

In a minute or two the railway tracks came into view. Two freight cars stood on the siding. A confused knot of black figures swarmed around the cars. Some were running away. As the truck skidded to a stop, others fled down the embankment. Still others crouched beneath the cars. There were women and children among them. The train that brought us to Seratsi the night before carried two cars loaded with sacks of grain. The floor boards were hardly more than slats with wide spaces between. Thrusting knives, broken glass, and the jagged edges of tin cans through the spaces, the people had ripped open the sacking. They held baskets and big straw hats to catch the grain pouring out.

Todd, roaring like a bull, caught an old woman around the shoulders and flung her bodily down the embankment. She rose to her knees, scraped a handful of grain from the ground, and fled. In a wink the major threw another woman and a man away from the car. They offered no resistance except to cling to the baskets and hats filled with grain. It was all over in a brief moment. Breathing hard, Todd ordered the men to set buckets under the rivulets of grain streaming down from the two cars. Then he turned furiously on two men with rifles. It was not necessary to understand Chinese to recognize a Homeric chewing-out in the manner of the marine corps. "They either went to sleep or they're in cahoots with the people in town," growled the major. "My fault for not putting on an extra man last night. That business about the *pai-tou* made it slip my mind. Well, let's get going . . ."

Back at the compound the cook said: "How you likee eggs? Fly, boil, mixslup?" The major and George ordered fried eggs. "Mixslup" turned out to be scrambled. Todd swallowed ham, eggs, toast, and three cups of coffee in what seemed like a single co-ordinated motion. Then, having ascertained that I could drive the truck, he rose and said: "Let's get going."

"Let's go. Let's go." A hundred times a day he murmured it, often talking to himself.

From Seratsi the road led across twenty-one miles of flat plain to the Yellow River and the point where the mouth of the canal would open. It was little more than a track, cut by the carts and trucks, running straight except to veer around sand dunes and enter the villages dotting the route. Here and there it passed stunted trees, listless and drooping, as though hunger had blighted them, too. In the clear morning light the jagged mountains looked deceptively close. The sun was barely over the horizon, but already the rays stung the back of my neck, and the Dodge began to smell of hot grease. It was harsh and forbidding country, yet with a savage beauty. The major breathed in deeply. "Great country," he said. "Can't you go any faster?"

The road curved into a miserable little village. It smelled of death, as they all did. Todd found the local *pai-tou*. They walked over to a mound of grain bags covered with straw matting. The major counted them and scribbled some figures in a notebook. While they were talking, a man plodded toward them, pushing a wheelbarrow. He moved painfully. When he reached the grain, two other men lifted a bag from the pile and set it in the wheelbarrow. Each lifted one handle and trundled the wheelbarrow across the yard to a hut. The first man, meanwhile, slumped against the bags. His arms fell limply in his lap and his head hung down. All three were famine victims just beginning to work a few hours every day. They were barely strong enough to push a wheelbarrow. As food came into Suiyuan the year before, the first step had been to get coolies back on their feet. Obviously nothing could be done until some strength flowed into them again. Then the contractors assigned them to light work—pushing a wheelbarrow and odd chores. Gradually they put them on heavier work. At a given stage of recovery, depending on the judgment of the contractors, they took shovels and went to the canal to dig. The more they could do, the more grain they earned. It sounds heartless, a reversal of logic. Surely a weak man should receive more than a strong one. There was a reason, however. As the starvation point passed, the farmers began drifting away from the labor gangs on the canal. They simulated weakness, received their grain rations, and tilled their own fields.

Todd stopped at three more villages. The procedure was the same in each—a discussion with the *pai-tou*, an examination of the grain and counting of the bags, an eagle-eyed look at the people, not only the men, but the women and children as well. Then a strange sight appeared ahead on the road, a vision so startling I thought it must be a mirage. A walled city rose from the desert. Crenellated towers were spaced at regular intervals along the walls. Behind them a slim Gothic spire shimmered in the sunlight. "Paotow," said the major. "A nice fellow lives here. Belgian priest. He built those walls."

Paotow was bigger than the other villages. It looked a little more prosperous and therefore was a regular target for the bandits. Todd said the priest erected the walls many years before. He modeled them after the only form of fortification he knew—the castles and battlements of medieval Europe. He had blended Norman forms with Chinese features. So, there in the heart of Mongolia stood a medieval European town. The stone tower, completely Gothic, rose above a long, one-storied Chinese building. Gothic arches framed the windows and formed the entrance. This was the church—a handsome, symmetrical spire dominating the town. In the low Chinese building the priest lived in a cell and took his meals in a refectory, which I came to know well. From the battlements the Paotow people could fight off frontal attacks. But in the age-old maneuver against walled cities the bandits hid a man or two inside the town during the day and expected them to open the gates after dark. "They get in cahoots with somebody in town," said the major. "You can't trust anybody any more."

Not far from Paotow we came to a section of the main canal. The floor at this point was twelve meters wide, and the banks sloped backward, making the surface width considerably greater. It ran straight as an arrow toward the river, farther than I could see. Hundreds of coolies were digging, filling *shun dze,* wicker baskets, with dirt and toiling up ramps cut in the banks to carry it away. They took two baskets at a time, using carrying-poles. While Todd talked with a foreman, I walked down the ramp to the floor of the canal. A coolie had just filled both baskets. I put my shoulder under the carrying-pole, lifted them, and took one step. That was all. The weight seemed to be crushing my collarbone. I staggered and set the baskets down. The coolies guffawed. Millions of tons of earth had been cut, lifted away, and carried to dumping points by human muscle. China may lack machinery. But an all-powerful government able to concentrate unlimited human labor on a given project doesn't need bulldozers. People are cheaper.

Tattered rags covered some of the coolies. Others wore only a G-string. Still others, oblivious of the women passing the scene, were stark naked. Here there were no signs of starvation any more, no emaciated faces or protruding ribs. These men had been among the first to receive food from the International Famine Relief Commission. Little by little they had grown strong enough to walk, start light work, and come at last to this crushing labor.

Not all were working, however. Squatting in a field not far from the lip of the canal a circle of men sat talking. Each held a brass pipe with a long, slim shaft and a tiny bowl at the end. They were smoking opium. They had already forgotten the famine. If they understood the purpose of the canal—to guard against the next drought—they no longer cared. Todd spotted them and strode toward the circle, snarling. They quickly put away the pipes and picked up their carrying-poles.

When we had got into the truck again, he asked why the coolies had laughed.

"Just wanted to see how much the baskets weighed," I said. "I sure found out. That's why they laughed."

"Don't ever let 'em get away with that," he said seriously. "If one of 'em ever laughs at you again, knock him down." He meant it, too. Later on, Oliver Haskell, a mild-mannered student of sociology, had a dispute with a gang foreman. The men dropped their shovels and walked off the job. "You know what to do," Todd said as he rushed up. He found the *pai-tou* and knocked him down himself.

"Here's the picture," he said to me that first day. "We pay the contractors, and they get the men from the villages to do the digging. They can have either money or grain for wages.

A year ago most of them wanted grain. Things are better now and they're not so hungry. Still, there is a lot of grain going out in payments. We've advanced the wages to the contractors, and some of them are trying to welsh out. I know what's happening, of course. The coolies want to go back into their own fields before they work out the advances we've made. They're not going to get away with it."

My job, he said, would be to meet the train that came twice a week from Peking to the terminus at Seratsi. Sometimes it would bring two carloads of grain, sometimes one. I was to load the bags on the truck and distribute the grain throughout the villages between Seratsi and the river, a specified number of bags to the *pai-tou* in each place, and get a receipt.

"Now that won't keep you busy all the time," said the major. "When you're not distributing grain, you will take a couple of men and build roads."

"I never built a road, Major," I said. "Not sure I know how."

"You know how to fill up holes and take out ruts, don't you? It's plain shoveling. Can't make any time when the road's in this shape."

All afternoon he kept urging me to drive faster. On a straight stretch I put the accelerator down to the floor boards. The light truck leaped. It whipped into a curve. The right front wheel hit a patch of loose sand and the truck went out of control. It flipped over on its side and flung the major and me into the ditch in a shower of dust and sand. I expected him to explode in a blast that would rattle the windows from here to Peking. He staggered to his feet and stood for a moment, wiping his eyes and slapping dust out of his clothing. "I thought you said you knew how to drive," he said mildly. Some coolies righted the truck and pushed it back on the road. "Let's go," said the major. "We're losing time."

At last the river, the mighty Huang Ho, came into view. A camp stood beside it, a cluster of huts and the usual mound of grain bags under yellow straw matting. Coolies were digging in the canal near the point where its mouth would be opened to the river. A barge loaded with granite boulders rode at anchor above the place where they were erecting a weir, a submerged dike in the river bed, just high enough to back up the water, raising the level to help push it into the canal mouth. The chunks of rock were so big that it took four and five coolies to tumble them into the water. Still other workmen were fitting stones into the cement facings on the banks of the river. In common with many such giants, the Yellow River often jumps out of its channel. The low banks of clay and crumbling sand cannot hold it in flood times. It escapes and goes roaring through villages and cities, tumbling houses downstream like ping-pong balls, drowning thousands of people. "China's Sorrow." If it were to veer away from Todd's canal, the whole grid work of ditches and laterals would become a dry waffle.

The engineers' office and sleeping quarters were in a flimsy wooden shack with sandbags stacked around the walls and half covering the windows. Two engineers, an American named Deane and a Swede named Olafsson, came outside as the truck rolled up in front. They all shook hands.

"Have a good trip, Major?"

"Fair," said Todd. "Got some college boys who claim they want to work. See that they do. You'll have most of 'em here."

Inside he quickly checked their figures on the volume of water in the river, the saturation of silt, the average employment, and some charts I did not understand.

"It's going too slow," he said. "We'll have to push 'em harder."

"More and more of them are quitting," said Deane. "They won't stay on the job. The *pai-tous* say they want to plant opium poppies."

"Sure," snapped the major. "It's the poppy season and they're not as hungry as they were. But the *pai-tous* have got their payments and they'll work out the contracts if I have to kill a few. By the way, somebody killed the *pai-tou* at Seratsi the other night."

"We heard about it," said Deane. "One of the engineers, that kid named Tai you got in Tientsin, is windy. He wants to talk to you. I think he's going to quit. Said he saw some *tu fei* [bandits] across the river the other day. You ought to be carrying a gun."

Todd snorted. He lifted a cartridge belt and a pistol from a peg in the office and handed them to me. "Don't let anybody take this away from you, sonny," he said. "Guns are valuable, and remember, those grain sacks are money."

When we turned out the lanterns that night, Olafsson set a loaded rifle against the wall beside each bunk.

Twice a week coolies shouldered grain from the freight cars on the railroad siding in Seratsi and stacked the bags in the pickup truck. While I drove a load to the compound, Tai Yulin stayed behind to keep an eye on the men. Poor Tai; no matter how he tried, some grain always vanished. A bag would be found slit. Tai said he couldn't be everywhere at once. A sack would break, spewing grain. Tai said he stood over the coolies while they scooped it from the ground, yet somehow the bag would be half empty when they finished. "It is all my fault," he would whimper, wringing his hands. "I cannot understand how they stole it, but it is all my fault. I shall frankly admit it to Major Todd."

Of course, he never did.

Tai was the engineer from Tientsin who wanted to quit after the murder of the *pai-tou*. It had taken the major only a scowl and a whiplash remark to make him change his mind. He had gulped, blinked behind his large, horn-rimmed spectacles, and said nothing. He was not a graduate engineer. He had had some training, but it was his father's connections with a Kuomintang official that got him his position with the Famine Relief Commission. Evidently he had expected a genteel assignment in Peking rather than in the drought area. Still, he said, he had come to Suiyuan to save lives, to help the poor, "to do rather than talk about doing," as he put it. China swarmed with people like Tai, principally students and intellectuals, who burned with the desire "to do." Verbally, at least, a missionary-like zeal fired them with high purpose. Some, like my friend Martin Fong at Lingnan, were sincere and no doubt worked effectively when the time came. But Tai Yu-lin (he had not taken a foreign first name) represented the much larger group who quickly lost flying speed in the hard realities of "doing something." Tai said he had a delicate stomach. The northern diet, with wheat instead of rice as the staple, did not agree with him. The sun and heat in Mongolia hurt his eyes. A day jolting over the roads in the pickup truck, he said, gave him such pains in his back that he could not sleep. He was deathly afraid of typhus. At sundown each night we made everybody strip—the cook, the kitchen help, the yard coolies, and ourselves. Buckets of kerosene stood by. Everyone looked for the fleas and lice that carry typhus. The coolies examined each others' backs. If they found a louse, they touched it with a kerosene-soaked cloth. It shriveled instantly. Tai said the body odor of the coolies made him sick, but he liked having his own back examined through a magnifying glass.

The major assigned him to ride with me in delivering grain to the villages. It was like serving a milk route—so many bags here, so many there. Tai talked to the *pai-tous*, translating. Most of them had fallen behind on the work. Each, remember, had contracted to cut a given section of the canal or laterals for a specified sum. More and more there were reports of men leaving the digging in order to plant their poppies. "He says the work will have to stop until next year," Tai said after one such interview. "I replied, and very sternly, mind you, that he must fulfill his agreement with Major Todd. I said also that he should make the village people understand that the irrigation system will protect them in another drought. It is for their own good. Oh, I gave him a good piece of my mind, never fear." (I'll bet you did, I thought.)

"Todd Almighty will wring his neck," I said.

"Yes, Major Todd is very firm. Perhaps too firm at times. It is wrong to strike the men. I have heard them talking. They say foreigners treat them like cattle because they are Chinese. Pardon me. I hope I have not offended you, but that is what they say."

"Sometimes they're right," I said. "I don't like to see a foreigner kick and slap a ricksha boy, either. My boss on the newspaper in Shanghai calls those people 'shit heroes,' and there are too many of them. On the other hand, Todd is hellbent to finish this job. The men are driving him crazy."

The day came when I hit a coolie myself and knocked him down. It was a searing experience, and perhaps every man should have it once to teach him forbearance. On the days when we were not trucking grain to the villages, Todd told me to take two men and mend the road. One day, an extremely hot day even for that country, I was trying to dig out the shoulder of a dune to straighten a curve. Every few yards of sand and dirt removed caused more sand to tumble down from the side, so that after an hour or so of digging, the road was in a worse condition than when we had started. One of the two men was fat, round-faced, with jet black hair. He kept talking constantly. From time to time both laughed. Finally, when one big slide swept off the dune into the road, the fat one said something and they both leaned on their shovels, helpless with mirth. An instant later, feeling the pain in my knuckles, I was sick with self-loathing. Another "shit hero" striking a coolie.

On the days when we delivered grain, I tried to time it so that the truck would arrive in Paotow at noon. Father LaFond, a Belgian priest, always asked us to stay for lunch. He was a fascinating man. Robes tend to make a man look tall, but even in his long brown cassock Father LaFond was still short. His beard matched his eyes, deep brown, hypnotic eyes filled with wisdom and gentleness. A quiet smile never left his face or his eyes. He spoke in a low, quiet voice. If he had any inner conflicts, they never showed. He looked like a man at peace with himself and the world, quietly sure he could call on the Lord whenever necessary. In the tradition of his predecessors, Father LaFond was well grounded in the practical sciences. During the seventeenth century Jesuits at the imperial court instructed officials, and often the Emperor himself, in geometry, mathematics, astronomy, medicine, and military ordinance. Their positions gave them security in China at a time when foreigners generally were barred from the country. Father LaFond had designed the beautiful stone spire and supervised the building of his church, his living quarters, and the city's walls. He laughed when I said that from a distance Paotow looked like a medieval city in Normandy. "Not Normandy," he said. "Bruges. I was a young man then, still remembering Bruges." When I met him, he had been in China thirty-four years, most of them in the northwest. He said that during this long span he had returned to Europe for an operation and a long convalescence. Europe tasted like weak wine by comparison with China, he said. "I was impatient to come back to my work here. Of course, in the ideal we are supposed to arrange matters so that we ourselves become superfluous. To work ourselves out of a job, as you say in America. However, I pray nothing will take me from here again."

And I pray that he went to his reward before the Communists took China and the torturing began.

You were strongly tempted to impose on his time, to linger in the cool, dimly lighted refectory, asking questions. You could not be long in China without forming some opinions about the missionaries. You could not wholly agree, either, with the foreign businessmen and Chinese students, the ma-

jority of whom sneered at missionaries and their work. Father
LaFond was an inexorable realist. He said Chinese nationalism probably would make the missionaries' position more difficult. He faced the fact that the Chinese tended to identify all
Christian converts with the foreigners. Tactfully he veered
away from the question of whether the Christian churches
should support the Chinese in their drive to revise the "unequal treaties." Nor did he ever discuss the Protestants and
their works in China. The comparisons of Catholics and Protestants, the differences of approach, of philosophy, methods,
schools, landowning, numbers of converts, numbers of back-
sliders, numbers of Chinese clergymen—comparisons often
flavored with little sarcasms and heavy-handed ironies—never
rose to Father LaFond's lips. He seldom talked about converting the Chinese, but he waxed enthusiastic in describing ways
of helping them. He made it all seem simple and crystal clear.
You love, therefore you help.

Not long after we left Paotow, on a return trip to Seratsi
the motor in the truck gagged and stopped. I examined the
carburetor and the spark plugs and ascertained that the gas
line was not plugged. Whatever the trouble, it was beyond me.
There was a village nearby. "Skip over and get some horses,"
I told Tai. "We need to be towed home." The wind had started
to rise. By the time he came back, leading two Mongolian
ponies, pillars of dust twisted across the plain. Gusts of hot
wind sent the sand flying. It stung like buckshot. The side of
my face began to feel raw. "This is terrible," said Tai. "It may
last a long time and the dust makes me ill." He covered his
mouth with a handkerchief. During certain seasons the wind
blows for days in Mongolia. The low moaning goes on and on.
Tempers fray. You become nervy, depressed, unable to eat,
beset with a nameless anxiety. To step out of doors into the
abrasive sand and dust is an ordeal. Foreigners especially
dread the coming of the winds.

That day, however, we had reason to be grateful for it.

As the ponies plodded around a dune, straining against the wind, Tai suddenly gasped: *"Tu-fei!"* He pointed. A mile or so ahead and to the right of us were eight or nine men. They wore round Mongol hats and long rough coats. They were walking the ponies, moving at an angle that would soon bring them to the road. Tai stared with wide, mesmerized eyes. He tried to speak, but the words rattled in his throat.

"How do you know they're bandits?"

"The guns," he gasped. "See the guns?" Each of the horsemen carried a rifle slung across his back. I had to admit that harmless farmers would hardly be riding to the fields carrying rifles.

Tai jumped out of the truck and ran, crouching, around the shoulder of the sand dune. "I hope they did not see us," he said, panting. "Oh, I hope so."

"Probably didn't with all this dust. Anyway, if they rob us, they won't get much. They're welcome to the goddamn truck."

"Your gun," he said. "They will kill you to get it."

In detective stories it says that the feel of a gun, the weight and the hard metal, gives a feeling of assurance. It may be. But the more I thought of it, the less I liked having the pistol. Tai was right. I wrapped it in a bandanna and buried it with the cartridge belt in loose sand.

Then I crawled to the top of the dune to watch the horsemen. In a stage whisper Tai asked what they were doing. They had tethered the horses in a clump of trees and were squatting on the ground. Tai moaned. "They are waiting for the wind to stop," he said. "They may wait all night. Oh, what shall we do?"

"Perhaps we should go on. Pay no attention to them. They might not bother us."

Terror froze his face. "No, no. They probably would let you go, but they would hold me for ransom. Let us leave the truck and run away from here. There are better places to hide."

An hour passed. The men stayed under the trees. Then the

wind began to die down. The dust thinned and the air cleared.
Low on the horizon the sun was a bright orange. One by one
the horsemen got up. Still walking the ponies, they crossed the
road. A few minutes later they were out of sight behind the
dunes.

"They've gone, Tai," I said. "We can—"

He was gone, too. Later the major said Tai had been seen
in Peking. "Good riddance," he snorted.

When I undressed that night I felt something move in the pit
of my arm and a slight itching. Ordinarily it would have sent
me rushing for a kerosene-soaked cloth. But the stinging in my
cheek from the sand made me overlook it. I put more cold
water on my face and fell into the bunk. A week later I
wakened during the night. The room seemed unusually hot.
Then a chill shook me, and I pulled the sheet up to my chin,
shivering. My head ached. There was a hot iron behind my
eyeballs. Little else in the next two weeks is clear, except some
images, real and unreal. One of the images is of a large,
square, almost bovine face bending over the bunk, and a pair
of incredibly dirty hands. It is linked with the memory of
some bitter liquid. This was Dr. Gao. The "Dr." was probably
literary license. As for his pharmacopoeia, it seems improbable
that any chemist ever stocked it. For all I knew or cared, it
was a brew of spider webs and powdered serpent skulls. The
other image is of George Gambell sitting beside the bunk,
and hearing a voice that must have been mine asking: "Is it
typhus?" I slipped into unconsciousness without hearing his
answer.

The delirium began. I saw the house in Shanghai where
those ten murders had taken place. The corpses merged into
the Communist meeting. Lola Liang's head lay on the floor

and she was saying something. Then I was in the Pearl River, gasping for breath, tasting bitter water, and frantic because the river crawls with germs. I tried to swim, but something held my arms like a heavy weight, and it turned out to be an ocean-going junk with Dr. Gao's eyes in the prow.

At last a morning came when the table where George and I played casino, the two chairs, and the other objects in the room stood still, clearly in focus. I felt paralyzed, but, no, my fingers wiggled when I tried to move them. There was a great weariness and yet a warm blur of peace. I fell asleep. When my eyes opened again, it was night and I felt hungry. Strength slowly returned. Dr. Gao brought a bowl of chicken broth, and I tried to hold the spoon, but dropped it. His hands were still incredibly dirty, but deft and gentle as he held the spoon. A grin split his broad, cowlike face. "Okay, now," he said.

The major flung open the door. He talked a moment with Dr. Gao, then turned to me. "You're out of the woods," he said, "but you won't have much strength for a while. Sending you back to Peking. Appreciate your help and—" He glanced at his wrist watch. "Holy smoke, look at the time! So long, and good luck."

A busy man, the major.

In Peking I added a long section to the report on Suiyuan mentioned earlier. Here are passages from it:

"Hundreds of farmers have quit the canal to seed their own poppy and grain fields. The work has stopped in many places. Having been fed, they either refuse to work or apply the screws in a hundred ways to squeeze more money from the Commission. Wages have been doubled and re-doubled and bonuses are offered. It has little effect on the farmers. Next year, between harvests, they may return but not this year.

"As a typical example of the disillusioning actions, when a crew reached the water-table, they all quit. They believe working in a few inches of water makes them sick. The digging stopped until special pumps could be brought from Tientsin.

"Murders take place in spite of assurances of protection from local authorities. Not a hand is lifted to find and arrest the murderers, who are not always bandits but sometimes the farmers . . . Some of the *pai-tous* say they are being threatened for higher wages . . . In villages where the Commission has offices, funds needed for the canal are being used to pay special guards.

"The books at Seratsi are a tangle of bad debts, broken contracts, graft, 'squeeze' and plain thievery. . . ."

In a special way the Suiyuan story is illuminating.

We have seen some of the government officials, national and local, before this, along with the war lords and the Chinese merchants in Shanghai. We know what to expect of them. During the worst stages of the famine no government authorities rushed in with effective action. On the contrary, war lords and minor military satraps refused to spare any railroad cars to carry supplies to Suiyuan. Moreover, merchants and speculators held back stores of wheat and grain as long as the prices kept rising. These gentlemen teach us nothing new.

Then the International Famine Commission came into the picture, bringing assistance in several forms. A foretaste of the American experience on the Ledo Road and other supply routes to China during the Pacific War quickly developed. The aforementioned graft and "squeeze" rode in on the freight cars. For example, a section of the report in my Peking notes added: ". . . the mysterious loss of an average of 3½ catties [about four pounds] of grain per sack along the route."

Finally, the Chinese farmer himself, the peasant, joined in the peculation wherever he could. When he no longer needed the assistance, the grain and the employment that enabled him to buy food, he dropped his shovel. He was oblivious to commitments, untroubled by any sense of duty or responsibility. As an ignorant man, condemned to a precarious existence, fiercely intent on survival for his family and himself, he may be forgiven. Still, it was another aspect of China at another moment in history.

The dog-eat-dog aspect.

Chapter XIX

THE

GLORY OF THE AGES

MANY THOUSANDS of years ago in a distant part of China a nobleman prepared to go to Peking. At the last moment his wife asked him to make a small purchase for her—a comb. She specified a wide, crescent-shaped comb. Knowing her husband's weaknesses, as all wives do, she said tactfully: "You have so many important matters, it may be that you will forget the comb. To remember, you need only do this: look in the eastern sky at the new moon."

Sure enough her husband forgot. "However," he said to a merchant in The Street of the Happy Phoenix, "I do recall that my wife told me the moon would remind me. It is curious, but that is what she said." Together the two men stepped outside the shop and looked at the sky.

Directly above the Tien-an Men a full moon was rising. Instantly the shopkeeper said: "But of course! Your honored lady asked that you bring her this new thing—a mirror."

"How clever you are," said the nobleman.

"And how fortunate you are," said the shopkeeper. "You could search all of Peking and not find a mirror. It so happens that I have one."

In that distant time, as the shopkeeper said in all truth, mirrors were a new thing. Few people had ever seen one. And so, when the nobleman's wife first looked in the mirror, she uttered a cry of surprise and grief. The poor woman burst into tears. "My husband has a mistress in the city," she said to her mother. "I have found her portrait. She is younger and prettier than I am."

"Let me see the portrait," said her mother. At a single glance she laughed scornfully. "Jealousy has made you blind. Why, this woman is even older and uglier than I am."

Now, with this Chinese story as a preface to remind us that feelings color vision and that we all look at the same object through different prisms, let us see Peking.

I begin with a flat, unqualified assertion: Peking is the glory of the world.

It is one gigantic object of art, pure beauty and grace, distilled over the centuries from the genius of architects, painters, decorators, landscapers, city planners, and gifted artisans. No other city in the world is so nobly conceived, so majestic. Peking is beyond comparison.

This is an extravagant view, and by no means does everyone share it. To one pair of eyes the double-roofed temples and the great gates, which are really buildings, appear overmassive. The brilliant colors seem garish to some. Depressed by the April windstorms that harry Peking, people came away with a visual memory of a drab, dust-coated city. One day a couple sank into chairs beside me on the veranda of the Hotel des Wagons Lits, and the man said: "Well, we've looked at all the palaces and temples in the joint, and you can have 'em." His wife said: "Too much clashing colors for my taste." And there was the party of tourists at the Ming Tombs, and the man who called out: "Come on, boys, let's give 'em the old Chicago yell. The whole place is dead."

The descriptions of Peking written by Englishmen and Hollanders who saw it in the seventeenth and eighteenth centuries are brief and matter of fact. To be sure, they had their minds fixed on trade, and the splendor of the city may have translated itself into visions of the enormous fortunes to be made in China. The fact that the emperors thought the white men came bearing tribute, as did the Indians, Mongols, Tonkinese, and Tibetans, probably colored their view, too. They were kept waiting beside the five marble bridges over the River of Golden Water, in the first courtyard of the Forbidden City, until a bell summoned them to the presence of the Son of Heaven. More often than not he sent them home empty-handed and with a picture quite different from the one left by the indefatigable Venetian, Marco Polo. The later emperors had ceased to emulate Kublai Khan. The Khan's great partisan, Ser Marco Polo, says that in his day there were twenty-five thousand courtesans in Peking and he reports:

"When ambassadors arrive . . . it is customary to maintain them at His Majesty's expense, and in order that they may be treated in the most honorable manner, the captain-general is ordered to furnish nightly to each individual of the embassy one of these courtesans, who is likewise to be changed every night, for which service, as it is considered in the light of a tribute they owe the Sovereign, they do not receive any remuneration."

To me Peking is a white city, a paradise of alabaster. This is a subjective impression, a sensibility, not entirely a literal fact. True, the Ivory Bridge is white, and so are the expanses of marble courtyards and conduits, the Bottle Pagoda, and many other structures. Someone else, however, might well see it as a blue-green city because of the Jade Pagoda, the flashing glazed tile roofs of those colors, and the lovely parks where little lakes reflect the trees, doubling the image of green. To still another person the yellow-orange tiles on other palace roofs and the yellow dust spilling down the sides of the Tartar Wall might make Peking a yellow city.

However, the majority image is of a red city. (I am speaking of color, not politics.) The Chinese architect loved flaming red pillars, deep crimson columns and porticoes with gold inlay to accentuate the red, and he put red lacquer on gates and doors. The walls of the Tien-an Men, "Gate of Heavenly Peace," are blood red. Thousands of red flags flutter in the streets. And, of course, in the political symbolism all of China now is Red. Since the dawn of time, red has been the symbol of prosperity in China. It will be interesting to see whether the people will still think so after a few more years of Communism.

In a word, Peking flames with color—red, blue, green, yellow, and white—so much color that you tend to choose unconsciously the one dominant shade in the whole montage. To me it is white.

Structurally Peking is a pattern of squares. It is impossible to resist the simile of a nest of Chinese jewel boxes, one inside another with still smaller ones inside the major squares. The heart of it is the Forbidden City, "The Great Inner Enclosure." Here the Emperor and his ladies lived. It is surrounded by the Imperial City, which was nearly as sacrosanct. Princes, nobles, and the high officers of government lived here with their families. The Northern or "Tartar" City encloses the Imperial City, and the Southern or "Chinese" City is locked into the complex by the outermost walls. Boxes within boxes. The almost inexorable symmetry was no accident. Here again is the admiring Marco Polo:

"The whole plan of the city was laid out by line and the streets in general are consequently so straight that when a person ascends the wall over the gates and looks right forward, he can see the gate opposite to him on the other side of the city. All the allotments of ground upon which the habitations were constructed are square and exactly on a line with each other, each allotment being sufficiently spacious for handsome buildings with corresponding courts and gardens.

"In this manner, the whole interior of the city is disposed in squares so as to resemble a chess board, and planned out with a degree of precision and beauty impossible to describe."

Poor Ser Marco! Even now, seven centuries later, you can still feel his bewilderment as, staggered by such splendor, he struggles to find words to describe Peking. It is a crushing task. Again and again painters, poets, and writers have been overwhelmed by the profusion of palaces, temples, tombs, pagodas, graceful bridges, carved lions and dragons, and the miraculous combinations of mass and airiness. It is not only the number of buildings that is impressive, but the exquisite artisanship visible in the harmonious forms and colors. "Impossible to describe." Let us hope that the Lady Golden Bells, of whom Donn Byrne wrote, really lived, or at least that another as beautiful stood by to lighten the labors of Messer Marco Polo.

Yes, it is impossible to describe Peking; still, the attempt to picture the city should be made. For Peiping, to use the city's present name, is again the seat of frightening power in the world. You will see it appear more and more in the newspapers. Hugh Willetts, in his truly remarkable book *Chinese Art* (published by Braziller in 1958), adds: "As William Empson has remarked in conversation, the Forbidden City was a biological device for ruling the world. And, however ineffectually it may have regulated its own internal affairs, there can be little doubt of its capacity to reduce outsiders to a state of supplicatory awe." One of these days, I believe, Americans will again be standing inside the Forbidden City. In the meantime the effort must be to evoke an image, however imperfect, to go with that dateline in the news—"Peiping."

A special interest attaches to the two major parts of Peking —the Northern City and the Southern City. Kublai Khan built the Northern City, Tai-du, in 1270. The other already existed. Then, says Marco Polo, the Khan's astrologers forecast a rebellion among the Chinese, and he reports: "All of those inhabitants who were natives of Cathay were compelled to evacuate the ancient city and take up their abode in the new." Some four centuries later the process seems to have been reversed. The Manchu emperors gave over most of the Northern

City to their troops for residence. Once again the Chinese began moving, now back to the "Chinese" City.

Perhaps this turbulence—endless cycles of war, pillage, death, destruction and rebuilding, wave after wave of foreign conquerors—may account for the words meaning "peace," "tranquillity," and "harmony" that recur so often in the place names. Listen to them: The Gate of Unity within Harmony; The Palace of Earthly Tranquillity; The Gate of Heavenly Peace; The Tower of Truth; The Pavilion of Sweet Sounds; The Gate of Prosperous Harmony; The Gate of Several Harmonies; The Gate of Peace in Old Age. Music to soothe the savage breast?

Or it may be the other way around. Before the Communists came, there really was a sense of peace and harmony in the air of Peking. Perhaps the mellifluous titles reflect it. Anyway, the atmosphere there was quite unlike that of any other city I ever knew in China. The broad avenues, the parks, and the view from the hills all contributed to a feeling of tranquillity, as though you were in tune with the universe. The sense of quiet happiness contrasted greatly with the frantic gaiety of Shanghai and the moiling quality of cities like Canton and Hankow.

Apart from the physical beauty, the very essence of Chinese art, other factors would account for the feeling of serenity (in spite of the noise and dust) in Peking. It was the center of culture and learning. It was the Athens and Rome of China, and indeed of the whole Orient. Magnificent schools blossomed there, not the least of which were two American institutions— Yenching University, with its lovely campus and buildings, and the medical college established by the Rockefellers.

Never having been a Treaty Port, a Western preserve, the relationships between Chinese and foreigners seemed easier in Peking. The superior-inferior pattern was less pronounced. (This is an uncomfortable relationship, no matter which end of the stick circumstance thrusts into your hand.) The northern Chinese is specially attractive. He tends to be tall, easy-going, given to quiet laughter. The ever recurring "erh" and "sher" sounds make his speech softer. He is quite different in manner and appearance from the fiery, darker-skinned Cantonese, and the stocky, thick-set Szechuen people. He is not "sulky as a Lolo," one of the wild mountain tribes, or as excitable as the Hakka. He makes a wonderful companion. He and Peking deserved each other.

Today in the antlike Communist society, with its regimented drive, that special quality of the great city can scarcely be expected to survive. The population probably has doubled to around three million. New buildings—government offices, hospitals, and factories—in the grim, blocky Communist design rise beside architectural treasures. Toadstools beside a jewel box.

Still, Peking has lived through many catastrophes. Perhaps the instinct for beauty that created it will preserve it through this one.

꽃

The student in the next room began playing his favorite record, "*L'Après-midi d'un faune*." Another student, coming down the corridor from the shower room, was singing a classical Chinese song and easily reaching the soprano notes. Both melodies, the one French and the other Chinese, worlds apart in time and space, blended as though written for each other. Nothing ever jangles in Peking, I thought.

A humid breeze rustled the trees on the university campus and puffed through the dormitory window. It flipped up the sheet of paper in my typewriter. Page forty-eight. "Report from Suiyuan." Many more pages of that story remained to be written. In my description of the disaster and the efforts to meet it, a picture of the Chinese peasant was emerging. It was not a pretty picture, not the idealized one drawn by the students and missionaries. In Suiyuan the peasants preyed on each other exactly as other classes of Chinese preyed on them. They malingered, stole, and murdered, taking wherever possible, giving as little as possible. Karl Marx did not know the Chinese peasants firsthand. However, everything he wrote about this class applied, doubled in spades in China. Marx said that the peasant's first loyalty is to his land. He said that the peasant will join a revolution, or any communal effort, so long as it coincides with self-interest. Then, he warned, the peasant will desert. If Marx had been driving the old Dodge truck in Suiyuan in 1930, he could not have been more accurate. Today the Communists probably have given the peasants more food and clothing than they have had for a long time, but the great communes and all the other marks of iron control indicate that Communism has not changed the fundamental nature of the Chinese peasant. *Tant mieux!*

In any case, a "people-are-no-damn-good" thread ran through my "Report from Suiyuan." Writing it was a catharsis. The beauty of Peking was like a tonic after Suiyuan. I looked at my watch. Time for the bus to the city. Page forty-eight would have to wait.

Outside, a bright sun brought out the colors of the university buildings and set diamonds shimmering in the lake. Yenching University was an American mission school, a gem of architecture and landscaping. The buildings surrounded a lake which was bordered by banks of uneven white stone and dotted with islands, bits of green in the water. An American architect, Henry Murphy, combined Chinese and Western forms in the buildings. The walls were white. Flaming red pillars supported Chinese roofs and porticoes, upswept at the eaves. On a peninsula jutting into the lake stood a miniature of the bigger buildings, a lovely little shrine with red walls trimmed in white and the same curling eaves. A circular resthouse on one of the islands echoed the Temple of Heaven, except that it had only one roof instead of three. Just as Peking is a geometrical entity, from the Ming and Manchu tombs in the Western Hills, fifteen miles away, to the innermost chamber of the Forbidden City, so the plan of the university, the shapes of the buildings and their relation to the grounds, formed a harmonious whole. In every way Yenching was worthy of Peking.

On the way to the city, after passing through a few miles of open country, the bus came to a bridge and stopped. A herd of geese choked the bridge from parapet to parapet, regally indifferent to the cries of a boy herder and the advice of the bus driver. To the Chinese two geese symbolize marital bliss; it seems more substantial, somehow, than the Western symbol, two doves. A bamboo frond is the Chinese counterpart of our symbol of peace, the olive branch. Instead of saying "Let's bury the hatchet," they say "May the bamboo wave." The omnipresent bamboo. It is the coolie's carrying-pole. It provides a construction foreman with scaffolding strong enough to hold any number of men. Hollowed out, it can be converted into a pipe for carrying water. The carpenter shreds it into matting, and the cabinetmaker builds bamboo furniture without nails. Bamboo filaments serve the Chinese artist in the brush with which he paints or writes. By no means least important, the shoots are delicious when eaten separately or when used in flavoring a thousand-and-one dishes. What would the Oriental do without bamboo?

The bus nudged the last indignant goose off the bridge, turned left, and passed through a village. Now the glow of tile roofs, blue, green, and yellow glaze, shimmered in the sky above Peking. The topmost stories of pagodas came into view, shining through the trees. The bus passed a small stone bridge. Its architect, more concerned with beauty than comfort, built the arch so high that it formed a perfect circle with its reflection in the water. Silvery bells pealed in the streams of rickshas. This, too, was typical of Peking. In other Chinese cities a ricksha runner warned pedestrians out of his path with a harsh shout—"*Wa-a-a, waa.*" The Peking ricksha carried bells, which were attached to the plunger beneath the passenger's foot. A high note would be sounded first, immediately followed by a lower note. If you first touch C and then G-sharp on the piano, you will hear something like the bell music that sounded in the streets of Peking day and night. The music echoed the city's rhythms. Some cities have an aura, a personality as distinct as a human personality. You can feel San Francisco long before you pass the city limits. Mukden at first sight gave me a feeling of dread; I had the same feeling about the Red Fort in New Delhi. Singapore is a tennis player in white shorts. Moscow has steel teeth. Rome is a crystal chandelier with tinkling prisms. Hanoi and New Orleans are half-brothers. A physical connection between the ruins of Angkor, in Indochina, and those of Palenque, in southern Mexico, seems highly improbable; yet the two ghost cities speak the same language. In appearance Bali and Peking could be on separate planets, but the spirit of each, the serenity and lightheartedness, was astonishingly alike. To the Balinese, creation of an object, not its value or use, is an end in itself. A Chinese saying expresses somewhat the same feeling—and adds a snapper: "We invented the compass, but prefer to stay in Peking. We invented paper, but do not publish newspapers. We discovered gunpowder, but made no firearms." And for the benefit of Americans they often would add: "We built the first ocean-going junks, but did not use them to discover America."

Peking was one of those cities where you walked for the sake of walking, without any compulsion to reach any objective or do anything when you arrived. The pure pleasure of observing the dappled pattern of sunlight and shade on a marble wall was enough. Or you could stroll around the Thieves' Market, which was stocked for the most part with articles actually stolen, and pick up a tennis racket cheap, a Han bronze guaranteed to be a genuine antique, or a packet of pornographic pictures. There was a circus in Morrison Street, advertised by a huge sign in English: "Colossal! Amazing! Spectacular! Each act is better than the next!"

In the markets, as in other Chinese cities, shops stocked with the same merchandise rubbed elbows in the same street. Jewelry Street. Box Street. Gold Street. Silver Street. At one time the Chinese held gold and silver to be of equal value. The white man's fascination with gold amused them and was taken as another evidence of his uncultured tastes. But the price of gold went up.

Bronze Street. To cast a perfect bell, the Chinese once said, there must be a mating of the male and female principles. The Ying and the Yang. All life springs from the mating of the male sun and the female earth. The Chinese symbolize it in a round disc with intermingling patterns of dark and light. In the dim past, they say, to insure a perfect tone in the bell, the artisan and his wife threw themselves into the molten metal at exactly the right moment. Later, it seems, a wise man (you will note it was a man) discovered that inasmuch as the furnace itself embodied the male principle, there was no need for the artisan to immolate himself. His wife alone would do.

Jade Street. Why do we call an unchaste woman a "jade" and use "jaded" as a synonym for surfeit or weariness? No philologist would agree, I am sure, but it is interesting to consider the question in the light of the story of jade in China. More than three thousand years ago the Chinese ascribed magic powers to it. They used it in sacrificial rites. They carved stylized representations of the male and female principles in jade. Mysticism surrounded the strange stone, which was green or candle-grease gray. Then the Chinese endowed it with all the virtues—longevity, purity of soul, truth, and sincerity (sincerity because it does not conceal its flaws and in fact gains in beauty by revealing them). Then, perhaps around 100 B.C., jade began to lose this high estate. It was still the most precious of stones, but it came into use for ornamentation, worn by emperors and princes. Some five hundred years later a dam seemed to break. Jade articles in profusion came from the jewelers' shops—figurines, bowls, even hairpins. The Chinese still admired the beauty of the stone, and an emperor wrote in praise of it on a jade tablet. But the rarity and mystical qualities had gone. Like a "jade," jade retained its looks but lost its virtue, and perhaps the Chinese grew "jaded" from seeing it in so many forms.

In Ivory Street I entered a shop to resume an old argument and visit a singsong girl. A singsong girl was the Chinese equivalent of the geisha in Japan—an entertainer, more or less. The shopkeeper smiled and indicated by a nod that she was waiting in the usual place. She was about six inches tall and beautifully formed. Every minute detail of the carving was perfect—the folds of her robe, the flowing grace of her long sleeves, her plaited hair, and her arched, roguish eyebrows. She even had fingernails and dainty little feet, if you took the liberty of turning her upside down. A faint smile curled the corners of her mouth, although, depending on the light, her moods changed. The merchant knew he had me hooked. He could wait, the old bandit. His first price had been staggering. It went down a notch or two when I said: "Look, I'm not a tourist. I am a poor student at Yenching." Having been assured by the Old China Hands that merchants never gave the best price until a customer started to leave, I had turned toward the door. Nothing happened. He stood in the dim corner of the shop, smiling as he gently set the singsong girl on her low, teakwood base. He knew I would be back.

She was smiling now. Her face felt cool and silky. I put her on the black base again and moved away, trying to think of some new argument. Meanwhile, a man and woman had come into the shop. They were Americans. They sounded like tourists, but had some experience of ivory and carving. The woman kept asking about prices. "Seventy dolla'," said the shopkeeper. "This one a hunna' dolla'. Many people like this elephant. Eighty fi' dolla'." After a moment the woman said: "Everything is frightfully expensive. You are higher than the stores in America." The shopkeeper smiled, a bland, ingratiating smile. "All plices in Peking dolla'," he said. "Peking dolla' not so big 'Melican dolla'. Only half." The old highwayman! He knew exactly when to time this announcement and the effect it always achieved. Now, divided by two in quick mental calculations, nothing in the shop would seem expensive.

Then an awful thing happened. The man saw my singsong girl. He lifted her from the niche in the corner and held her in his profane hands. "Look at this," he called to his wife. "Isn't she a beauty?" The woman cautiously said the carving was rather nice. The merchant glanced at me, relishing the panic. "Call 'um singsong," he said. "Plenty good piece ivelly." They brought her into the light near the door. "I like her," said the man. "How much?" The old assassin glanced at me again, malice glittering in his eyes. He paused and shook his head. "She sold," he said. " 'Melican gennaman just have buy."

In Ivory Street I hailed a ricksha and told the boy to go to the Tartar Gate, carefully pronouncing its Chinese name. "Tata-gay," he said. "I know." Along the way, even when the street ahead was clear of pedestrians and bicycles, I kept treading on the plunger and ringing the ricksha bells from the sheer joy of being alive on a blue-and-gold autumn afternoon in the most beautiful city in the world and carrying the singsong girl wrapped in silk.

Then the Tartar Gate—massive as a fortress, light as a cloud castle. How had they achieved that marriage of mass and grace? The miracle surpasses even the sheer lace carved from marble on the monuments in the Western Hills. The twelve-

story pagoda in the Monastery of Celestial Peace and the Hall
of Annual Prayers in the Temple of Heaven are poems. The
Tartar Gate is an epic.

And now, to complete the picture and make it perfect, a
camel train approached the Gate. It came trailing clouds of
dust and sound—a chain of tawny beasts, out of the past into
the indubitable present. Red tassels and trappings swung from
the harness of the lead camel, red for prosperity and good luck
along the trail. Behind it came thirty more. They walked stiff-
legged, heads held high, the very picture of disdain for man
and all his works. Each carried a load of boxes and bales of
rugs or cloth roped to the sides. Food and bullets rode in some
of those boxes. Sun-blackened drivers walked beside the camels, urging them on with short, sharp cries. From Peking they
would head northwest, aiming at the heart of central Asia, one
thousand miles to Mongolia, half again as far to Urumchi in
Singkiang, still farther to Tashkent in Turkestan, across deserts
and mountains. Along the route they would encounter hospitality in the traditional greeting "Take rest and hot water with
us." And possibly they would meet with bandits, depending
on the size of the caravan and its relations with the wild
tribesmen in the wilderness. Rifles swayed in the baggage,
near the hand of each driver. The caravan was an impossibly
romantic sight.

One by one the camels passed through the Gate and were
gone, wraiths from the past returning to Samarkand and the
court of Timur the Lame. As the last camel vanished, a bull-
throated gong tolled in Peking. The deep tone rolled majesti-
cally across the city and echoed against the wall of the Tartar
Gate.

Peking is closed now to much of the world, a Forbidden City in the darkest sense. Of all the Communist crimes, this one is unforgivable. For Peking does not belong to them alone; it belongs to all men. Peking is a shining monument to the noblest instincts in the human soul. One day soon the gates will open again and you will stand before the glory of the ages.

Chapter XX

COCKPIT
OF THE ORIENT

"THERE IS probably nowhere in the world an actual parallel to this situation"—Lytton Commission Report on Manchuria, 1932.

In the northeast, in a region shaped like a crude arrowhead, the dynamics of history were furiously at work in the 1930's, fusing some of the elements of the Pacific War and preparing the pattern of Southeast Asia as you see it today. The crucible was Manchuria.

It resembles the American Middle West. Flat plains, relieved here and there by low hills, stretch for about a thousand miles on the longest east-west and north-south axes. The Khingan Mountains rise in the west like the Rockies. The Chenshan, "Thousand Hills," pile up in the south near the border of Korea. It is good farming country, capable of supporting countless millions of people. There is coal and iron in the ground. Ships can enter the warm-water ports throughout the year. Many men—statesmen, soldiers, and empire builders—have coveted Manchuria.

Between the two world wars it was the point where the interests and ambitions of three nations intersected. Russia sat entrenched in the north. Japan had a sphere in the south. The Chinese asserted that Manchuria was an integral part of China, basing the claim on population and a very debatable interpretation of history.

All three had to reckon with the war lord Chang Tso-lin, the "Old Marshal," and later with his son, Chang Hsueh-liang. These men physically controlled Manchuria during that critical period. Maintaining power with a private army estimated at seven hundred and fifty thousand men, they performed all the functions of an independent government. The "Old Marshal" leaned toward Japan in his dealings and made a try at seizing power over all China during the War Lord Era. His son, the "Young Marshal," hated Japan, but otherwise was largely unpredictable in his politicking. Over the years, Manchuria had become a cockpit of schemes, intrigue, and contending Powers.

Hovering around the edge was still a fourth force—the United States. At one time American financiers framed plans for railroads and development, but never carried them out. Nevertheless, American statesmen came into the fray from time to time, particularly Secretary Stimson. In 1929 he attempted to intervene when Russia sent troops to Manchuria to chastize the "Young Marshal." Two years later he tried to prevent Japan from taking the country. On both occasions he called on other governments to join against the aggressors. To politicians accustomed to formulating policies on solid considerations of trade or economic interests, Stimson's grave concern was baffling. Since the United States had no concrete interest in Manchuria, they put his actions down to unwarranted meddling. The only result was aggravation.

On an autumn morning in 1930, having left Peking, we came to Manchuria and an astonishing reception.

Had we been members of the Senate Foreign Relations

Committee, the Chinese, Japanese, and Russians could hardly have spent more time and attention on us. The Chinese kept us for a full day, the Russians for two days, and the Japanese, whisking us around south Manchuria in their efficient trains, for nearly a full week. The daybook records interviews with the Chinese president of the Chinese Eastern railway, the Japanese manager of the South Manchurian railway, executives of the Soviet railway, a provincial governor, a former governor of Siberia, educators, scientists, engineers, and public-relations men from the three governments. It was overwhelming. I suppose they felt that any Americans, even an obscure group of students, were worth the time and effort. The purpose behind their reception appeared in the phrase, repeated again and again: "When you get back to America, tell them . . ."

The Russians, as always, were charming and plausible. They made an extremely good case. "The Soviet government has no political interest whatever in Manchuria. When the arrangements are complete, we will turn over all our interests to China. . . . That has been stated as the official intention of the Soviet Union. . . . The days of Tsarist imperialism are ended. . . . The peaceful policies of your government and ours are identical. . . . When you return to America, tell everybody that we wish to be friends and would be glad if diplomatic relations were restored."

We were charmed.

The Japanese talked little; they exhibited. They led us to the edge of a gulch, a great black gash in the ground so wide and deep that the trucks below looked like toys. This was the Fushun coal mine, the largest open-cut colliery in the world. Then they showed us the shale plants . . . the Anshan steel works . . . a locomotive swinging overhead, carried by a traveling crane in a railway plant ("We make the complete train here, everything from the bolts and washers to the all-steel passenger cars") . . . laboratories analyzing earth and seeds to increase the acre yield of farm products . . . freighters and tankers lining the docks at Dairen. The atmosphere in south Manchuria crackled with Japanese energy.

They let the enormous stake speak for itself.

Then, with thinly hidden emotion, they showed another form of their heavy investment in the country. They took us to the site of the siege of Port Arthur in the Russo-Japanese War. In a museum, on a scale model taller than a man, they outlined the maneuvers in the capture of the Russian fortifications. Later, standing on the summit of "203 Metre Hill," one of the main bastions in the system, the Japanese public-relations officer said quietly: "Japan lost ninety-two thousand men in this battle alone."

The Russians had arrived first in the nineteenth century. Then, after the war with China in 1895, Japan attempted to get a foot in the door. Three European governments frustrated the move. The great Chinese statesmen Li Hung-chang obtained a secret treaty guaranteeing help from Russia in case of another Japanese attack. Li, like his successors to this day, had no illusions about his new Russian allies. Prophetically, he wrote in his diary: "If Russia did not desire to control us in all our home affairs, what a powerful alliance would be possible between us."

In short order, as Russian historians note, "Manchuria was well on the way to becoming a Russian province." Railroads, the heart and sinew of this development, spread rapidly across the plains. The Russians built Harbin, a new district in Mukden, the ancient capital of the Manchus, and they transformed an indolent Chinese town into a great port city, Dalny, more commonly known by the Japanese name "Dairen."

When John Hay promulgated the Open Door doctrine, the Japanese thought they saw an opportunity to check the Russians. They asked if the doctrine applied to Manchuria. Would the United States join any other government to uphold it by force? Hay replied emphatically: "No." So often American statesmen asserted a principle in international affairs, but would not, and usually could not, add: "And the United States will fight for this principle if necessary."

Thereupon, Japan entered an alliance with Britain (the British were glad to have Russia diverted in the Far East) and prepared to open the door to Manchuria in their own way. They did so in the Russo-Japanese War.

At this point Chang Tso-lin, a fascinating little man, came on stage. He ran Manchuria for more than ten years and with a little luck might have become master of all China.

Chang was an illiterate peasant. He worked as a laborer on a Russian railroad, but became a bandit when he was about twenty-one. When the war began between Russia and Japan, Chang, by then the leader of his gang, joined forces with the Japanese. His forces grew considerably, doubtless with Japanese arms and money. Afterward he professed loyalty to the Chinese government—but kept his "army" intact. After the Revolution he was appointed governor of Feng-tien, his native province. Five years later he became the boss of all Manchuria. In 1921 he declared his fief independent.

He was barely more than five feet tall, physically delicate, the antithesis of the hard-drinking, hard-riding, wenching members of the war lords' club. He held his audiences in a darkened room, his small figure lost in a huge thronelike chair flanked by two tigers. Some of the biggest tigers in the world breed in the Khingan Mountains. In the dimness a stranger could not be sure whether these were alive or carven images. It happens that they were stone tigers. Nevertheless, they had a certain unnerving effect on people who came to negotiate with the "Old Marshal."

Chang maintained comparative peace and quiet in Manchuria during his years of power. The soldiers were paid regularly. Taxes were geared to a farmer's ability to pay and still live. Chang permitted a certain amount of currency manipulation, because in China this was considered a semilegitimate operation. "But," said one of his advisors, "if it got out of hand, the 'Old Marshal' would call in the money people and tell them to slow up or heads would roll. He cut off a few heads to show he meant business."

As a result, Manchuria escaped much of the bloodshed and chaos that plagued China proper in the period between the fall of the Manchus and the rise of the Nationalists. Every train that came through the Great Wall into Manchuria was loaded with Chinese peasants, riding on top of the cars, hanging perilously from the sides. The flood approached a million a year, Chinese seeking peace and a measure of security.

The Japanese dealt with Chang for concessions, and their arrangement with him, by no means perfect, was at least satisfactory. They told me the deals often fell through after a time. Chang would send word that he had "miscalculated" his share of the take and wanted a new agreement. They said he also angled for an American "loan" of $50,000,000, promising to keep Manchuria independent and guaranteeing to make American interests predominant in the country. He coveted the Chinese Eastern railway and harried the Russians wherever he could. So, on the whole, he was a useful figure to Japan.

Nevertheless, a Japanese bomb blew him to bits on his private train.

The case was typical of Japan's difficulties with her military men. A group of army officers hatched a plot in which the assassination of Chang was to have precipitated an all-out attack on his army, followed by the seizure of all Manchuria. The General Staff in Tokyo had no knowledge of it. Higher authorities succeeded in countermanding the general advance after the "Old Marshal's" death.

Had this happened in the U.S. army, there would have been an investigation. The officers involved would have been court-martialed. The commander on the scene probably would have been fired. No such thing happened in Japan then, nor was the government able to control the army later, for this reason: The Japanese constitution at that time specified that the

Minister of War and the Minister of the Navy must be a general and an admiral on active service. It gave the army and navy the power to block a premier designate from forming a Cabinet. For example, the Emperor designates Mr. X, well-known political figure, as premier. Mr. X, forming his Cabinet, requests Admiral Y and General Z to serve as ministers of the armed forces. But the army and navy do not approve of Mr. X's known policies. The word goes out, and no admiral or general will consent to serve in his government. Mr. X has no choice but to request the Emperor to excuse him.

Thus, in the middle 1930's, as the armed forces and super-nationalists determined to take action in China, there were two "Japans." One was represented by the civilians and the harassed and unhappy diplomats, the other by the military. Willy-nilly, to reach the highest office, a politician had to be in good standing with the armed forces. The quirk in the constitution was a bludgeon, and the military used it to push through the policy they wanted.

"The Secretary feels that something should be done"—the unpublished diaries of William R. Castle.

The "Old Marshal's" son and successor, Chang Hsueh-liang, precipitated the miniature "Manchurian Incident" in the summer of 1929. Russian troops moved into the country and could have taken it two years before Japan made her fateful move. The events that led up to it were these:

The "Young Marshal" accused the Russians of using their offices in the Chinese Eastern railway and their consulates to spread Communist propaganda. He raided a number of Soviet offices, seizing documents. The Soviets retorted that this was merely a pretext for him to take over the railroad. Russian troops invaded Manchuria and smartly spanked Chang's forces.

In December he signed a new agreement, restoring the Soviet position in his domains.

The incident foreshadowed far more serious events yet to come. It brought the first effort to organize what is known to-day as collective action to preserve peace. The United States took the lead in this through the actions of Henry L. Stimson, Secretary of State.

When the fighting began in Manchuria, Stimson reminded Russia and China that they had signed the Kellogg-Briand Pact, a treaty renouncing war. None of the other signatory na-tures showed any great concern. After all, it could be argued that Manchuria was not an integral part of China, and also, as a New York newspaper said, the controversy was "none of our business." Stimson, however, insisted that a treaty was the highest form of contract and must be respected. Again and again, in spite of the hard realities of American public opinion, of the reluctance of other governments to act, and of the com-plexities in the Far East, he would insist that treaties must be honored. It may have been unrealistic, but Stimson's devotion to the law impelled him to try to use the Kellogg-Briand Pact as an instrument for keeping the peace.

Thus, on July 23 Edward R. Castle, then Assistant Secretary of State and later Undersecretary, wrote in his diary:

"The Secretary has been appealing to China and to Russia, through France, basing his action on the Kellogg Pact. One reason for this was to prevent a declaration of war on the day the Pact is to be declared effective—tomorrow. It may have a definitely good effect if the world can be made to believe that, through respect for the Pact, war was averted. This will not be true but that does not matter if the world believes it true. It will make the Pact a real thing and something to be called forth in the future."

Castle added to that day's entry a realistic appraisal reflect-ing the spirit of the times in the United States:

"The only thing that worries me at all is that other nations may get the idea that we, as a depository of the Pact, must act every time there is a threat of war."

The American people were not prepared to have their government play the role of international policeman. To talk was one thing, to act was something else again.

Four months later Russian troops began moving into Manchuria, and there was sporadic fighting. Castle wrote in his diary:

"The main question is what, if anything, to do about the Russian advance in Manchuria. It is making the Kellogg Pact look like 30 cents . . . The Secretary feels that something should be done."

Stimson asked Britain, France, Italy, and Japan to join in a joint appeal to China and Russia to stop fighting. Japan declined. Joint notes from the other four governments were sent on December 2.

China replied that she had not violated the Kellogg Pact. (The Nationalist government did not rush to assist the "Young Marshal" and was perhaps not unhappy to see him chastized.) Moscow blandly replied that Stimson was "misinformed" about Russian troops having crossed the border. Direct negotiations were taking place, they said. Then, with obvious relish, they professed "amazement that the government of the United States, which by its own will has no official relations with the Soviet, deems it possible to apply to it with advice and counsel."

Three weeks later a new agreement was signed and the incident closed.

Stimson, though obviously rebuffed, professed to believe his prompt action had averted trouble. He said "public opinion of the world is a live factor which can be promptly mobilized and which has become a factor of prime importance in the solution of problems and controversies which may arise between nations."

Actually, the Russians did not withdraw out of respect for

the Pact or for world opinion. They withdrew only after the "Young Marshal's" signature went on the dotted line of a new agreement.

Castle's diary records a conversation with Undersecretary of State Joseph Cotton on December 7:

"Cotton and I agreed in thinking that the Secretary's démarche to China and Russia in behalf of the Kellogg Pact was unfortunate, at least in its timing . . . The general impression outside and in the press is that the Secretary made a flop and his expressions of satisfaction that the results have been good are not taken with any particular seriousness."

Some newspapers applauded; others did not.

The New York Times said: "Here was a little war that might grow into a large one starting in Manchuria . . . any serious threat to peace will bring into place some such machinery as Mr. Stimson improvised on this occasion."

The New York *Herald Tribune* said: "It appeared to be none of our business . . . The only possible way of acting effectively would be the use of arms. Obviously nothing could be more fantastic than an effort to exercise our will over two such vast areas."

Time said: "The U.S. press rallied surprisingly . . . against Secretary Stimson as a Meddlesome Mattie."

The Hearst newspapers said: "In the first real test, the Kellogg 'Peace' pact proves a peace disturber."

The 1929 "Manchurian Incident" was a prelude to the more serious one of 1931. As the decade ended, war returned to the world. Public opinion might deplore, but could not stop, the fighting. It is open to question whether Stimson, again insisting that treaties be honored without trying to determine why they were broken, did more harm than good.

Chapter **XXI**

THE NOBLEST ROMAN

"FOR WORLD PEACE . . . ," writes Spengler in *The Decline of the West*, "involves the private renunciation of war on the part of the immense majority, but along with this it involves the unavowed readiness to submit to being the booty of others who do *not* renounce it."

In the autumn of 1931 the Japanese army set out to seize Manchuria and speedily did so. The somewhat anomalous relation of Manchuria to China proper, and Japan's huge economic and strategic stakes there, already have been described. On several counts, therefore, some experienced American and British analysts took the position that there was considerable justification for the Japanese action, or at least that the case was not all black and white.

The Manchurian Incident laid some direct questions, big questions, in the lap of the warless world:

Had the nations in fact renounced war as an instrument of policy? Did the treaties, the Kellogg-Briand Pact, the Nine-Power Treaty, Locarno, have any true substance or validity? If challenged, were nations prepared to act together to implement these documents? What, in short, could be done if one government, for any reason, violated the treaties?

The world would face these questions again and again until the final explosion at the end of the decade.

Secretary of State Stimson wrote in his diaries: "I am afraid we have got to take a firm ground and an aggressive stand toward Japan."

Henry L. Stimson came into public life as United States Attorney for the southern district of New York. He approached the problems posed by the Manchurian Incident like a prosecuting attorney. The Law, in the form of treaties signed by Japan, had been violated. The malefactor must be brought to book. It was as simple as that, on paper. Unlike the southern district of New York, however, the world possessed no policemen to apprehend lawbreakers, no power to enforce decisions, and little disposition to do either. There lay the complication. What could be done?

Stimson began by exhortation. He again sought to arouse world opinion, as he had done in the little "Manchurian Incident" of 1929. In the conviction that Japan feared the military power of the United States, he wrote a series of tough notes to Tokyo. Then his thoughts turned toward economic sanctions, boycotts, and embargoes, recognizing the danger that they might lead to war with Japan. He appealed to other governments. He pulled the United States into a closer relationship with the League of Nations. Finally, he could only propound a doctrine, the policy of not recognizing political changes achieved by force. He went on speaking of punitive "measures short of war."

Although Stimson referred to the Open Door, considerations of American interests in Manchuria were not the primary motivations in his thinking. (The Japanese and the rest of the world would have understood his concern very much better if it *had* been based on some tangible interest.) The total American trade with Manchuria, imports and exports, amounted to only about thirty-three million dollars a year according to consular figures. Americans had no large investments in the country. No American military bases stood on Manchurian soil. The physical safety of the United States could not be directly affected by anything that happened in Manchuria. In a word, the welfare of the average American was not involved in any way by the Japanese action. In fact, as more than one American businessman and financier had reported to Washington, the Japanese had brought peace and stability to the part of Man-churia they already controlled. It could be assumed that the whole of Manchuria would be better off in Japanese hands. Stimson, however, was not looking at the practicalities. He saw this as a test case of what he called "the higher motives and higher policies."

Moreover, he seems to have seen it as his own special, personal problem, almost a personal affront, as though he were the custodian of world peace. The italics are mine in these passages of his diary:

"*My problem* is to let the Japanese know we are watching them." "I told him he must remember that *I faced* the fact that these actions by the general officers might affect the safety of the world." "After their promises to *me* . . . I feel like kicking the whole thing over and publishing the whole record. It makes me feel that I cannot trust the sons-of-guns now." "I instructed *my* ambassador in Tokyo . . ." "I cautioned the Japanese ambassador that *although I was making every effort to save Japan's face* . . . they must settle it mighty quick."

This is especially curious in light of the calmness of other governments and the attitudes of other Cabinet members and technicians in the Foreign Service. Britain said it saw no reason to act, although, considering her military installations in China and the possible effect on the huge British stake in China proper, a strong line might have seemed justifiable. The sympathies of some officers of the Foreign Service inclined more toward Japan than toward the Chinese. In a Cabinet meeting,

Stimson reported, Secretary of War Hurley expressed the feeling that "we were making a mistake to get into it at all."

Henry L. Stimson was a strong man with strong convictions.

❦

In his memoirs Herbert Hoover said: "I was soon to realize that my able Secretary was at times more of a warrior than a diplomat."

The Secretary of State looked like a Roman senator. His face was wedge-shaped, tapering from a powerful forehead to a square chin. Two vertical wrinkles were etched between his deep-set eyes. His nose was prominent. His mouth and jaw signaled firmness. He wore a small mustache. White hair fringed his large, round head. When he smiled, which was not very often, his wide grin reminded people of Theodore Roosevelt. Mostly his expression was grave, even troubled.

His ancestors were New Englanders—clergymen, soldiers, and businessmen. His mother died when he was nine and his grandparents reared him. At Phillips Academy in Massachusetts he learned discipline, hard work, and scorn for creature comforts. Reporting on facilities there he said: "Winter life there was neither soft nor enervating." His classmates at Yale and at Harvard Law School called him "Stimmy," and some of them ragged him for being so meticulous in all things. Since he took himself seriously, others took him seriously. He was not entirely humorless, but in his voluminous writings the light touches are as rare and widely separated as oases in the Sahara. He had a volcanic temper, which, for the most part, he kept on leash.

His great friend, and perhaps unconsciously his model, was Theodore Roosevelt. He smiled like "T.R." and sometimes affected his hearty manner. He often quoted the famous line "Speak softly and carry a big stick." (By some curiously inverted reasoning, Stimson convinced himself that his notes to

Japan conformed to the Roosevelt maxim.) The title of the biography he helped write, *On Active Service in Peace and War*, has the whiff of El Caney and the Rough Riders. Like Roosevelt, he believed in the strenuous life. He rode to hounds, played golf, tennis, and squash, enjoyed deep-sea fishing and climbing mountains. He wrote with relish of hardships in the Rockies and of a long, arduous vacation in the mountains of northern Luzon in the Philippines. "Ethical principles tend to become simpler by the impact of the wilderness and by contact with the men who live in it," he wrote. "More problems are divested of the confusions and complications which civilization throws around them."

His outward appearance, solid Vermont granite without any intrusions or striations, belied his nervous system. In the middle of the conflict over the Manchurian Incident his friend, Dwight Morrow, died. Stimson wrote in his diary: "I really have been hardly able to pull myself together since. It is a staggering blow. I was in no condition to think of one [a statement for the newspapers] for myself." Sometimes, looking down on cities from the cockpit of an old single-engine airplane, he would philosophize about the works of man. When he was under stress, insomnia often attacked him. On one occasion "some heavy reading on China" kept him from sleeping. On another, when he was particularly angry with the Japanese, he wrote: "This churned me up so much during the evening that I found it rather difficult to get to sleep." Vice versa, when he had a "good night" he gratefully recorded it in his diary.

Regardless of whether he had a good night or a sleepless one, he often started work at six in the morning.

When he was twenty-five he married a tall, dark-haired Connecticut woman, Mabel Wellington White, descendant of a family that goes back to the Revolution. No children were born to them. Affectionate references to "M.W.S." appear often in the thousands of pages of Stimson's diaries. . . . They spend a quiet evening alone in their home outside Washington. They have a quiet week end at "Highhold," their estate on Long Island. They take a long walk through the woods in the afternoon. She reads to him after dinner. When he is exasperated with men and events, he lets off steam at home. "M.W.S." outlines the plot of a play she intends to write. In conformity with Washington protocol they often attend official dinners. . . . Stimson's nephew, John Rogers, of New York, recalls an occasion when they canceled a visit to the Japanese embassy after having accepted the invitation. It was during the period when Stimson was writing his notes to Tokyo. He felt that one of the steps taken by the army broke promises made to him shortly before. Rogers said his aunt described Stimson's anger and added: ". . . and therefore we did *not* dine with the Japanese ambassador."

Stimson became United States Attorney when he was thirty-nine. Four years later he was defeated as the Republican candidate for Governor of New York. ("Victory would almost surely have opened to him a strong possibility of great advancement," says his biography, "even toward the White House.") At the age of forty-four he became Secretary of War, at sixty Governor General of the Philippines, at sixty-one Secretary of State, and at seventy-two again Secretary of War.

Two qualities in his character jut out like crags. One is the lawyer's insistence that nations as well as individuals abide by the legalities. Concerning his actions before the United States entered the First World War, his biography says: "In 1915, it was not war-making, but *illegal* war-making that he attacked." During the Manchurian Incident he wrote in his diary that Hoover called the treaties "scraps of paper." Stimson replied: "We have nothing but scraps of paper. They (the Japanese) are parties to these treaties and the whole world looks on to see whether the treaties are good for anything or not, and if we lie down and treat them like scraps of paper . . . the peace movement will receive a blow that it will not recover from for a long time."

The other quality was a conscious combativeness. "When I had to deal a blow," he said, "I believed in striking hard." He recorded a conversation with Elihu Root, his predecessor as Secretary of State, contrasting his methods with Herbert Hoover's. ". . . the President, being a Quaker and an engineer, did not understand the psychology of combat the way Mr. Root and I did." He illustrates his psychology of combat by citing a great law suit in which he said he kept his opponents under unrelenting pressure so that they had no time to recover. "I finally forced a settlement . . . and a surrender on all points." His biographer described Stimson as "an advocate and a fighter," and says: "Stimson preferred to choose his main objective and then charge ahead without worrying, confident that aggressive leadership would win followers."

These tactics appear in a somewhat different light in the diaries of the Undersecretary of State, William R. Castle:

"The Secretary is feeling very belligerent and nobody can blame him for his fury against the Japanese, but he must be restrained from saying things which we have got to follow up, no matter where they lead. He is tired just now and his mind does not work well."

Stimson applied his "combat psychology," his "unrelenting pressure," and his "charge ahead without worrying" against Japan. But, unlike his experience in the law courts, they neither won followers among other governments nor forced "a surrender on all points."

A Japanese diplomat once said to Ambassador Joseph C. Grew: "It's easy to be an idealist when you're not in trouble."

The Japanese operations in Manchuria began September 18, 1931. At first Stimson took a calm view. He rightly judged that the army had taken the bit, unsanctioned by the Japanese

Prime Minister, Baron Kijuro Shidehara, and in defiance of his peace policy. An excerpt from Castle's diary notes says: "The Secretary was looking at the whole thing very sanely and was not planning to take any such precipitate action as that which perhaps unfortunately he took two years ago when there was danger of a blow-up between China and Russia."

Very soon, however, Stimson's attitude changed. Manchuria became a personal issue.

"Sept. 22. My problem is to let the Japanese know that we are watching them and at the same time to do it in a way that will help Shidehara, who is on the right side, and not play into the hands of any nationalist agitators on the other."

Like a headmaster with a recalcitrant schoolboy, he lectured the representative of a major Power.

"Sept. 23. I cautioned the Japanese ambassador that although I was making every effort to save Japan's face, and to give them time to settle this by themselves with China, they must not think this did not indicate that I thought the situation was very grave, for I did; and that they must settle it mighty quick."

He seems to have overlooked the provocative actions by the Chinese and taken the view that it was a one-sided case.

"Oct. 8. The situation there seems to be rapidly getting bad. I am afraid we have got to take a firm ground and aggressive stand toward Japan. It is a very ticklish situation and I am much troubled by it.

"Nov. 6. *The news is getting very dark.*"

"Nov. 7. It looks now as if the military element in Japan might get control of the situation and oust the government at any time. So the President and I discussed eventualities; what we would do under such circumstances. Any such thing as an embargo or an attempt to put on pressures he ruled out on the ground that it was a step which would be provocative and lead to war. I concur with him on the danger of a blockade leading to war."

On the same day, however, he gave an order to his staff:

"I directed them to get together a lot of statistics and facts which we are short of now relating to the reliance of Japan on the rest of the world."

The idea of economic pressure on Japan evidently firmly gripped his mind. Although he knew Hoover's position on the matter, he returned to the attack on November 27:

"I pointed out to him again and asked him to reconsider without any direct recommendation on my part, certain elements which lie in favor of an embargo. In the first place, probably an embargo, if joined in by all the world against Japan, would be a very brief event. She would have to surrender very quickly."

Hoover remained adamant, and Stimson added: "The poor old President is in a bad plight. As he says, he has been making speeches against sanctions of force all this time and he cannot reverse himself."

All through the autumn months the notes poured out: a strong protest over the bombing of Chinchow, identical notes to China and Japan; approaches to Britain and France and to the League of Nations. He turned a deaf ear to (a) opinions that Japan might have some justification for her actions and (b) that he might be leading the United States into trouble, or at least a diplomatic rebuff.

Castle's diary: "Late yesterday afternoon, Perkins, counsellor of the Legation at Peiping, came in to say goodbye and discussed the Manchurian situation. To my great surprise, he said his sympathies were far more with the Japanese than with the Chinese. He said he did not believe the present situation in Manchuria was due to any one incident but that it was the cumulative effect of a long series of Chinese irritations."

Stimson's diary: "Rather to my surprise, Mr. Root is more sympathetic with Japan than with China and he is very fearful lest we do not recognize her real claims to Manchuria." He added that after an assistant explained the State Department's position, "he backed us up 100 percent on what we had done to date."

Castle's diary: "We have no idea how to weigh the relative merits of the Japanese and Chinese propaganda. The Secretary is inclined to take many of the Chinese statements at full value and to discount the Japanese statements." And in a later entry: "Of course, there is always in the back of one's mind the thought that probably in the long run the world would be better off if Japan really and completely controlled Manchuria."

Stimson's diary: "At Cabinet this morning, Hurley, the Secretary of War, gently turned to Manchuria and suggested that we were making a mistake to get into it at all; that the Japanese were going to seize Manchuria anyhow, and we were simply letting our country in for a rebuff and a loss of prestige. He did it gently but gave the army view which he had evidently been getting from some of the generals.

"So it was necessary for me to give a pretty thorough talk in reply, which I did with some vigor; and the President backed me up very thoroughly." (Reading this passage later, Stimson penciled on the margin: "Hurley vs. H.L.S. H.L.S. gave broad statement of policy on *sanctions*.")

These opinions, the coolness other governments exhibited in response to his line of policy, and reports from the embassy in Tokyo on the temper of the Japanese people, appear not to have swayed Stimson in the slightest. On the contrary, they only hardened his determination. At this point what appears perilously close to wishful thinking, pure self-hypnosis, enters the picture. In a man of such integrity and mental clarity, it is difficult to understand. However, these points surfaced:

1. He somehow concluded that Japan was afraid of the United States. "I thought we had a right to rely upon the unconscious elements of our great size and strength. I knew Japan was afraid of that, and I was willing to let her be afraid of that

without telling her we were not going to use it against her."

Castle recorded a message that Stimson must have seen. "A telegram from Peiping said today that the Japanese General Staff is war-mad and would be quite willing to take on the United States."

2. Stimson came to believe that his notes were having a salutary and sobering effect on the Japanese generals. "The evidence indicated this morning a little bit that Japan is getting scared and is trying to be conciliatory . . . *probably she is beginning to feel the effect of the cables which I sent with regard to the bombing of Chinchow,* which represent public opinion pretty thoroughly." Later, when Japan agreed to an investigative commission, he wrote: "Apparently, it has been *the result of the stiff tone which I have taken* with Shidehara and with Debuchi and in the two messages which have been sent to Dawes" (italics mine).

Between the dates of these two entries, however, he wrote in his diary: "The worst news concerns the attitude of the Japanese people at home. They are getting more and more excited and more and more militaristic."

Months later, after Japan had been under pressure from Stimson for a long time, Ambassador Joseph C. Grew commented in his diary on a forceful and definitive message he had sent to Stimson. "I don't want to be sensational but I do want to go on record—continually—that the Japanese Government intends to proceed with its program in Manchuria unless prevented by superior physical force . . . American policy should be framed with a precise knowledge of these facts."

3. Stimson convinced himself that an embargo would quickly bring Japan to her knees. The figures compiled by his staff, he said, "show that she could not stand it more than a few days or weeks." In a conversation with Roy Howard, editor of Scripps-Howard newspapers, Stimson said: "I told him that the real thing that would hold back the businessmen and the army of

Japan was the fear of losing our trade in raw silk and I gave him the figures."

Here, surely, is a pure case of self-delusion (or else Stimson was hoping that Roy Howard would write this as his own opinion).

For in a problem as big and intricate as the economic strength and weaknesses of a major Power, statistics are extremely tricky. They can be interpreted in different ways. It is a matter of selection and emphasis of one fact as opposed to another. The Paley Commission showed, for example, the dependence of the United States on a list of minerals and raw materials. By stretching a point here and there, you could argue that the United States would not be able to fight a major war for very long if deprived of these imports. In 1937, when the "undeclared war" began between Japan and China, one of my colleagues fell into this ditch. I never knew where he got his figures, but he soberly reported that Japan's gold reserves and financial condition generally were such that she could not fight on a major scale for more than six months! Nations have demonstrated that they can continue to fight a long time in spite of economic strangulation. To say that Japan "could not stand it for more than a few days or weeks" was drawing a very long bow indeed. As for the collective embargo against her, maintained "by all the world," the thought undoubtedly fascinated Stimson, but he could hardly believe it would ever materialize.

Evidently Stimson did not put it quite this way in his efforts to persuade Hoover. The President wrote in his memoirs: "He argued that the sanctions, if applied by the United States alone, were 'only pressure' and Japan would give way before them."

4. Finally, and most important, Stimson reached the conviction that public opinion in the United States was thoroughly aroused against Japan and that the American people were supporting him in every step he took.

"The revulsion of public opinion in this country against her has been very manifest," he told his diary. He asked the Japanese ambassador to tell Tokyo that "both the government and the American people" were taking a serious view of Manchuria. In different words he rephrased the view that "American opinion would be very seriously aroused." A friend who had just come to Washington from Denver dined with Stimson, and the Secretary wrote that he "thinks that it was rather general that they [Americans] felt that *the responsibility of policing the world was now on us, and that we should build a big navy*. The Manchurian matter will certainly clinch those opinions" (italics mine).

If you read the newspaper comment of that day, you will find very little such sentiment. Personally, I can remember very little interest of any kind. Having been in the Orient just before, I naturally followed the reports more closely than most of my friends. Their general interest, if any, usually took the form of a question. "What's it all about?" On the whole, and with little knowledge of the details, they tended to feel that "the Japs" were picking on the Chinese. But this was hardly "revulsion" or a condition of being aroused to the point where they thought the United States ought to take steps to stop Japan. Americans generally were mainly concerned with food and jobs during the depths of the Depression, and I do not recall anyone clamoring to have their taxes used to build a bigger navy.

In fairness to Stimson it must be said that the Washington picture of the rest of the United States is frequently, if not usually, a little out of focus. Rivers of information come into Washington, but they come from observers who, like all of us, are more or less fallible. The sentiment in Kansas City or Phoenix, you discover, is not exactly what you were told in Washington. So, Stimson, sitting in the State Department, might very well have believed man-on-the-street sentiment stood solidly with him, on the basis of what he considered reliable reports from around the country. Also, there is always the possibility that subordinates in the Department told the Boss what they knew would please him to hear.

Reports to the contrary and criticism of his policy put him in a fury. He called an editorial in a New York paper "treasonable." He did not hesitate to pick up the telephone and bawl out Washington correspondents when their reports displeased him. With a few exceptions he seems to have mistrusted that nonexistent monster, the Press. "In spite of my admonitions on Monday about the necessity of going slow with publicity during these negotiations, the press boys had planned very carefully before hand to jockey me into saying something," he noted in his diary. "They didn't get very far." He raged about an Associated Press dispatch which included what is known as "explanatory" passages in a report of one of his press conferences. Such material, also known as "interpretive," is simply background and explanation. Editors know that the average reader cannot, and does not, keep abreast of the day-to-day details in a complicated story. So, to make it intelligible they often link up the statements and events of a given day with what was said and done last week. "Explanatory writing" in a news story simply points out the background and meaning of an event or a statement. It is not editorializing or opinionating. Stimson, however, took the position that the correspondents were not to interpret him. His hypersensitivity is reflected in a note about a conversation with Walter Lippmann. Stimson wrote: "We ended up with a talk about Manchuria. He approved very enthusiastically my policy in Manchuria, which was a great relief to me." His over-all attitude, however, shows in this passage: "It is a pity that we can't get a greater sense of responsibility into the heads of these newspaper boys and what is still more important, their employers . . ."

He selected a group of Washington correspondents, some fourteen or fifteen in all, for special attention. He called them his "Elder Statesmen of the Press." From time to time they were invited to his home for dinner and an off-the-record briefing. This is an old Washington gambit. It is designed to explain, and often to sell, the policy of an officer in government—but without quoting him or attributing his statements to him in paraphrase. The format is usually an informal dinner followed by the session. "Well, gentlemen, let's take down our hair now and talk candidly. I want to tell you what I'm trying to do and some of the inside. This is purely for your information and to help you evaluate developments. You'll see why I can't put this out generally or be quoted. . . ." It is flattering to be taken into the confidence of an important man, and very useful to be able to question him in private. You acquire an immense amount of sensitive information in this way. Also, it is a means of informing the American people of a situation that cannot be discussed openly in a press conference. However, it frequently is plain brainwashing, as well. The official tries to sell you on his policy and hopes to see it appear in print under your byline, without your having disclosed the source.

In his diary Stimson described one session with the "Elder Statesmen of the Press." He gave them dinner in his home and then brought up the question of Manchuria himself. He asked them if there were aspects of it they would like him to discuss. Apparently they did not feel any burning public interest in Manchuria. He reported that they asked him to assess the policy of the French statesman Pierre Laval on quite another matter!

The Japanese completed the conquest of Manchuria on January 2. Five days later Stimson sent notes to Japan and China stating what later became the doctrine of nonrecognition. The United States would not recognize political changes brought about by force. The notes mentioned the long-standing American doctrine of the Open Door in China. They added: "The United States does not intend to recognize any situation, treaty or agreement which may be brought about by means contrary to the covenants and obligations of the Pact of Paris of August

27, 1928, to which Treaty both China and Japan as well as the
United States are parties." If he hoped that this declaration
would speedily become a rallying point for other governments,
especially the British, he was to be disappointed.

Three weeks later help came from an unexpected quarter—
a Japanese admiral. A Japanese bluejacket was murdered in a
suburb of Shanghai. The admiral ordered marines into action
against a Chinese army stationed nearby. So began the famous
struggle in which the 19th Route Army, commanded by flat-
nosed General Tsai Ting-kai, won what amounted to the first
Chinese victory over the Japanese in modern times. For forty
days the 19th Route and two units of Nationalist infantry
fought the Japanese to a standstill. Planes and naval artillery
pounded them, but they held their positions until forced back
by heavy reinforcements, which gave the Japanese numerical
superiority. No action so greatly heartened the Chinese or won
more applause and sympathy for China in the United States.
(It also produced some of the weirdest war correspondence in
history. Floyd Gibbons, the Richard Harding Davis of his day,
took the first line of a popular song and began a dispatch thus:
"Climb up on my knee, Sonny Boy, and let me tell you about
the Battle of Woosung." An opposition editor, fearing Gibbons's great reputation, wired his correspondent for a report on
Gibbons's movements in the battle zone. The correspondent
answered: "Gibbons in Cathay bar sipping pink lady. Shall I
cover, please?")

Shanghai was eight hundred miles from Manchuria. This was
China proper, and no ambiguity about the political status of
this battlefield muddled the issue. Far more important, shells
and bullets whizzed around the biggest foreign city in China.
Foreign lives and property were in danger. Fears arose that the
Japanese might use the International Settlement for a base.
Bells and nerves jangled in the great chancelleries of the world.
Castle wrote in his diary:

"The Secretary is in a high state of excitement about the situ-

ation in Shanghai which certainly looks as though it might be
bad. The Japanese have too many troops and too many ships
on hand to make one feel comfortable . . . If they try to carry
out their full purposes by moving into the International Settlement, the possibilities of trouble seem limitless. It is not Manchuria again because the Japanese have no treaty rights in
China which are being violated. On the other hand, they have
undoubtedly had to stand a lot in connection with the boycott
which has been made effective through murder and arson, the
Chinese police looking calmly on."

The League of Nations now acted. As a result of the fighting
near Shanghai, the Assembly eventually adopted a resolution
bringing the League in line with Stimson's nonrecognition doctrine. The United States, although not a member of the League,
moved toward closer co-operation with it. Charles Beard wrote
(in *American Foreign Policy in the Making*, published by Yale
University Press in 1946): "American internationalists had seen
in Stimson's operations a chance to 'implement' the Kellogg-
Briand Pact by inducing the United States to join or use the
League for the purpose of thwarting Japanese imperialism."

American newspapers disagreed sharply about the desira-
bility of this development.

"More power to Stimson," said the Milwaukee *Journal*.
Strong approval came from the Baltimore *Sun*, the New York
Herald-Tribune, the Washington *Post*, the Newark *News*, the
Jersey City *Journal*, the Springfield *Republican*, the Cleveland
Plain Dealer, the Richmond *Times-Dispatch*, the Pittsburgh
Post-Gazette. The Brooklyn *Eagle* called it "the most important
single development in American foreign policy since 1920."
Walter Lippmann wrote: "The theoretical debate which has
lasted ten years as to what we would do and would not do in
case war threatened and in case the League intervened has
been answered conclusively by Hoover and Stimson."

On the other hand, the Detroit *Free Press* said: "While Stimson's activities may have been proper enough, the wisdom of

his going much further in that direction is another matter." The New York *Post* said: "Stimson is being thoroughly unfair to the people of the United States . . ." The Chicago *Tribune* and the New York *American* agreed. The New York *Daily News* said: "Let's shinny on our own side of the street . . . we have no right to sit on the safety valve of Japanese expansion." The Philadelphia *Record* called Stimson's doctrine "muddled statesmanship, unwise and ineffective." Also in opposition, the *New Republic* said Stimson was heading the United States either to war with Japan or to "a thumping diplomatic defeat." The Hearst newspapers generally disapproved. So did the Minneapolis *Tribune,* the Seattle *Times,* the Dallas *News,* the Memphis *Commercial Appeal,* the Atlanta *Constitution,* the Miami *Herald,* the Cincinnati *Times-Star,* the St. Louis *Globe Democrat,* the Denver *Post,* the San Francisco *Chronicle,* and the New York *Sun.* To make the record complete—although it is a little difficult to determine whether the editor was with or against Stimson—the Communist *Daily Worker* shrieked: "Hands off China! Defend the Soviet Union!"

For better or worse, a step had been taken. Stimson stood in a much stronger position.

✌️

A passage from Stimson's diary says: "It may be a case of having outstripped the world by taking too high a position. Who knows?"

The developments arising out of the Manchurian Incident did not usher in an era of law and order, instead of war, for the settling of disputes between nations. The world was not yet ready for that.

A League of Nations commission investigated and censured Japan. The Japanese answered legal arguments with legal arguments. Nor were they alone. A highly qualified American diplomat, J.V.A. MacMurray, erstwhile Minister to China, later wrote:

"Although we may not sympathize with, or condone, the harshly aggressive course that Japan has followed in Manchuria and seems bent on following elsewhere in China, we must, if we are to comprehend the motives actuating Japan, understand that it was in large measure the result of the challenges that the Nationalist Government offered—that China, in effect, 'asked for it.' "

Unwilling to retreat, Japan pulled out of the League. The chief delegate, Yosuke Matsuoka (who was American-educated and a long-time resident of the United States), led the Japanese representatives from the great assembly hall in Geneva in one of the most memorable scenes ever enacted there. Very quickly Japan renounced the Washington and London naval treaties. Not long after, she signed the first treaty with Nazi Germany. Walter Lippmann observed with sadness and accuracy: ". . . moral force physically disarmed is not sufficient . . . injunctions and resolutions are ineffective . . . at this stage of the world's development, the Western Powers are not prepared to take the risks of enforcing peace."

Stimson wondered in his diary whether he had "outstripped the world by taking too high a position." In Tokyo Ambassador Grew recorded a conversation with a Japanese diplomat and quoted him as saying: "It is easy to be an idealist when you are not in trouble."

The national election of 1932 brought Franklin D. Roosevelt to the Presidency.

Grew wrote:

"The Japanese press is unanimously pleased with the election results, first because they foresee a tariff policy more favorable to them, and second because it means the passing of Mr. Stimson whom they consider personally responsible for most of their troubles with the world over Manchuria."

This was no understatement. In Japanese eyes Stimson had

become the embodiment of American hostility to Japan. Some hoped he did not represent the majority in America, only the vehemently anti-Japanese and pro-Chinese sections of it. The militarists, however, made effective use of his name and memory. Whenever they needed to whip up chauvinistic feeling, whenever they lacked a respectable explanation for their China policy, they simply recalled Stimson, in the sure knowledge that the people would react as they wished. For years the characters in Japanese which transliterate Stimson's name, *su-ti-mu-so-n,* continued to reappear in Japanese newspapers. He was their most useful whipping boy.

As Roosevelt prepared to take office, the technicians in the American section of the Foreign Office in Tokyo undoubtedly dug out of their files an article that had appeared in *Asia* in July 1923. It said: ". . . American sympathies have been pro-Chinese rather than pro-Japanese. Perhaps, however, we are appreciating now a little more readily than formerly the Japanese point of view." It went on to say that Americans were beginning to understand Japan's need for markets and raw materials in China. The article was signed by Franklin D. Roosevelt.

However, those who hoped that Stimson's policy would pass with him were doomed to disappointment. Before the inauguration he talked with Roosevelt at Hyde Park. Soon Roosevelt was saying to him: "We do pretty good teamwork together."

In his book *After Seven Years* (published by Harper & Bros. in 1939), Raymond Moley, who was then one of the closest advisors of the President-elect, said Roosevelt committed himself to maintaining the whole of Stimson's Far Eastern policy. He said that he and Rexford Tugwell, another close advisor, pleaded with Roosevelt:

"On January 18th we spent hours with Roosevelt at the 65th street house explaining, as a starter, why we felt it was a tragic mistake to underwrite the Hoover-Stimson policy in the Far East. Rex, always more fluent and excitable than I, elaborated the argument with all the clarity and passion of which he was capable. I listened intently, trying to discover from F.D.R.'s re-action what had motivated him."

They got the same answer that Roosevelt would give to many other Americans in the turbulent years to come—his ancestors.

"Roosevelt put an end to the discussion by looking up and re-calling that his ancestors used to trade with China. 'I have al-ways had the deepest sympathy for the Chinese,' he said. 'How could you expect me not to go along with Stimson on Japan?'"

Moley commented: "The damage . . . had been done."

In the long view Stimson's policy may be adjudged in two ways.

He confronted the world with the great question: to settle disputes by orderly processes, or by the law of the jungle? Had the nations really renounced war? Would they set up ma-chinery to keep the treaties? He demonstrated, probably with-out meaning to, that moral suasion without physical strength and courage is useless. Could nations with a concert of in-terests, if only in a way of life, afford not to act together? Obvi-ously not if they hoped to survive. The lessons of the 1930's clearly answered these questions. Today, as a result, the democ-racies are far better equipped, physically and morally, to meet the elephantine strength of Russia and China than they were to meet the menace of the Dictators. As an instrument, the United Nations represents at least a small advance from the be-ginning made by the League of Nations. A tiny sliver of respect for concepts of law and order between nations may, just may, have evolved.

In the context of this progress, Henry L. Stimson showed great foresight and made a tremendous contribution.

But, in having "outstripped the world," in having insisted on the legalities while disregarding the facts of life, in having taken a position without the power to back it up, he was dan-gerously unrealistic. The Law, as such, existed in Dodge City a century ago, but the sheriff still had to carry a gun. I think it is fair to ask whether the half-measure, which was all Stimson could take, was not more damaging than no measure at all. In the seizure of Manchuria the United States could either refrain from action on the ground that it was none of our business, or it could oppose Japan and be prepared to take the ultimate consequences if necessary. The middle course, nonrecognition and hectoring, achieved nothing. It did not stop Japan or set a precedent. It only poisoned the atmosphere in the Pacific and brought the United States and Japan one step closer to war.

Chapter **XXII**

THE TICKING CLOCK

DAY AND NIGHT the *"banzai* parties" escorted soldiers to the trains. Cheers and shouting echoed and re-echoed through Tokyo Station. The departing man went directly into the car and stood stiffly at attention in front of the open window. His family, friends, neighbors, and co-workers at the office crowded close to the window. Individuals made little speeches of exhortation. After each one the group would shout *"Banzai"* three times in unison, waving the white flags with the blood-red ball in the center. The soldier neither smiled nor spoke. His face was a mask. From time to time he saluted and bowed. The farewell might go on for as much as an hour. Finally, when the train slowly moved, a fierce explosion of *"Banzai"* thundered in the station. The whole length of the boarding platform became a snowstorm of thousands of fluttering flags. It felt and looked like a football rally, the send-off for the Big Game. This ceremony bade the Japanese soldier not Godspeed but glory in China. He carried with him into combat the image of the glowing faces of people to whom already he was a hero.

This was the summer of 1937, the year when the "undeclared war" began between Japan and China. I was in Tokyo when the fighting started, having been sent out as the correspondent for the Associated Press. No other assignment ever seemed so intoxicating. Here was the biggest story in the world to be writing about. For the first time, I experienced the greatest reward a newspaperman can have—the sense of being in the center of history. Japan seemed infinitely more attractive than when I had seen it before. (Nations usually are more vital, more exuberantly alive in time of war than when they are at peace.) I liked the country, the people, the excitement. And I admired the other correspondents, men of many nationalities. For the most part they were cultured, well-trained newspapermen, far better equipped than I. At times I felt hopelessly inadequate in comparison with them. So, I took lessons in Japanese, read history, and raced around, trying to cultivate sources of information, eternally harried by the fear of being beaten on something in the news—a fear that materialized more often than I like to remember.

The office was a one-room cubicle on the seventh floor of the Japanese news-agency building, Domei. (The postwar name of the agency is Kyodo.) Sometimes the elevators stopped running. There was no heat until a fixed date in November, regardless of the weather. In the frequent earthquakes the building swayed perilously. These were minor inconveniences, however, beside another consideration: also on the seventh floor were the United Press; the British agency, Reuter's; the pre-war French agency, Havas; the German D.N.B. office; correspondents for some individual European newspapers; and, for a time, the offices of Tass, the Soviet agency. The seventh floor, in short, was a goldfish bowl. From the hallway it was not difficult to overhear a telephone conversation in one of the offices. At any moment your opposition might walk in while you were checking a story; if you locked the door, he would be even more suspicious. The office boy was strictly enjoined against showing a dispatch to anyone in the elevator while he was taking it down to be transmitted. Being so highly competitive myself, I probably imagined more of these hazards than actually existed. But they added zest to the game.

Because of the war we often stayed in the office overnight. Reports from the fronts usually reached Tokyo, via the War Office or from Japanese correspondents in the field, before they reached our offices in Shanghai, Peking, and Hong Kong. As the friction steadily developed between Japan and the United States, the lights burned late in the Foreign Office. Word would come that they were writing a reply to the latest American note. We had to wait for it. There were frequent changes of government due to changes in policy caused by the war. From the time that we heard the first rumor of an impending resignation until the Emperor appointed a new Prime Minister and he completed his Cabinet, we worked around the clock. The changes took three to four days on the average. Finally, as Tokyo is fourteen hours ahead of New York in time, most of the cables from the Foreign Desk—queries and informative messages—came in between midnight and two o'clock. If I had gone home before then, the night man would telephone and I would have to go back. More often then not I spent the rest of the night on the office couch. It was a marked improvement over the times in Shanghai when I had slept on the desk.

My pet on the staff was the chief translator, a sweet little old man named Kubo-*san*. He was well under five feet tall, so small that even the Japanese remarked about it. He had been with the Associated Press since 1914. In that day, he said, the correspondents covered Tokyo wearing morning coats and high silk hats and riding in a coach-and-four. Kubo-*san* still kept his high silk hat in the office. It pained him to see the correspondents of my generation so informally dressed. He had a sly wit, more American than Japanese. Late one night, while we were waiting for a Foreign Office note, some correspondents came in to play hearts. I lost steadily. Kubo-*san* looked at the clock and said: "I hope that note comes out pretty soon." I asked if he was getting sleepy. "No," he said, grinning. "I am afraid you are going broke." He took his life in his hands several times during the dangerous "February 26 Incident," when two army units rebelled and Tokyo became an armed camp. Again and again he went into the streets to help cover the story and repeatedly passed through the lines, ignoring warnings from both the rebels and the loyal units confronting them. His chief task was to read the Japanese newspapers and that section of the Domei report written in Japanese. He had an acute news sense, better than mine, in fact. One day he found and translated an item from the papers about a hen that had laid a fantastic number of eggs in a year.

"What do you expect me to do with this?" I asked.

"File it," he said. "Every farmer in America will be interested in that hen."

A typical day began with the English-language newspapers at breakfast. Then in the office a stack of overnight Domei dispatches would be waiting, along with the Okuyama translation service—a digest of the newspapers, trade journals, and magazines, translated into English. After that, a series of telephone calls had to be made to government offices and various embassies. My best sources were not among the officers at the American embassy but among those at the Canadian, British, French, Belgian, and Dutch Embassies. In my experience, the American embassy anywhere in the world is usually a poor source for American newspapermen. It is not that the Foreign Service officers are badly informed. On the contrary, they are as good as any in the world, especially today. But for some reason, State Department policy, perhaps, they are generally very cautious and close-mouthed with reporters. One of the Secretaries of State—Cordell Hull, I believe—is supposed to have said that American correspondents should be considered adjuncts of the embassies. That may be the policy on paper, but in practice they play it very close to the chest, indeed.

The embassy in Tokyo was no exception. The ambassador, Joseph Clark Grew, was a career diplomat, very experienced, a handsome, affable man, universally liked and admired. He was always accessible. I had no hesitation in telephoning him at any hour of the night with a question. Invariably, finishing a conversation in his office, he would ask: "How are you fixed for cigarettes?" Out would come a carton of unprocurable

American cigarettes. He was exceedingly careful in what he said and how he said it. Frequently he spoke off the record on matters that seemed innocuous to me. Not until after the war, when I read his book *My Ten Years in Japan,* did I discover how much he left unsaid.

He had a remarkable staff. At that time a great number of socially presentable tea hounds and cookie pushers found their way into the Foreign Service, I suppose because it is a genteel trade, often conducted in white tie and tails. (Since World War II this has changed radically.) But the staff in Tokyo, from the ambassador down to the code clerks, was highly competent. The counselor, Eugene Dooman, and the chief secretaries, Edward S. Crocker and Cabot Coville, were brilliant diplomats, experts in getting information and evaluating it. Naturally military information about Japan was highly important. In the offices of the naval and military attachés were three officers who were to write glorious chapters in the story of American arms. One was the late Frank Merrill, who led "Merrill's Marauders" in the Burmese jungle. One was a sharp-eyed young lieutenant commander, Edward T. Layton, now an admiral in the Naval Intelligence School. He is the officer who put together stray bits and pieces of information that led to the destruction of the plane carrying Japan's top commander in the Pacific War, Admiral Isoroku Yamamoto. And the third was a handsome, dark-haired young army captain, who even then was notable for doing everything well. This was Maxwell Taylor, erstwhile Army Chief of Staff.

From time to time I had the impression that the embassy officers did not see eye to eye with Secretary Hull on the policy the United States was following with respect to Japan. Naturally that was a subject they could not discuss openly. Some of them, I know, felt that the State Department was dangerously pro-Chinese. They could clearly see where the line was leading. Neither the surprise at Pearl Harbor nor the events that led up to it resulted from any failures on the part of the embassy staff to report and evaluate the events in Japan.

The only routine in Tokyo was a press conference at the Foreign Office three mornings a week. An official identified in dispatches as "a Foreign Office spokesman" answered questions, but volunteered very little information. Always he took a negative approach. He had little to say. In answering a question, he seemed evasive. His manner plainly indicated that the conference was painful to him and that he was anxious to be finished with it. The only possible result could be to create the impression that the Japanese themselves were unable to justify their position in China and their case in the disputes with other governments.

During the summer, page boys brought iced tea to the Foreign Office conferences. The Tass correspondent, Naghy, was a big, dark-haired Russian of great charm and a wicked sense of humor. When the spokesman said something unusually fatuous, Naghy achieved a sound effect closely resembling a minty Bronx cheer by burbling up the last drops of tea through the straw. I suspect it was about the only fun he ever had in his job. Tass recalled Naghy that year, and the correspondents gave him a farewell party. A note in the daybook I kept says: "He claims to be glad he is going back to Moscow, but he didn't look it." Some months later a Japanese correspondent returning from Moscow reported that Naghy had been executed. He may have been caught in the great purge of Soviet officials in the Orient and the high-ranking officers of the Far Eastern Red Army.

The foreign colony was Suburbia in a white tie. Everyone knew everyone else. The main groups—embassy people, businessmen, and missionaries—tended to cluster together socially. Still, you saw pretty much the same faces at every party. And because protocol usually dictated the place cards on the dinner table, the same two people might find themselves seated together night after night. They entertained a great deal, mostly in their own homes. At irregular intervals, using phonograph records because there were no orchestras, the American Club held a dance. Each nationality celebrated the national holidays of the others—the Fourth of July, Bastille Day, Empire Day, St. Patrick's Day. In so close-knit a little community, a hostess felt compelled to devise some special motif for her dinners. She transformed the veranda into a Western saloon or gave a Hawaiian *luau* in the garden. Her guests went to great trouble to assemble the appropriate costumes. Next morning a detailed account of the party would appear on the society page of *The Japan Advertiser*. The argus-eyed Japanese servants could have added some interesting details, but the paper couldn't have published them. In short order, however, these details became common knowledge via the kitchen-door grapevine. As in Suburbia everywhere, gossip traveled at the speed of light.

The partying slacked off during the *nyubai*, a hot, damp period in early summer. The humidity goes so high that mold quickly forms on books and shoes, and you have to keep an electric light burning to dry out the clothes closets. In the very hot weather later, most of the wives and children moved to a mountain resort, Karuizawa. (It was on a tennis court there that the present Crown Prince met the commoner he has since married.) The husbands joined them on week ends.

I took a little Japanese house in a fishing village and commuted to the office. There I watched the best economic system in the world. The fishermen, each in his own boat, rowed out into the Inland Sea at dawn. At sundown they returned with the catch. Japanese housewives from around the countryside waited on the curving, golden-sand beach to buy fish. The fishermen, unhampered by union cards or a government agency to meddle in their business, agreed among themselves on prices. These changed almost daily according to the abundance or scarcity of a given fish. There were no middlemen, no marketing problems, no credit cards. The consumer got the article and the producer got his money then and there, on the beach. The system had the beauty of utter simplicity. They appeared to be the happiest people on earth, with the possible exception of those on Bali. A psychiatrist would have starved in that village.

It was most interesting from another point of view, too. In a beautiful pine grove a mile or two from the village stood the Emperor's summer palace. Still farther away the great naval base, Yokosuka, looked out to sea. Neither was visible from my village. Nevertheless, the police carefully warned people not to point a camera in the general direction of either the palace or the great naval base. The tragedy that overtook one of my colleagues, a story which developed a little later, originated on the seashore where he had taken a summer house near a sensitive area.

In the effort to do what is called "enterprise reporting"— that is, to develop stories auxiliary to the hard news—I stumbled into trouble with the New York office. Early in the China Incident I decided to try to sample Japanese public opinion with respect to the fighting. On the surface the people seemed to be solidly supporting the army. But what did they really think? I put together a questionnaire. It was carefully worded. In some of the questions the stereotyped phrases from editorials in the Tokyo newspapers were incorporated. I intended to mail a thousand of these to people in all walks of life. Before doing so, I sent a copy to the Foreign editor in New York. A crisp cable came: "Disapprove questionnaire." His letter arrived later. "The Associated Press does not manufacture news," it said. Today we go to very great lengths to test public opinion with questionnaires and plain doorbell ringing. But twenty years ago these procedures were considered "manufacturing news." Time marches on—fortunately.

Thereafter I confined myself to interviewing Japanese as often as possible. Thus I met Baroness Shidzue Ishimoto, the famous "Margaret Sanger of Japan," that country's first advocate of birth control. She is a beautiful woman, educated in the United States. She was immensely brave at that time to attempt to establish clinics for dispensing information about birth control. The army, naturally, wanted more births, not fewer.

Twice she went to prison. Once, she talked her way out by notifying the police that one of her sons was about to be presented at court. "As his mother, it is my responsibility to see that he is properly dressed," she said. They released her. I was never able to write the Baroness's story. It would have put her back in prison. But I learned a great deal from the thousands of letters that Japanese women wrote to her. Overpopulation, the problem she confronted in the 1930's, still plagues Japan. But again, time marches on: today the government has met this problem head on with information clinics and legalized abortions. Well over a million abortions a year are performed legally. Last year when I was in Tokyo I was told that the total number of abortions, estimating the many not reported, may reach close to two million!

For another interview I went far out to the suburbs to see General Sadao Araki, erstwhile Minister of War. It was a bitter winter day, and his house was unheated. For two hours the old soldier, with his stern, *samurai* face and flinty eyes, sat on the floor talking. A thin kimono left his chest and arms bare. He said Japan should finish with China as soon as possible and then go all out against Russia. He said that unless there was a showdown, Japan could never come to terms with China. He developed his reasons. He put no faith in treaties or promises. Considering the Comunist tactics as they developed soon afterward, Araki showed remarkable foresight.

Kubo-*san* translated the interview. In the taxi on the way to the office he said Araki had used such elliptical language and semimystical expressions that it had been difficult to follow the line of thought, much less to translate it.

"But he does want war with Russia," I said. "There is no question of that, is there?"

The little man nodded gravely. "Oh, yes. That is what he said." Kubo-*san* thought for a moment and added: "I think he is right, too."

When the American papers published this interview, the Soviet embassy protested, asserting that the Tokyo correspondent of the Associated Press was trying to foment a Japanese attack on Siberia.

A strange and fascinating man in Tokyo would soon notify the Kremlin that Japan had no intention, for the moment, of moving against the Soviet Union. He was the master spy—Dr. Richard Sorge.

Chapter XXIII

RICHARD SORGE,
SUPERSPY

ABOUT ONCE A WEEK or so, usually around midnight, the telephone would ring in the office. A laughing, slightly alcoholic German voice would say: "What are you doing? If it is a big scoop, I demand a copy."

"I'm reading about the difference between Fascism and Communism, but I can't understand it. Got any ideas?"

"Give it up. I have something more important with me. Join us for a drink at the Silver Slipper."

That would be Sorge.

The Silver Slipper was a small bar in an alley in the Nishi Ginza, a gay area just west of the famous Ginza. It had become a rendezvous for foreign correspondents. Theoretically, it closed at eleven o'clock. In the campaign to sober the people about the war in China, the police had ordered all bars to close at that hour. The door of the Silver Slipper would open slightly, however, if the proprietor knew you. Inside, a single dim light burned. The waitresses, all wearing elegant evening gowns, brought the client his drink and then, if he wished, sat and talked with him. In the murk you could hear low-pitched voices —in the darkest corners nothing at all. For this reason some of the correspondents never went to the Silver Slipper until after eleven o'clock. Sorge, however, would bring his own girl, seldom the same one. When I came in and looked for him, he would bellow, disregarding the warnings for silence. Then he would bang the table until the glasses jumped. "Bring my friend your cheapest bottle of beer."

Sorge was above average in stature and big all over, a great rock of a man. He had very broad shoulders, powerful arms, an athlete's torso, fists like boulders. Every feature suggested strength—the craggy forehead, the lines around his chiseled nose, the firm lips and chin, the wide, piercing blue eyes, all framed with curly black hair. Most of his photographs published after the war show a sinister, Mephistophelean face. They must have been retouched to create the effect, a sinister picture to go with a sinister story. Occasionally his expressions became deeply thoughtful, but never sinister. Most of the time Sorge was roaring with laughter.

He was wonderful company—cultured, amusing, and a sparkling conversationalist on any subject, but especially politics and women. He drank a great deal. When his left eyelid began to droop, it signaled that he was far gone in drink. This happened often. Yet the next day he would go careening around Tokyo on his motorcycle, wearing his black leather coat, apparently as good as new. I liked him very much and I am glad we did not suspect his true mission in Japan. The Japanese police discovered it during the Pacific War.

Sorge, although a German, organized and directed the great Russian spy apparatus in the Far East. He was at his peak in the years when the world moved toward a general war, reporting accurately to the Kremlin. He was about forty when I first met him. He was born in Russia, the son of a German engineer working in the Russian oil fields, but educated in Germany. He was a university student in 1914 when World War I began. He volunteered for the army, was wounded in Belgium in 1915 and left for dead on the battlefield. Not many soldiers are fit for combat after a terrible wound. Sorge spent months in the hospital. Then he returned to the infantry, this time on the Russian front. Again he was wounded, more seriously than the first time. The old imperial army was stingy with medals. Sorge came out of that war wearing most of the good ones.

Whenever possible, I nudged him into reminiscing about the Kaiser's army. Distant wars, the ones you haven't seen, are far more interesting than those you have seen, particularly when infantry goes into action in spiked helmets or, as in the case of the St. Cyr cadets, in full parade uniform. "*Ja,* the old army was great, the best in the world," Sorge said one night, "but the new one, Hitler's *Wehrmacht,* is better."

"Heil Hitler."

"Don't try to be funny," he said. "War is not funny."

"There is a Maginot Line now," I said. "The French say it is impregnable. You can't use the Schlieffen Plan any longer."

"Good infantry can go through any line," he said. In a flash his mood changed. "Let us forget the war," he said. "You Americans have never seen the thousands who go away and never come back."

He often touched this chord: "We must do away with war."

Now, surely Sorge's brilliant war record indicates that he was a patriotic German and loyal to the Kaiser. Had he been a Communist during World War I, it seems unlikely that he would have risked his life for the imperial Hohenzollerns. When did he change?

We go on with the story, based on the very little he told me as compared to the great deal he told the Japanese after they caught him.

When the war ended, he joined a German Socialist party. There were several that arose out of the chaos in postwar Germany. The Communists took over the one to which he belonged. By that time he had received a degree as a Doctor of Social Sciences. He never mentioned his political philosophy, but he did say one night: "When I went back to the university,

I began thinking seriously for the first time in my life. I thought of the endless series of wars that had washed back and forth across Europe for centuries. Having been in one, I began thinking what these wars had meant to the people who were caught in them. It is terrible to imagine."

He came back to this point in another conversation. We had again been talking about the First World War, specifically about Hindenburg's astonishing victories in the Masurian Lakes campaign. Sorge, of course, had not been on that front at the time. He came later to the Eastern Front. He again dwelt on the suffering of the people, the soldiers in both armies and the civilians.

"I came to the conclusion that something must be done to stop this for all time," he said. "Obviously, Socialism is not the answer." He recalled that in 1914 the German and French Socialists at first had attempted to remain united, until the assassination of Jean Jaures, which was followed by the vote by both the French and German parties to support their respective governments in the war. "That was the best hope," Sorge said, "and it came to nothing. They could not stop the war."

His left eyelid was drooping. He became morose. "There is nothing an individual can do," he said. "I no longer even think of it or try to do anything. The best thing is to remain clear of all parties and politics. None is worth ——" He uttered an obscene word and ordered another drink.

Obviously the last statement was untrue. As a dedicated Communist at the time, Sorge was extremely busy.

After receiving his university degree, he had gone into the coal mines, first in Germany and later in Belgium to convert the miners to Communism. In the late 1920's he was taken into the Russian Communist party, as distinct from the German party. He asked to be relieved of his work as a propagandist and to be trained in intelligence. Evidently, he impressed the Russians. They trained him thoroughly and sent him to China as a spy. He organized a ring there, and then transferred to Japan. All this he set out at length in the confession he made to the Japanese police.

In Tokyo he found himself in a perfect position, with a perfect "front" and perfect pipelines to secret information about both Germany and Japan. Consider the situation:

Ostensibly, like the rest of us, he was a correspondent. He wrote for a number of German newspapers and magazines. He concentrated on heavy political analyses and economic reports of the type so cherished by many European editors. On an occasion when I needed some economic statistics on Japan and China, he translated one of his articles for me. I read it, copying the figures, and then said: "This is heavy going for the customers, Sorge. You ought to try to get more sex into your stuff." He grinned. "Sex is too important to waste on newspapers," he said. The Japanese police claim that Sorge consorted regularly with some thirty women in Tokyo. Drinking with him at night, I always found him with a different woman. Most of them were Japanese, occasionally a European. He boiled over with energy, a hard-drinking, hard-living man. In all probability, however, haunting the bars and chasing women were a calculated part of his masquerade. He created the impression of being a playboy, almost a wastrel, the very antithesis of a keen and dangerous spy. He knew, as we all did, that the Japanese police watched every move we made. The time came when I felt more than reasonably sure that even the wastebaskets in the office were searched. At night, taxi drivers were ordered to keep the dome lights burning in the cabs so that the police could see the passengers. But Sorge took no precautions. He rode his motorcycle everywhere, and how he kept from being killed on it after drinking so much is a mystery. One afternoon when I was with him, he made a telephone call from a box almost directly in front of the Soviet embassy. Obviously no Red undercover agent would do that!

So there was the "front," an amusing, somewhat alcoholic

correspondent who spent his evenings (but not all of them) in the bars or chasing women. When he disappeared from the bars, the police doubtless assumed he was in bed with one of his mistresses, not that they ever went looking for him at the time.

Then he strengthened the "front" greatly. He became intimate with the German ambassador, a Major General Ott. Ott was a pleasant, hard-working man, a professional soldier, not entirely at ease in diplomacy, I often thought. When World War II started, he made Sorge a temporary member of his staff! Sorge then knew everything about Hitler's plans that Ott knew and almost as soon as the ambassador knew them. Now he was inside the embassy, a patriotic German with a great war record, apparently a loyal Nazi carrying a Nazi party card. It is almost hilarious to recall his mock dismay when he said: "I have to be here every night. When am I going to have time for drinking and doing my own work?" As the Japanese military, dazzled by Hitler's victories, moved Japan closer to an outright alliance with Germany, Sorge naturally became highly *persona grata* in Japanese circles.

His pipeline to Japanese secrets was at least as good and perhaps better than the one to Berlin. His chief Japanese lieutenant was a man named Hosumi Ozaki. Ozaki also had been a newspaperman. (No wonder the Japanese came to the conclusion that all reporters must be spies!) After the start of the Chinese War, however, Ozaki became an advisor to the Cabinet. He was on excellent terms with the Prime Minister, Prince Fumimaro Konoye. When Konoye went out of office the first time, Ozaki took a high post in the South Manchuria railway. There, naturally, he continued to be in touch with military information of the highest order. For the railway, as I have pointed out, was not merely a commercial operation. It was an organ of government. Besides, Ozaki had many friends in high places after serving as advisor to the Cabinet. They had no reason to suspect him.

So, there was Dr. Richard Sorge in the late 1930's in position to discover the plans of Russia's two chief enemies, Japan and Germany, almost as accurately as if he had been in the chancelleries and War Offices when they were being formulated. Surely no other spy in all history ever succeeded so brilliantly in his mission.

His service to the Kremlin at that particular period in history was invaluable. It cannot be overemphasized. Without the information he sent to Moscow in that decade, the whole story of the Far East and perhaps of the Second World War might have been different.

He was able to tell the Russians that Japan would move into Southeast Asia, not Siberia. The importance of this news is obvious. Two of Japan's finest armies were stationed in Korea and Manchuria, based where they could strike at Siberia. Opposing them was one of the finest Soviet forces, the Far Eastern Red Army. If the Japanese plan called for a southward move, instead of northward, units of the Russian forces in Siberia could be withdrawn for service elsewhere. Apart from these strategic considerations, Sorge's reports affected Soviet political planning.

He also flashed accurate advance information to Moscow about the impending Nazi attack which came in June 1941, some two years after Hitler and Stalin signed a nonaggression pact.

Finally, it appears that Sorge knew that Japan was drafting the plan to strike without warning at Pearl Harbor. There is some question as to whether he had the accurate date, but it seems that he discovered the plan and the conditions under which it would be set in operation.

These were the three monumental pieces of information, each a turning point of World War II, that he sent to Moscow.

It is ironic that the Japanese, who were among the most spy-conscious people in the world, suspected perhaps every other member of the foreign press corps in Tokyo, but not Sorge.

Nor, as we have seen, did the Germans with whom he was working.

Even before he went into the German embassy, I sometimes asked him for help when I wanted information from there. He played it very cleverly. Once or twice, when the facts were not important, he put through a telephone call in my presence and told me truthfully what the embassy people said. On other occasions he reported that he had been unable to get the information. In the supremely important moments, when Japan was about to join the Axis in a full alliance late in 1940 and when we were all scrambling frantically for every shred of information, he gave me a useless mixture of fact and fiction. I saw him rushing out of the D.N.B. office one night, rode downstairs in the elevator with him, and questioned him briefly as he straddled his motorcycle.

"I don't know any more about it than you do," he said. "This fellow Stahmer is here, but if anything about an alliance is going on, they must be doing it all in Berlin, not here."

"I'm not asking you to give away any secrets," I said. "The rumors are flying. The story has been reported as a rumor in Shanghai. All I want is your opinion. Do you think there is any foundation for them?"

"It's all on too high a level for me," he said. "I'm just a glorified office boy up there, doing press work. I don't have an opinion. There is one thing—" He broke off and thought for a moment, as though weighing a big question. "I can tell you this much for what it's worth. It will get me in very hot water if you say I told you."

"Don't worry about that. You know better."

"Well," he said, "I do know that some of them in the embassy don't want the Japanese in the alliance."

"Does that include Ott?"

"I don't know about him."

"Why wouldn't it be useful to have the Japanese as allies now?"

"Some of them feel that these people are too involved in China to be of any use to us. And there are some who have a poor opinion of their army. You understand, these are just conversations I've had. I don't know that any actual reports or recommendations along this line have gone to Berlin," he said.

After the war I saw reports indicating that Hitler himself had this opinion of the Japanese. He appears to have rated them as a potential nuisance value to the Russians but little more, and was as startled as the rest of the world by their rapid victories in Southeast Asia after Pearl Harbor.

In his turn, Sorge never asked me for information. The other German correspondents occasionally came into the office and asked an assessment of some event, but he did not. Perhaps he had better sources. Or perhaps he assigned that task to his aide, Branko Voukelitch, a member of the Havas staff, down the hall. "Voukie," a pleasant little man with a Cheshire-cat grin and a high-pitched voice, frequently asked if we could throw some light on American policy or attitude. It appears that this type of work, quizzing the other foreign correspondents, was his principal assignment from Sorge. I never entertained any suspicions of him, either. Curiously enough, there were two correspondents whom I *did* suspect might be something more (or less) than reporters. One, I thought, was working for the Germans, the other for the Japanese.

In hindsight the long conversations in the bars with Sorge appear in a different light than they did at the time. You can read into them meanings not apparent then, weather vanes pointing to his politics.

It puzzled me that he invariably refused invitations to my home. Two or three times I asked him to dinner, but he gave excuses. His own personal life, I knew, was unconventional, to say the least, so I put it down to that. For the same reason, it seemed natural that he never asked me to his home. He did ask me to the home of one of the German embassy attachés for an after-dinner drink one night. The daybook records solemnly:

"The attaché assured me Germany's relations with Russia are good and getting better all the time. Sorge kidded me about looking under the bed for wars."

He surprised me on one occasion with some remarks about the Italians. After Hitler and Mussolini swore "eternal friendship," the Germans and Italians in Tokyo generally maintained the fiction of being close personal and professional friends. An Italian economic mission came to Japan in 1938. After the conferences, the head of the delegation met the correspondents in the Imperial Hotel. He was a pouter pigeon, a pompous little man who evaded questions about his negotiations with the Japanese by long digressions about the glory of Mussolini and the Fascist regime in Italy. After some twenty minutes of this, Sorge whispered: "Let's get out of here before I lose my temper and hit this oilcan on the spout." Leaving the hotel, I needled him for talking about his "loyal allies" in that manner. Usually, and for reasons that are obvious now, Sorge didn't seem to mind sarcastic references to the Axis. More often than not he would simply laugh. This time he snarled. "Bad people, the Fascists," he said. "They are worse for the Italian masses than the old monarchists." There was such venom in his voice that I refrained from saying that it was difficult to detect any difference between the Fascists and the Nazis.

Not long after Pearl Harbor the Japanese caught Sorge and rounded up those of his assistants who were still in Japan. The romantic version of the story is that a discarded Japanese mistress betrayed him to the police. The Japanese, however, told me that they picked up one of the members of his apparatus. In the usual fashion, he had organized it in a pattern of concentric circles. Apparently the man they caught was on the outermost circle, an operator of little importance himself. However, he led them to others, who led to others. Finally, to their stunned astonishment, they came to the innermost center of the organization, Richard Sorge himself. Voukelitch was apprehended along the way. He died in prison. Sorge made a complete confession. He was tried during the war, and the Japanese said he died bravely on the gallows.

In the sense that we now recognize the Communists as enemies, Sorge was an enemy. Nevertheless, he was a charming, attractive man and a good companion. Spying, to use a cliché, is a dirty business. At least it must be said of Sorge that he undertook that dangerous trade out of deep conviction. He was an educated man. His personal experience and the conclusions he drew from it led him to becoming a dedicated Communist. He risked his life for something he believed, and that is something, as the French say.

Earlier I mentioned that the Japanese put me through a long examination on a question of espionage during the months while I was interned in Indochina. They often used the word "spy" or the phrase "when you were spying." It seemed preposterous that they could believe this. In one way or another I told them so.

What I did not know, however, was that Sorge had been discovered and that both he and Voukelitch were then in prison. The police in Tokyo found references to me in Sorge's diary and of course knew that Voukelitch often came into my office.

In one stage of the examination, when I protested against being called a spy, the officer produced a pencil. On the sheet of paper in front of him he wrote two Japanese characters on opposite sides of a vertical line. One was the character for "spy," the other for "newspaperman." He looked at me solemnly.

"Same road," he said.

Chapter XXIV

QUARANTINE

In Chicago on the night of October 5, 1937, President Roosevelt threw a switch, one of the series that put the United States on a collision course with Japan. He said:

"War is a contagion, whether it be declared or undeclared. It can engulf states and people remote from the original scene of the hostilities . . . It seems unfortunately true that the epidemic of world lawlessness is spreading. When an epidemic of physical disease starts to spread, the community approves and joins in a quarantine . . . Peace loving nations can and must find a way to make their wills prevail."

This was the famous "Quarantine Speech."

In Tokyo the following night there was a Foreign Office dinner, one of the more or less regular functions to which some foreign correspondents were invited occasionally. I happened to be a guest that night. As I came into the room, the spokesman who presided at the press conferences, Tetsuo Kawaii, rushed up to me. Kawaii seldom showed his emotions. He would remain poker-faced, apparently undisturbed in the face of the needling type of questions that occasionally were addressed to him. Now he was extremely agitated. He asked if I had read the speech.

"Only the resumé," I said. "Domei didn't file a full text."

"What does it mean, in your opinion?"

"I haven't the faintest idea," I said. "Judging from the abstract I read, it sounded pretty much like the usual respect-for-treaties statement."

"No, there is much more to it than that," said Kawaii. "We are wondering what he means by a 'quarantine' and whether this is a way of announcing some change in American foreign policy."

"He didn't mention any governments by name."

"No, but he spoke of wars 'declared or undeclared,'" said Kawaii.

"So you think he had Japan specifically in mind?"

"What other interpretation could there be? If you would like to have a look at the text, we have it in the office."

After the dinner I went to the Foreign Office and read the speech. Then I went to the American section and found a technician, the late Seichi Motono, with whom I had become friendly. I asked if they had received an assessment yet from the embassy in Washington.

"We asked them for one," he said, "but it hasn't come in yet." He smiled. "Apparently Mr. Roosevelt is going to put a 'smallpox' or 'measles' sign on our door."

In the United States the President met the correspondents. They were clamoring for him to spell out the meaning of the "quarantine." The memorable exchange took place between him and Ernest Lindley, chief Washington correspondent for *Newsweek*. Lindley is a distinguished journalist. He had known Roosevelt as Governor of New York, traveled with him during the presidential campaigns, and wrote several definitive books about the President and his works. In short, Lindley, in questioning the President so sharply, was not acting in the manner of an "unfriendly reporter." Politicians, when they read something in the papers unfavorable to them, sometimes attribute it to an "unfriendly reporter." Lindley's questions show that he was convinced Roosevelt had some specific plan, that the word "quarantine" must represent concrete action in some form. Roosevelt began to twist and evade. His answers, in fact, seemed almost to minimize the importance of the speech. He did say that he was not thinking of either sanctions or international conferences. Lindley raised the question of the Neutrality Act. He wanted to know whether the proposed "quarantine" would entail a revision of the law.

"Not necessarily," said the President. "That is the interesting thing."

"You say there isn't any conflict between what you outline and the Neutrality Act," Lindley continued. "They seem to be on opposite poles to me, and your assertion does not enlighten me."

"Put your thinking cap on, Ernest," said the President.

His answers to all the press-conference questions indicated that he had formulated some idea of how to help the peace-loving nations find a way "to make their wills prevail." But he said he would not give the reporters any clue. For some reason, moreover, he put the conference off the record.

Americans were very much under the spell of the illusions that "measures short of war" could be taken against a nation without any risk. The Los Angeles *Times* reflected this strange view. It called the speech a "warning" and commended Roosevelt for having uttered the warning. Then the paper said it supported any effort for peace "that does not involve the United States in active hostilities or commit us to a dangerous course of action."

Men whom Americans had every right to consider authoritative fostered the idea. They assured the people that the government could take punitive action without risking war.

In a letter to *The New York Times* two days after the speech, Stimson urged a boycott on Japanese silk and embargoes on the sale of oil and rubber to Japan. "Let me make it perfectly clear," he wrote, "that in my opinion this is not a case where there should be any thought of America sending arms to participate in the strife going on in Asia."

The Chairman of the Senate Foreign Relations Committee

agreed and assured a quick, painless result. "War is not necessary," he said. "The quarantine would be successful in itself in stopping the Japanese invasion of China in thirty days."

The American Federation of Labor called for a boycott. The Federated Council of the Churches of Christ in America backed Roosevelt.

To this day the speech remains a mystery. Did the President have some plan in mind? If so, the details never came to light. Was it a trial balloon to test American public opinion? On balance, the reaction was favorable. Was it connected in any way with the down turn in business in 1937 after the partial recovery from the Depression? Did the President expect to deter Japan with words? If so, his speech backfired.

In Tokyo the newspapers waited several days before making any full-scale analyses in editorials. Some no doubt held back, waiting to see if the President would amplify his statement and clarify his position. Those newspapers that usually expressed the army point of view probably were waiting for word from the generals on the line to take. The first editorials of importance appeared in these chauvinistic papers. They all asked: "Has American foreign policy changed?" They warned that sanctions or boycotts would only strengthen Japan's "firm resolve" to press ahead in China. Her "immutable purpose," one editorial said, would not be deflected "by threats on the part of the United States." Stimson's name reappeared in print as the papers recalled the friction and resentment aroused by his notes of six years before. The editorials made it plain that Japan no longer considered herself bound by the Nine Power Treaty. In the same vein they asserted that Japan would not negotiate within the framework of the League of Nations or in a joint conference of the signatories of the Nine Power Treaty. In a word, they expressed the hope that the "Quarantine Speech" did not represent a revival and extension of Stimson's policy, and warned that trouble lay ahead if it did.

From the moment of the speech a tide began to run in Japan.

You could feel a certain change. In his personal relationships with Americans the individual Japanese never showed any enmity, nor did he later when relations between the two governments had almost reached the breaking point. But the Japanese who had looked upon Britain as the principle source of opposition in China now began to see the United States in that role. From time to time some development created a temporary illusion that relations might be improving. In the main, however, after October 5, 1937, relations moved along the same course—a collision course.

Aggravations piled up on both sides of the Pacific. From the window of my office overlooking Tokyo Bay it seemed that a sheen of paranoia was settling over the great ocean.

In December of 1937 Japanese naval aircraft sank the American gunboat *Panay* on the Yangtze River. Never before nor since have I seen such consternation, such unbridled expressions of emotion on the part of a people who try to conceal their deepest feelings.

The news reached Tokyo on a Monday. I had gone to the American Club for lunch and was looking through a batch of newspapers, newly arrived from home, when Kubo-*san* telephoned. The tone of his voice told more than his words. "Something terrible has happened in China," he said. "Japanese have sunk an American warship." That was all he knew. A press ban had been put on the story. An American cruiser and other war craft were stationed off Shanghai. It might have been any of them. I asked him to try the Navy, War, and Foreign offices for more information. Then I found a taxi and raced up to the embassy.

The ambassador's face was gray. He had little to add, except that the ship had been the *Panay* and that she had been bombed and sunk by Japanese planes. "I'm afraid five years of my work here has gone down the drain," he said. "Everything we have been trying to do finished with one stroke. Don't quote me on that." Later he wrote in his diary that he had immediately begun planning the details for a quick departure in case the United States broke off relations with Japan. He didn't mention that.

A somewhat mysterious Japanese named Kumesaki was waiting in the office when I returned. I say "mysterious" because although ostensibly he was merely a businessman (with a hobby for collecting idiomatic English expressions and American slang) he appeared to have something like carte blanche at the Admiralty. If you wanted to see an officer there, including the Minister of the Navy, it was quicker to ask Kumesaki than the navy spokesman. He burst into a torrent of personal apologies and expressions of regret now. "This is the worst day of my life," he said. "I can't tell you how we feel." He was completely fluent in English, but it failed him now. He could not find the words he wanted and repeated again and again that it was the worst day of his life. "Of course, it was an accident," he said, "but an officer at the Navy Office has just said he felt like committing suicide. Would you come over there with me right away?"

I ripped out a quick cable containing everything I knew and went to the Admiralty. Kumesaki's description of the atmosphere there was, if anything, understated. Officers came up to us, bowing, murmuring apologies. Men hurried in and out of offices, half running. Behind the doors the hum of voices sounded like a dynamo whirring. Messengers came and went. Evidently details of the incident were still coming in. Kumesaki led me to an office and bowed himself out. I shall never forget the astonishing spectacle of a Japanese admiral in tears as he related the details of the sinking and offered apologies.

The incident, of course, was no accident. The Japanese naval pilots were fiery supernationalists, as fanatical as any of the direct-actionists in the army or in the secret societies. They were not typical of the navy, generally. On the whole, possibly because they had seen more of the world, the naval officers were less insular in their views and less chauvinistic than the army men. The pilots, however, were nationalistic maniacs. It appears that they attacked the *Panay* on their own, either to "chastise" the United States, or to provoke an outright break in relations.

In the days immediately following, individual Japanese men and women stopped Americans on the streets in Tokyo to apologize. You didn't need to know Japanese to understand the import of what they said. The Foreign Minister took the rare step of going to the embassy to see Grew, reversing protocol. School children took up collections to send to the families of the *Panay* victims. The navy, maintaining that the attack had been an accident, brought officers from the scene and showed the correspondents, with charts and diagrams, how it happened. People came to us with letters and poems and requested that we cable them to "the American people." It was an emotional binge of the first order.

I believe most of it was genuine. The scene at the Navy Office that night could hardly have been play-acting. The behavior of civilians on the streets left little doubt of their feelings. The reaction in Tokyo came, not from fear of war with the United States, but because, as they put it, Japan had been "disgraced."

Out of this and other incidents there developed in the American mind a cartoonist's picture of a grinning, brush-mustached little man saying "So sorry" while preparing the next piece of deviltry. The Japanese at home indeed were "so sorry," both for the damage to their relations with other countries and because the incidents demonstrated, with increasing frequency, that the government was losing control over the armed forces. Grew wrote in his diary at that time: "War may very easily come from some further act in derogation of American sovereignty or from an accumulation of open affronts. Therein lies the danger, and it is a real danger which no one with any knowledge of the irresponsibility of the Japanese military, as distinguished from the Japanese Government, can eliminate from the future picture."

The *Panay* case was settled, but the scar remained.

As the fighting progressed and spread in China, a mountain of reports, major and minor, piled up in the State Department about damage to American property. A missionary establishment was bombed; the army said the Chinese placed artillery close beside it. Soldiers broke into a mission school looking for Chinese girls; the War Office said the men would be punished. American businessmen flooded Washington with complaints about restrictions on business generally, and specifically the closure of the Yangtze to shipping; the Japanese replied that strategic considerations dictated the restrictions and besides that they did not want another *Panay* case. Americans were injured in the fighting; the Japanese said all civilians had been warned to leave the area.

Frictions increased, the wearying, frustrating series of complaints and answers, charges and countercharges.

On October 6, 1938, and again in December the United States addressed strong notes to Japan. They protested the damage, restrictions on trade, monopolies, violations of assurances that the Open Door would be respected. Tokyo replied that conditions had changed and said, tartly, that to attempt to apply the pre-Incident concepts "does not in any way contribute to the solution of immediate issues and further does not in the least promote the firm establishment of enduring peace in East Asia."

It seemed to me, sitting in Tokyo, that the United States was taking an impossibly unrealistic position. Long before, if you remember, John Hay had told Japan the United States was not prepared to use force to maintain the Open Door. Moreover, in American territories, the Philippines and Puerto Rico, the

Open Door policy was not honored. Most important, however, was a more recent fact. Since 1931, when Japan took Manchuria, the Open Door had ceased to exist there. The Japanese had long since demonstrated that they did not propose to follow the old concept. For more than seven years the American government, in fact, acquiesced to the new situation.

From a material point of view, from the standpoint of dollars and cents, relatively little was involved for the American people. It could be argued, in fact, that the trade with Japan, the Japanese portfolio bonds held in the United States, had greater value than the American investment in China. But even assuming this were not a fact, was the game worth the candle?

Previously I have referred to the analysis of the factors in the Far East and the American relation to them, set out in great detail by J. V. A. MacMurray. Two years before the "undeclared war" he set this view before the State Department:

"In the changed situation since 1931, China has ceased to be for us a field of unlimited opportunity and seems in the way of becoming a waste area. Japan on the other hand has become a jealous and irascible and dangerous claimant to the estate. So it may well be questioned whether in the absence of any present prospect for substantial advancement of our material interests in China, we should not make up our minds to write off our claims to leadership, forego the attempt to assume initiatives or otherwise take a decisive part in current problems relating to China.

"We might in our minds (1) abate somewhat the rather exaggerated zeal with which we have been accustomed to afford 'protection' to citizens whom we are no longer actually in a position to protect. We might (2) let the other most interested Powers carry the heavy end of the log, go along with them as best we may, and take no marked initiative of our own. While having it in mind (3) to take our superfluous military forces out of China, we might let them dwindle by attrition until there comes a time at which to remove them without antagonizing others or breaking too obtrusively without our own practice. And (4) our Asiatic Fleet might similarly be reduced, ship by ship, kept more and more away from Chinese waters and perhaps indeed (now that the Philippines are entering a phase of qualified independence) withdraw practically in toto from the Far East."

This is hard thinking—cold-blooded, if you like, but realistic. Americans like to be on the side of the angels.

As to Japan, MacMurray continued:

"We can deal with them fairly and honorably and in a friendly spirit, and we can dispel some of their groundless suspicions—since China is no longer a game worth the candle to us—we can so deal with that situation as to remove all ground for the jealous fear that we are secretly inciting the Chinese against them; and we can similarly let our conduct make it evident to them that we are not intriguing to egg Russia on against them."

No such advice would or could be taken, however, for a number of reasons.

First, it soon became apparent, even watching developments from so great a distance as Tokyo, that American public opinion had hardened against Japan. The war had taken the image of a black and white case. China had been attacked, therefore China must be all in the right and Japan all in the wrong. The provocations, what MacMurray called "asking for it," either were unknown to the man on the street in America or were not admitted. The long series of official protests, going all the way back to the Stimson notes, helped shape American sentiment. Americans assumed that their government must be protecting some vital *American* interest in the Far East, not just the "higher motives" and "higher principles" of the treaties and the Law, as enunciated by Secretary Stimson. Indeed, in later years the stronger term "American rights and interests" was advanced to justify the later series of notes and protests.

Second, Japan's armed forces shocked Americans. The sinking of the *Panay*, the rape of Nanking, the damage to American property and restrictions on American business, and the obvious intention to establish monopolies in China—all these actions touched sensitive nerves in all classes of Americans.

Third, there were the assurances from prominent Americans that the United States could take action against Japan, "measures short of war," without incurring any risks. It was a kind of 1937 "brinkmanship."

Finally, and most important, there was the powerful voice of the American missionary.

Of all those raised in condemnation of Japan, his was the most influential. He asserted his right to remain in combat zones and he demanded in no uncertain terms that the American government protect his person and his property, churches, hospitals, and schools. Politically he wielded great power. No congressman or senator could afford to ignore the protests of the missionary, amplified a thousand times by the churches supporting the missionary. Through resolutions and statements, and more directly through letters to friends and letters read in church services, the missionary reached and shaped American public opinion.

Having lived in their homes, studied in their schools, and seen them at work, I think I can claim some knowledge of the missionaries. The majority were sincere, dedicated, hard-working men and women. They believed what they were doing was necessary and right. China and the mission field represented fulfillment and answered a deep need for many of them. Like the foreign concessions, the missionary establishments rose out of the chaos and political disintegration in China during the nineteenth century. Bayonets had opened the way for them and bayonets secured their continued stay. The latter-day missionary came to deprecate that fact; his predecessor had justified the means by the end. The missionary, like the businessman, regarded China as a great fertile field for tilling. The Open Door in this case meant a guarantee of the right to work freely among the Chinese.

Obviously the U.S. government could not physically protect them. It had not been able to safeguard the missionaries, especially at remote points in the interior, during the Chinese civil wars. Chinese troops killed missionaries and destroyed mission property as late as 1927. During the disturbed times, missionaries fled to coastal cities where foreign troops and gunboats *could* protect them. Further, they did not seem to feel the same compulsion to remain at their posts during the Chinese-versus-Chinese disturbances as they did during the Chinese-versus-Japanese fighting. The State Department advised them to leave in 1937 and again in 1940. Thousands of Americans sent their wives and children out of the Far East. The majority of missionaries did not go. They stayed in the danger zone with "the people to whom we have been sent." They called on their government for action to halt Japan and for protection of their lives and property—demands which would have carried great weight with any administration.

Meanwhile, letters and reports from missionaries flooded into America, were read from pulpits, and were reprinted in newspapers. Many and perhaps most could be described as eyewitness accounts of the war in China, firsthand and factual, but not necessarily written from an unbiased point of view.

So, the missionaries stayed and the inevitable happened. I do not imagine the Japanese troops or bomber pilots took any undue precautions to keep it from happening. They could hardly be expected to veer away from a building from which the American flag floated. Especially when that flag became more and more a symbol of hostility.

Incidents multiplied and received expression in the form of more notes and protests. And more indignation in America. Indignation, however, is not the same as a willingness to have your son put into uniform and sent to China to fight for American "rights and interests." During that period a traveler newly arrived from the United States brought some information.

He came into the office in Tokyo and introduced himself as John Foster Dulles, a lawyer from New York. He said he was in the Far East on a holiday and would like to ask some questions about Japan and China. It was not an unusual request. Travelers often seek out the resident correspondents in a given country for a quick briefing. This one, I soon discovered, had more background and knowledge of American foreign policy than the average. He asked a number of pointed questions about the war, the public opinion in Japan, the militarists, and how the Japanese were reacting to the policy line then being followed by the United States. I told him the Japanese were not likely to pull back now no matter how many notes came from Washington. "Now let me ask you a question," I said. "It looks as though there will be a war in Europe any day now. If so, will we get into it?"

"I should think so," he said. "Public opinion in America is against war anywhere right now, here or in Europe. It's purely a question of how long it takes Roosevelt to bring Congress and the people around to his position."

The conversation jolted me. If Dulles's assessment were correct, it explained actions taken in Washington that had seemed so puzzling. After Dulles left, I wrote Brian Bell, chief of the Associated Press Washington office, and put a carbon of the letter in the office daybook.

Brian replied in one of his typically terse notes. "I think the gentleman exaggerated the picture," he said. "Not even F.D.R. could get Congress to back him on going to war. Besides, a presidential election year is not far off. Wars and rumors of wars will take a back seat during the campaign."

The tide ran ever faster. By the end of 1939 the drift became so pronounced that a collision seemed all but inevitable.

In 1938 a "moral embargo" went into effect against shipping airplane parts and bomb components to Japan. There was no official nor popular reaction in Japan to the news. What, after all, is a "moral embargo?"

Next, Washington notified Tokyo that it intended to abrogate the Treaty of Commerce and Navigation of 1911. Six months later the action was taken. This opened the way to putting restrictions on selling certain types of war material to Japan. However, in spite of such measures Japan continued to buy well over ninety per cent of her total iron and steel scrap in the American market. For example, in 1939 the total figure was 2,550,000 metric tons; imports from America accounted for 2,175,000 tons. In the next year the total was 1,391,000 tons, 1,116,000 of which were bought in the United States. (Statistics from the "Japan Iron and Steel Industry.")

The most fateful year was 1939.

In August Hitler and Stalin signed a nonaggression treaty. The news shocked Japan. No military alliance yet existed between Japan and Germany, but they both had signed the Anti-Comintern Pact, an agreement to combat Communist propaganda and subversion.

Further, Japanese geopolitical planners had long asserted that another war with Russia would be necessary someday. The army's grand objective was to drive the Russians from the island of Saghalien and to slice off a piece of Siberia beyond Lake Baikal, due north of Mongolia. With Germany as a counterpoise in Europe, if only as a threat, to Russia, these schemes had seemed entirely feasible. The Japanese had been probing.

In 1938 and 1939 they engaged the Russians at several points

on the ill-defined border between Mongolia and Siberia. These
were no small skirmishes. The Japanese learned a good deal
about Russian artillery, armored divisions, and the air force.
Reports of great air battles reached Tokyo along with results
that sounded ridiculous . . . Six Japanese attacking one hundred Russian planes and shooting down thirty-eight . . . Japanese pilots, vastly outnumbered, dispersing Red airmen with
lopsided losses day after day. An interesting insight in Japanese
psychology developed out of these reports. Some other correspondents were reading the stories in my office one day, and we
all had a good laugh. When they left, little Kubo-*san* turned
to me. He was an intelligent man, well-informed and certainly
no Nationalist fanatic. Nevertheless, he said in all seriousness:
"Do not laugh at those reports about the pilots, Morin-*san*. You
must understand that our Japanese spirit makes such things
possible when we fight."

The civilians in the Japanese government at the time, the
navy, and the leading industrialists in Japan did not favor an
attack on Siberia. Still, had it not been for the events in Europe,
I think the army would have had its way. The nonaggression
pact between Germany and Russia, speedily followed by the
beginning of World War II, changed everything. Very soon
the militarists saw rosier visions in the sky.

The German victories in Poland dazzled them. There followed the lull called "the phony war," long months while the
Germans were regrouping. On May 10, 1940, the blow fell. German panzers, clanking and clattering, overran Holland and Belgium. The French reeled. The British wrote a glorious page of
military history on a dreary stretch of beach—Dunkirk. France
collapsed, and Adolf Hitler danced like a clumsy sugar bear
at the news. Silence settled over Europe.

If the Japanese had been dazzled before, they became in-
toxicated now at the vistas that seemed to open. To the south
lay a treasure trove in the great colonial regions—oil, bauxite,
and rubber in the Dutch East Indies, rubber and tin in Malaya,

rice, sugar, and minerals in French Indochina. References to the colonies as "motherless children" began appearing in those Tokyo newspapers which, as I have noted, represented the army point of view. Very soon they spoke openly of Japan's "golden opportunity." Holland, France, and Britain could not defend the colonies. The United States warned that she would not remain indifferent (that diplomatic cliché) to any action affecting the Indies. The warning carried little or no weight in Tokyo. The "golden opportunity" gleamed and shimmered in the bright tropical sun.

The air in Tokyo began to throb in the summer of 1940. The decision, however, was not easily taken. Some of the biggest businessmen were dubious. As a purveyor in World War I, Japan had profited richly. Some industrialists saw this recurring on an even greater scale now. Some Foreign Office people advanced another reason why Japan should remain neutral— her bargaining position. They reasoned that both sides would bid high to keep her neutral and even higher for her active support.

In this complicated equation the greatest of all the "X-factors" was the United States. None of the other democracies was in a position to prevent Japan from going into Southeast Asia. The army did not fear Russia. The Nazis, no doubt working to make Japan a counterpoise to the United States, said Germany had no interest in actions taken to set up the "East Asia Co-Prosperity Sphere."

But what would the United States do? Both by word and deed the President already had aligned himself with the democracies. However, the Japanese could read public-opinion polls. One showed that over eighty per cent of the people opposed going to war. The power to declare war rested with Congress, and the grass-roots congressman well understood the sentiments of his constituents at home. The great battle over extension of the Selective Service Act was developing. (Congress would pass it by one vote!) The Democratic party platform of

1940 said: "We will not participate in foreign wars, and we will not send our army, naval, or air forces to fight in foreign lands outside of the Americas, except in case of attack." Roosevelt was to repeat and re-emphasize this in the "again-and-again-and-again" speech at Boston in October.

That all seemed clear enough. In addition, by the summer of 1940 many high-placed Japanese had become convinced, regretfully, that no room remained for an agreement with the United States. They felt that Washington had become so implacable that nothing short of a complete cancellation of their program in China would satisfy the United States. What was offered in return? What could they expect as a *quid pro quo* from Pennsylvania Avenue? "Peaceful and productive expansion which resulted in the expansion of Japanese commercial activities in other countries" was the way Sumner Welles summed it up for a Japanese diplomat. The generals and admirals in Japan were scarcely likely to consider this a suitable alternative to the "Co-Prosperity Sphere," which would achieve the same result in less time.

So, in Japan the equation seemed to have resolved itself into this form: the United States had expressed concern over any moves affecting the Dutch, British, and French colonies in the tropics. But the President and his party had given the strongest pledges not to go to war "outside the Americas, except in case of attack." Germany was about to win the war in Europe. And Germany had given Japan a green light to go ahead with the "Co-Prosperity Sphere." Therefore, why not line up with Germany and get on the band wagon?

In the autumn of 1940 a special envoy from Berlin came to Tokyo—Heinrich Stahmer. He slipped into Japan so quietly that it was several days before we knew of his arrival. Deepest secrecy covered his mission. Then from Shanghai a message reported rumors that Japan was about to ally herself with the Axis. I began pounding the pavements and ringing doorbells. All my best sources failed. One man, surely in possession of the

information, said when I telephoned for an appointment: "If
you are coming over to ask about developments in our foreign
relations, I must tell you now that I can't even see you." I had
always believed that a persistent reporter, given the smallest
clue, could crack any story in the world. Now day after day I
came to a dead end. The best I could do was cable New York.
"Some reason to believe Shanghai rumors correct, but unable
confirm here." The office in Berlin was having no success, either.

On the night of September 27, a hot night when the air
seemed charged with electricity, the correspondents were summoned to the Foreign Office. It was about ten thirty. Fans
whirling overhead rustled a document in front of the spokesman. Around the long table, which was covered with green
baize, the German correspondents were already seated. They
looked quietly pleased. Outside the open windows the garden
was dark and still. With no preliminaries the spokesman said
Japan had signed a treaty of mutual assistance with Germany
and Italy. He would read the terms. Copies were available.
"If any one of the High Contracting Parties should be attacked
by another Power not now engaged in the European War or
the present hostilities in China, the other two will come to its
assistance with all . . ." Were there any questions?

Only the obvious one. "Who is it aimed at?"

The spokesman looked pained. "It is aimed at no nation.
Japan wants nothing but friendly relations with all nations."

"Would it be correct to say that this treaty applies specifically to the United States and the Soviet Union?"

He waved his big hands. "It does not apply specifically to
any nation. It is purely a pledge of mutual assistance, not a
threat."

The tide had become a rip tide. Soon afterward Japan protested to Vichy France that arms were reaching China through
northern Indochina, the French colony. Vichy, doubtless under
prodding from Berlin, agreed to permit Japanese inspectors to
station themselves along the route. To the Dutch East Indies

went a large economic delegation carrying a long shopping list, the top item of which was oil, specifically the type suitable for producing aviation gasoline. If the Dutch refused . . .

I was anxious to cover those negotiations in Java. A tragedy in the office next to mine opened the way.

Chapter XXV

ORDEAL

MELVILLE JAMES COX, the Reuter's correspondent, looked like the cartoon of John Bull in *Punch*. He was heavy, big-shouldered, square of face. He gave the impression of being a stolid, phlegmatic man, impassively watching the world from behind his thick spectacles with the heavy black frames. He had a dry wit. His English habit of understating supported the impression that nothing ever seriously disturbed his monumental composure. It came as a great surprise, therefore, to find him sunk in deep depression during the first year of the war in Europe. He would sit in his office, staring at nothing, speaking as little as possible. When he talked at all, it was always about the war. Evidently he thought of little else. He gave up the occasional rubber of bridge at the club after lunch and refused social engagements. He seemed to feel some personal responsibility for the British defeats in Norway and France. The tension of waiting for news of Hitler's invasion of Britain weighed terribly on him. He was too old to volunteer for fighting, as so many of his friends were doing. It might have been better if Jimmy had stayed drunk for a week, but he had never been more than a one-gin man.

Whether his state of mind played any part in the terrible fate that overtook him will never be known. It must be taken into consideration, however.

In the summer of 1940, as they had done for a number of

years, Jimmy and his wife rented a house on the beach near a town called Chigasaki. The big naval base, Yokosuka, stood nearby. I mentioned earlier that the Japanese police made it plain that this was a sensitive area. They did not like cameras, binoculars, and especially foreigners to be near Yokosuka. That year they were unusually touchy. Jimmy could not have known it, but the navy had scheduled large-scale air- and-sea maneuvers near the base.

Early on a Saturday morning in July the police arrested him in his beach house. They stated no charges. They took him to a military prison in Tokyo. The newspapers reported that the secret police rounded up twenty-two other Britishers the same day. A great espionage ring had been uncovered, they said. None was sentenced, so far as I know. The arrests seem to have been a manufactured scare designed to inflame the people against Britain and prepare the way for Japan's entry into the alliance with Germany and Italy. In the totalitarian state of that day such theatricalisms were wholly possible. Furthermore, the secret police were virtually all-powerful, as they are in Russia today. No court had any jurisdiction over them. The Japanese legal system did not embrace habeas corpus.

Mrs. Cox, a charming Belgian, immediately left the beach house and moved to the Imperial Hotel in Tokyo to be near her husband. The police permitted her to bring food and parcels to the prison, but I do not believe she saw him again until the day of his death.

The following Monday in the early afternoon Frederick Metzger, a Hungarian correspondent, burst into my office. "Something strange is going on about Jimmy," he said. "I have just come from the hotel. The police told Jimmy's wife to get over to the prison as soon as possible. But she had just come back from having taken some food to him there. I wonder if something could have happened."

I telephoned the British embassy and asked for Paul Gore-

Booth, a secretary. (He now holds a high place in the Foreign Office.) He sounded very agitated. He could say nothing. "Come to the embassy."

"Something is wrong," I told Metzger. "I'm going to the embassy."

Gore-Booth's face was white when he opened the door to his office. "Jimmy Cox is dead," he said.

"What happened?"

"We don't know. The *gendarmes* say he jumped out of the fifth-floor window while they were questioning him."

The police said they had resumed questioning after Jimmy came back from lunch, that he "tricked" them into letting him approach the window, which was open, and that before they could stop him, he jumped. They did not say how he tricked them. They produced a note addressed to Mrs. Cox, which began: "My dearest, This is the only way . . ." Mrs. Cox never saw that note. The police showed it briefly to a British consular officer who rushed to the prison. The embassy did not accept the note as authentic in spite of the tone that suggested a man contemplating suicide. There were several factual details that raised doubt.

When Mrs. Cox arrived, Jimmy was still conscious, badly mangled in the fall and screaming: "Let me alone, you bloody bastards. Take your hands off me." He died in a few minutes. His wife turned toward the officers, crying: "You killed my husband." Two younger men drew swords and took a step toward her. A senior officer ordered them to leave the room.

The police released only the barest details of the story. They said Jimmy had jumped from the window. "The suicide," an official source said, "is a confession of his guilt as a spy."

Here and there, from various persons, I pieced together the other parts of the case. Whether Jimmy killed himself, or was drugged and pushed through the window, could not be ascertained. Some of the circumstances supported both theories. I cabled everything I learned.

The funeral was two days later. I sat in the church, thinking of the gaps that had come in the correspondents' corps. First Naghy, the Russian, was reported executed. Then Frank Hedges was found on the street on a bitter winter night. Now Jimmy Cox. Who would be next?

When I came back to the office, Kubo-*san*'s face was grave. "The military police are angry with you," he said. "You may have to answer some questions."

My hands began to sweat. "What about?"

"I am not sure," he said. "I think they want to know where you got some of the information you sent."

While I was typing out a short cable about the funeral (and the few words came hard), the office door opened. Two men in plain clothes entered. It is a curious fact, but all over the world, regardless of the country, detectives look like detectives. I have been arrested or detained so often that I can almost identify a cop by the sound of his footstep. The two were *gendarmes*, agents of the secret police.

Kubo-*san* pulled up two chairs. The *gendarmes* shook their heads. I was to come with them. Kubo-*san* knew what to do— try to notify New York, notify the embassy, stay in the office.

The *gendarmes* put me between them in the back seat of the car. I offered cigarettes. They declined. I said it was nice weather, not too hot. They nodded, but did not answer. The car drew up in front of the *gendarmerie* building, the same building where Jimmy had gone through the window.

They led me to a large room, apparently a waiting room, empty except for two or three chairs placed against the wall. They went out. I sat on a chair for a moment, but then began to pace, wondering what this was about, trying not to wonder if that thought in church might have been too prophetic. Who would be next?

Suddenly, from somewhere near, a piercing scream ripped the silence. It was a man's voice. The scream shrilled again, twice. Then silence again. I told myself it was a piece of psychological mummery to soften me up for the examination or whatever lay ahead.

I found myself chain-smoking. When the two officers returned and signaled me to follow them, the floor was littered with butts.

They led me to an office. An older officer, also in plain clothes, sat on one side of a table. They motioned to a chair in front of him. It was then around six thirty in the evening.

The officer called an interpreter. I could understand most of the questions before he translated. It gave me a moment to frame the answers. The first questions were puzzling. For an hour or so the officer asked minute, apparently pointless details of personal history. The names of my grandparents, the name of my first grammar school, where I went to high school, what I had studied. A secretary appeared to be putting it all on paper. In this technique the easy questions, unrelated to the matter at hand, tend to put you off your guard. Once or twice the examining officer backtracked to some earlier question and to my answer. He pointed out slight differences between the first and second answers, unimportant but damaging to your confidence.

Outside, the sky darkened. A bright light directly above the table was turned on. Other officers stood around the room, darker shapes against the darkness. One, I noticed, stationed himself beside the open window.

Then the questions turned to Jimmy. For about three hours the officer asked seemingly inconsequential details. It occurred to me that the police had had no case against him. Perhaps the reason for bringing me here had been to obtain some shred of information to support the charge that he had been a spy. I began to feel relieved.

Toward ten o'clock they asked if I would like some food. I declined. My stomach was in knots. Tea? Yes, thank you.

Then abruptly the questioning became sharper. Who had told me about Jimmy's last words? His curses? Who had described the marks on his arms, apparently made by hypodermic syringes? How had I learned about his notes and the words "My dearest: This is the only way . . ." ?

In such instances the best thing is a faulty memory. "I talked to a great many people," I said. "As many and as quickly as possible. It is all very confused."

"You went to the British embassy on the day Cox jumped out of the window." It was more a statement than a question. They knew that and much more.

Whom had I talked to at the embassy? I said I had gone there so often that it was difficult to remember exactly which people I had seen on which days. Mr. So-and-so? Yes. The ambassador? No. Mr. So-and-so? Perhaps, but I could not be sure. He went virtually through the whole list of officers at the British embassy, naming men I did not even know. The grilling on my contacts there went on and on. From time to time he re-named those he had already asked about, checking the answers.

Toward dawn he seemed to have come to the end of the examination. Up to that point there had been nothing in his manner that could be considered threatening. Certainly no physical violence. The questions had come relentlessly, without interruption, but there had been no coercion. Now suddenly the officer turned ugly.

"You sent lies," he said. "You lied about Japan."

"Not that I know of."

"Why didn't you send the announcements issued by the military police?"

"I did," I said. "I cabled every communiqué from this office."

"That's a lie, too."

"No. The copies of the cables are on file in my office."

"Did you ever telephone the *gendarmerie* for information about Cox's suicide?"

"Not personally," I said. "But my assistants did. Several times."

"And did you put that information in your reports?"

Even at that hour of the morning, fuzzy-headed, tired, and oversmoked, the opportunity seemed too good to miss. "No, sir."

He looked pleased. "Why not? You preferred to report the lies they told you at the British embassy?"

"No, because we couldn't get any information from the military police," I said. "In fact, someone here told my assistants not to telephone any more."

Kubo-*san* had said it would be useless to call the secret police, but he did so, twice, and then was instructed not to telephone again.

The officer went to the door, taking the secretary and his notes. "Now we'll see what the commandant wants to do with you," he said.

The room was silent. The clock ticked on and on. The other officers still stood against the wall and near the window. They neither spoke nor moved. An eternity later the examining officer returned. "The commandant is not satisfied with this report," he said. My heart sank. I understood before the sentence was translated. "But he is going to be lenient. Sign this."

He pushed a sheet of paper across the table. It was in Japanese. Wearily I asked the translator what it said. "It's just a form," he said. "It states that you were not mistreated and that your answers were given voluntarily and without coercion."

I signed the document. The same two *gendarmes* led me out of the building. The dawn glowed like a promise in the eastern sky. The air felt cool. It was like wine, that fresh morning air. Above all, free air. I took deep breaths.

Two American embassy officers, Edward S. Crocker and Max Schmidt, approached from across the street. They had been working all night, trying to learn why I had been arrested. "Come up to the house," said Ned. "You look as though you could use a drink."

The following day the newspapers reported I had signed a "complete confession and apology." They fashioned a cloak-

and-dagger thriller pointing to the British embassy as a center of espionage and propaganda. This explained the intensive questioning about various officers at the embassy. Jimmy's arrest and mine were used to support the fiction of a British spy ring in Japan. Richard Sorge must have rocked with laughter.

To my amazement the incident seemed to have no effect on my relationships with the Japanese I knew. Nothing changed. Kubo-*san* never so much as mentioned it. In the morning the old cook, Kin-*san* (who by that time had the full story from all the delivery boys) merely glanced at me and asked what I wanted for breakfast. She scolded me when I couldn't eat. One anonymous postcard came, quoting a Japanese proverb— "Dark nights are made for dark deeds." Nothing ever illustrated so vividly the loyalty of the Japanese to friends.

Still, I could not help but feel that my usefulness in Japan had all but ended. A reporter should never be the subject of a news story, especially one so lurid as this. Kent Cooper, the general manager, deftly saved face for all parties. I had asked to go to Java to cover the economic negotiations through which Japan was putting pressure on the Netherlands East Indies government. Cooper waited several months after the night with the military police. Then he approved my request and instructed me to undertake a roving assignment in Southeast Asia.

On a December morning I stood for the last time in front of the house and looked out across the compound. The trees were bare. An icy wind shook the net on the tennis court. The net had become frayed and torn. The grass on the lawn had turned brown. Withered stalks of dead flowers rustled in the flower beds. The other houses around the crescent were silent. An early commuter train swept past, running swiftly on the tracks at the foot of the hill. The window in the upstairs bedroom rattled. The scene was homey and familiar and finished now. Finished more completely than I realized.

In December 1940, almost a year to the day before Pearl

Harbor, the car came to take me to Tokyo Station. As it turned in the driveway, I looked back for the last time at the old house.

One year remained before the storm.

Chapter XXVI

MINUTE BEFORE
MIDNIGHT

MANILA . . . Singapore . . . Tanjong Priok . . . Sarawak
. . . Palembang . . . Kuala Lumpur . . . Rangoon . . .
Bangkok . . . Pnom Penh . . . Saigon . . . Hanoi . . .
Over the whole of Southeast Asia the wind from the north
blew cold and menacing. White men knew, without knowing
where or when, that disaster in some form was coming. They
looked at the jewel-green islands with crescent beaches, at the
mirrored rice fields and enchanted forests, and told each other
the storm was coming. By the end of 1940 tension was mounting through Southeast Asia, the paradise islands and the beautiful mainland.

Would the Japanese come with warships and men? Or would
they succeed in wringing such economic concessions from the
Dutch that Indonesia would become the keystone of the "East
Asia Co-Prosperity Sphere?" How would that affect the neigh-
boring countries? Most important, what would the United
States do?

Vast decisions rumbled in the distance, and you could feel
them taking shape in Southeast Asia.

Manila. New Year's Eve. The Army and Navy Club.

The music stopped. Laughter and voices welled up in the
ballroom. Women in evening gowns, with camellias gleaming

in their hair, and officers in white-dress uniforms glittering with gold braid strolled off the dance floor. On the veranda the perfume of orange blossoms, camellias, and mangosteen floated through the soft night air.

The navy captain was a little drunk. Why not? It was New Year's Eve, the last hours of 1940. "My friend," he said, "you've been in Japan too long. Believe me, our problem would be simply to *find* the Japanese fleet."

His wife and another officer came to the table. She must have caught the last words her husband spoke. She frowned. "Please don't let's talk war tonight," she said. "We're having fun."

"Dearest darling," said the captain. "We're not talking war. We are talking about how long it will take the United States navy to find the Japanese fleet and blow it out of the water. After that"—he waved an airy gesture—"a couple of marine divisions will take care of the rest. That isn't a war."

"Oh, God," she said. "Why do we even have to talk about it?"

"I don't know much about the Japanese navy," I said, "but I have seen their army in the field, and it's—"

Both men started to speak at once. The junior officer gave way to the captain. "Oh, come now," he said. "Against what sort of opposition? Chinese who are no better than the Japs?"

"Against the Russians, too."

"No opposition," said the captain flatly. "The marines would go through them like a wet paper bag."

"They haven't got the oil and aviation gas to go on very long, either," said the younger officer.

"That isn't the point," said the captain. "The point is that the Japs have never run into a modern navy and army."

His wife rose from the table. "I'm going to get a drink," she said. "Let's have fun."

The captain said that was a good idea. He followed her. He never celebrated another New Year's Eve.

The attitude surprised me. It was not the captain's alone, or confined to the navy or the Americans. In Singapore the British had very much the same feeling. They were all supremely overconfident. The handful of Dutch in Indonesia, already under pressure, went ahead grimly preparing for the worst, but the oceans were wide and the Dutch expected help if they had to fight. If the Japanese moved, American warships would come swiftly from Pearl Harbor. Bombers were assigned to the Philippines. The big shore rifles of Singapore sheltered Malaya. The Australian fleet and the Asiatic fleet would cut Japanese shipping lines, beginning the process of strangulation. Against such sea and air power, how could the Japs hope to cross thousands of miles of the South China Sea to reach the Philippines and the colonies?

"You've been in Japan too long." The more I thought of the captain's words, the more it seemed he might be right.

But if Occidental military men generally believed that Japan's war machine was second-rate, the Japanese reciprocated with an even more serious misconception. Like their Axis allies, they had begun to believe that the democracies were soft and decadent. Had not France quickly capitulated? Britain would not long endure the pounding from the German air force. As for the United States, the government might recognize the necessity of fighting, but it was abundantly clear that the people would not authorize Congress to declare war.

On both sides of the Pacific in that critical hour military men had fallen into that most dangerous of all military errors—to underrate your enemy.

Hence, to Japan the risk of forcing matters in Southeast Asia did not appear overly dangerous. Although we could not know it in Asia, the Nazis were encouraging the Japanese in this belief, egging them on in order to distract American attention from Britain and Europe. It seems clear that for the time being Hitler wanted to avoid war with the United States.

After nosing around in Manila for a week, talking with military men and government officials, Americans and Filipinos, I cabled what is known as a "situationer." It was an analysis, pulling together the various aspects of the picture as it then appeared in the Far East. The cable was dated January 6. In essence it said that Japan could be expected to take some positive action in Southeast Asia within the year and that some authorities there felt war would be the result. The report received little or no publication in the United States. The Associated Press can only deliver information to its member newspapers. Editors pick and choose from the thousands of words they receive, taking this story, discarding that one. It puzzled me to see so little reaction to the analysis from Manila. Some weeks later the experience of another correspondent threw some light on the puzzle. He was a free-lancer who submitted material to a number of newspapers and syndicates in the United States. He had written a series of articles on the same subject and come to the same conclusion—"War with Japan may come this year." The articles were rejected, and he showed me the letter from the editor in New York. "We like the pieces and have every reason to believe in your judgment," it said. "However, as matters stand today, we could not sell them. The American people simply will not read any more bad news."

So, it seemed the issue was not to be faced.

The President had assured Americans they would not have to fight. He insisted that his actions, even then being taken, were designed to keep the United States out of war. Apparently he felt he could not tell them that the fall of France and the situation in Britain had altered the balance of power to such an extent that the United States might soon be standing alone. (Russia was not considered a potential ally, having signed the nonaggression treaty with Germany.) If the editor's statement was correct—"people simply will not read any more bad news"—then the President indeed had no other choice.

Still, the head-in-the-sand attitude could only increase the danger of an explosion in the Pacific.

❦

There lay the beautiful island, green as an emerald in the clear morning light. Graceful coconut palms beckoned from the shore. The swell of the sea was so gentle that only a ribbon of white surf gleamed along the golden beach. In the distance morning mist floated low around the walls of purple mountains and extinct volcanoes, cone-shaped and lovely. The sky above was a brilliant blue. The air felt fresh and soft. Pale blue smoke rose from the *kampong* nearby, the village partly visible through the trees. The smoke, acrid but sweet, came from burning palm oil. Beside the bamboo huts thatched with palm leaves men wearing sarongs and cherry-red fezzes squatted, talking. The women, dark, small-boned, and delicate in appearance, were washing clothes in the stream. Half-naked children played tag around the trees and splashed through the water like polliwogs.

This was Java, the beautiful island, unrivaled except perhaps by her sisters, Bali, Flores, the Halmaheras.

Many motives brought the white man to that serene and beautiful part of the world. The explorer hunted sea routes. The adventurer found excitement in strange courts and sometimes became a "white rajah." The merchant came for trade, the priest for converts. Finally, the Homeric struggles in the South China Sea and the Bay of Bengal were extensions of the wars in Europe. A four-sided elimination tournament began. When it ended, the Dutch controlled Indonesia for a time, except for a few bits on Borneo and Timor and Formosa. The Spanish had the Philippines. British rule settled over Malaya, Burma, Ceylon, India, and parts of Borneo. The Portuguese were all but blanked out. Japan came into the contest for a time, but withdrew to complete isolation. The French arrived to take Indochina. A great Siamese ruler, King Chulalongkorn, saved his people through political shrewdness and by profiting from the rivalry between Britain and France. This was the pattern at the dawn of the twentieth century.

For twenty years and more, especially since the end of World War II, "colonialism" has been an ugly word. Americans in particular have come to regard it as an unmitigated evil. The Communist, ever holier than thou, has profited hugely by keeping the memory green in the former colonial nations and causing Western idealists and liberals to hang their heads in shame. Morally, of course, it is wrong for one nation to impose its will on the people of another.

Still, I think we apologize too much today for the Colonial Era.

In the process of developing a country (generally for his own benefit, to be sure) the white man brought security and material benefits to underdeveloped people. He brought mercantile know-how, managerial and administrative ability, and concepts of government and public responsibility. Highways, railroads, and telegraphic communications brought a degree of physical unity never known before. Sanitation, public health, public works, water conservation—all these things and more were demonstrated to people who had only the vaguest and most primitive notions of them before. To cite one example, the population of Java increased in a century from about eighteen million to nearly fifty million. In Asia, population coincides closely to the available supply of rice. Without the vast water-conservation systems built by Dutch engineers, the rice simply would not have been grown.

In a word, in many parts of Southeast Asia the white colonists did a pretty good job. Millions of people there had a better life materially under colonial rule than they have today under their own governments.

The point is academic, of course. People want freedom even though it brings political dangers and economic penalties.

Nationalist movements began early in this century. Many tributaries flowed into the main stream. There were leaders such as Dr. José Rizal in the Philippines, Ho Chi-minh in Indochina, and Budi Otomo in Indonesia; the teachings of Gandhi, Tagore, and Gokhale came from India. Asians returning from universities in Britain, France, Holland, and the United States added momentum to the movement.

Nationalist impulses flowed from China in the lectures of Dr. Sun Yat-sen against Western imperialism and demands for the end of the "unequal treaties." In the 1920's, having organized in China, the Communists found fertile ground in the Nationalist movements in the south and gained some footholds among them. Even without the Pacific War, native organizations in all the colonial regions would have demanded more and more political autonomy and finally full independence. In Indonesia the Dutch saw it coming and already had made some concessions to it.

But the great catalytic force, the power that shattered the colonial structure physically and psychologically, was Japan.

First the Japanese set a series of examples for other Asians. They successfully resisted Western domination during the period when other Asian nations became colonies. They demonstrated that Asians could swiftly learn to use the weapons and techniques with which Western nations acquired colonies. Finally, they thrilled the Orient and coincidentally ripped away Occidental prestige when they defeated the armed forces of Russia.

Now in 1941 Japan was about to deliver the finishing stroke to the Western colonial system and set up one of her own in Southeast Asia. The first objective was Java. The first maneuver was pressure, not outright war.

In Java a critical but little understood contest took place between the Japanese economic delegation and a great Dutch statesman, Hubertus Johannes van Mook. The Japanese came demanding important economic concessions in Indonesia. These, if granted, would have formed the bases for setting up the "East Asia Co-Prosperity Sphere."

Van Mook's task was to gain time, to stall while the handful of Hollanders in Indonesia did what they could to prepare defenses and take measures to quickly destroy their oil fields if the attack came. In the bigger picture each passing hour gave the United States more time to get ready. Van Mook, a big, sandy-haired man, highly competent, with a great knowledge of the world and a great love for Indonesia, set out to prolong the negotiations. This he did. He gained a full six months, from January to the middle of June. Then, politely but firmly, he said it would be fruitless to continue the negotiations. The Japanese sailed for home. In Java we waited apprehensively to see what the next step would be. The word "force" had been appearing with increasing frequency in Tokyo newspaper comments on the talks in Java.

It was a major victory, for two reasons:

The democracies needed time. The United States was not ready. Defenses in Southeast Asia were weak and could only be shored up by American arms. Contrarily, Japan sought to lay the groundwork for the "Co-Prosperity Sphere" as speedily as possible. There was the treaty of mutual assistance with Germany and Italy. The treaty would come into effect, however, only if one of the three Powers were attacked. Who would attack if not the United States? As the year sped along, American warships clashed with German submarines. American tankers and freighters were torpedoed and sunk. Washington took economic measures against Axis assets and legislative action to open the way for more assistance to Britain. Watching this from even distant Java, it seemed inevitable that the United States would soon be at war with Germany. When the moment came, Hitler would call on Japan to honor the mutual assistance treaty and attack America. But if the foundation stones for the "East Asia Co-Prosperity Sphere" could be set in place without fighting, so much the better.

Meanwhile, almost every other day alarms rang like fire bells around the South China Sea. In February the Dutch and Australians suddenly ordered all their ships to stay south of Manila until further orders. A hush seemed to fall across the tropics. Then the crisis, if one actually existed, evidently vanished. In April Japan and Russia signed an agreement not to attack each other. Again a crisis atmosphere swept across the oceans. It could mean that Japan had sought this guaranty against trouble in the north as a necessary prelude for an onslaught to the south. We watched for signs in the sky. Next, there was a conference—naïvely described as a more or less accidental meeting in Manila—between General MacArthur, President Quezon, Admiral Thomas Hart, commander of the Asiatic fleet, Sir Robert Brooke-Popham, Air Chief Marshal from Singapore, and the Netherlands Foreign Minister, Eelco van Kleffens. In a curious interpretation of geography Tokyo newspapers said they were drafting plans to "encircle Japan." Threats crackled down the radio waves. Still nothing happened.

Then on June 22 an electrifying piece of news flashed through that tense, waiting region. Germany had attacked the Soviet Union.

I was on a ship bound for Singapore, having left Java soon after the end of the talks between Van Mook and the Japanese. A steward, sweating, panting, almost too excited to talk, burst into the ship's lounge. "Hitler has invaded Russia," he gasped. "The fighting has begun."

Someone asked where he had heard the news.

"It is coming in from everywhere—Berlin, Moscow, London. Hitler says the Russians betrayed him. Von Ribbentrop is speaking now and saying Stalin planned to attack Germany. *Ja*, it is true. I tell you so."

Cheers were rising all over the ship. People poured into the lounge, beaming, ordering champagne, toasting Stalin, toasting the Red army, toasting each other. It was the first piece of good news in many months.

One month later the next development canceled all the optimism over the turn of events in Europe. The Vichy government of France had agreed to let Japanese troops enter Indochina. "Protective Occupation," it was called. Between forty thousand and fifty thousand troops were to be stationed there. Now they had outflanked Malaya and were in position to attack Singapore from the rear if war came.

I hastened to Indochina and was on a bus between Pnom Penh, the ancient Khmer capital, and Saigon, a modern commercial city, when the first column of Japanese infantry came marching up the road. There they were again, the tough, dangerous little men in their ill-fitting uniforms. It had been one thing to see them in China and Mongolia. They had seemed to belong there. But in this serene and beautiful countryside (all of Southeast Asia has an enchanted, fairyland quality) they were a harsh note.

August: The President and Winston Churchill held the Atlantic Conference and issued a joint warning. "Any further encroachment by Japan in the Southwestern Pacific" could lead to war. A vaguely worded statement. What constituted "encroachment?" Had a line been drawn?

September: More Japanese troops poured into Indochina. They went into quarters outside the big cities, stationing themselves in jungle areas near remote villages. The newspapers in Saigon urged French women not to appear on the streets wearing shorts. Censorship reached the height of absurdity. I was not permitted to mention in dispatches that there were any Japanese in Indochina.

October: The Japanese began extensive maneuvers in the jungle. They were perfecting the techniques of fighting and infiltration in heat and heavy undergrowth, under conditions they would meet in the South Pacific. I spent a glorious week at the Angkor Wat. From the topmost level of this great temple palace I could hear the officers' commands and occasionally glimpse infantrymen moving through the trees.

November: Saburo Kurusu went to Washington to join Admiral Nomura in the negotiations. The sense of urgency grew stronger. I went to Hanoi in northern Indochina and from there by car over the mountains and across the border into China. The Chinese consul gave me an entry visa. Now, if need be, I could quickly escape Indochina into Yunnan.

In Hanoi I interviewed the Japanese ambassador, Kenkichi Yoshizawa, an old friend. He talked frankly. "Unless the talks in Washington succeed," he said, "the situation in the Pacific can no longer continue as it stands." He seemed a little sad. There was a sense of being dragged toward the edge of a waterfall.

Toward the end of November the Japanese envoys submitted a set of proposals to Roosevelt and Hull. They would send no more troops toward the south, but they did not offer to withdraw any. The proposal was rejected almost on sight. Henry L. Stimson, back in the Cabinet as Secretary of War, attended a "War Cabinet" meeting. He reported, and said he was surprised, that the President said "we" might be attacked soon, perhaps over the week end. He described the President's remarks in these words: "The problem was how we should maneuver them into the position of firing the first shot without allowing too much danger to ourselves."

In the lonely wastes of the North Pacific, far off normal shipping lanes, the Japanese First and Sixth fleets were cruising at a slow thirteen knots. They were 2,156 miles northwest of Hawaii.

At that moment only one fighting arm in the world could touch Japan. It was the mighty armada of ships and planes clustered in Pearl Harbor. With Russia at war, Japan no longer need fear the Far Eastern Red Army. Only one fighting arm on the whole globe . . .

Yet the die had not been cast. The Japanese task force had orders to turn back if they were sighted. Suppose some rusty freighter, blown far off course, had accidentally sighted the great, gray warships? Tokyo sent a message to Kurusu and Nomura, urging haste. Even at that eleventh hour the task force could be recalled. The apex of its arching course had been reached. Soon it would turn slightly southward.

Hull submitted American counterproposals. Japan must withdraw all troops from China and Indochina. Millions of men occupied the whole China coast and thousands of square miles in the interior. They had been fighting more than four years. Did anyone seriously believe Japan would agree? And in exchange for some promises of economic assistance?

The task force still cruised at thirteen knots. Course south-southeast.

The American counterproposal was read to the Privy Council in Tokyo. The preamble contained some qualifying words— "This is a basis for negotiation" and "This is a tentative plan."

A decade later in 1951 the diplomat and later Prime Minister Shigeru Yoshida disclosed that someone doctored the American note, eliminating these two sentences. "Not only were all those words deleted," he said, "but a portion covering the Japanese position was also deleted when the document was submitted to the Privy Council as the Hull Note. I was informed that only the American position was being maintained in a one-sided matter."

In short, here was an ultimatum.

Yoshida said that civilian administrators and some military leaders who were still reluctant to go to war with the United States now abandoned their opposition. They were now convinced, he said, that Japan had no alternative. The task force was on course for Honolulu. It could still be recalled.

On December 2 Imperial Headquarters radioed in code: "Aggressive action against the United States shall begin on 7 December." The famous "winds message," pulling the trigger, would soon be flashed.

In Tokyo, before the final week end, the American military and naval attachés burned their code books, records, and documents.

In Washington a news commentator analyzed the situation. "Having tried threats that did not impress the State Department, the Japanese are now giving soft answers." The Sunday morning newspapers published an advertisement for a forthcoming magazine article about the U.S. Pacific fleet: "Equipped with amazing new secret deadly devices that no enemy will ever know about (till it's too late) the biggest, toughest, hardest-hitting, straightest-shooting Navy in the world is primed and ready."

In the Pacific Ocean, two hundred miles from Pearl Harbor, the task force lay in darkness. Captain Fuchida Mitsue, commander of the flight groups in the First fleet, looked at his watch. The hands showed 5:00 A.M. Zero hour. In Saigon, because of the difference in time, it was approaching Sunday midnight. In the evening news broadcast from London a B.B.C. news analyst devoted his time to the talks in Washington. "If the Japanese would only stop shilly-shallying . . ."

I snapped off the radio and the lights in the hotel room. It was a hot night and somehow breathless. I went out on the veranda and looked down into the empty square beside the Hotel Continental. It was quiet. Then I went back to bed and again tried to sleep. A sound wakened me some time later, the whine of a siren on a Japanese staff car racing through the rue

Le Grand de la Liraye. It was exactly three o'clock in Saigon, eight o'clock in Honolulu.

At that instant the torpedo bombers burst through the clouds above Pearl Harbor and the first bombs left their racks.

EPILOGUE

THIS BOOK began in an internment camp in Saigon.

Early on the morning after Pearl Harbor a French correspondent burst into my hotel room. "The war has started," he said. The words hung in the air long after he had gone. The fact, so big, so brutal, was hard to take in. It was like the disbelief that comes when someone you saw an hour ago now lies dead. I sat on the edge of the bed for a long time, trying to understand.

A rifle butt banged on the door. A Japanese colonel, two soldiers, and a secret-police agent entered the room. In rickety French the agent said: "Our two countries are in a state of war and we have come to protect you"—a gentle euphemism meaning "This is an arrest."

Since they imprisoned only eight of us, the "camp" was a house. The guards warned us not to approach the gate or the garden walls. Otherwise, for the most part, they let us alone.

There was a garage behind the house. I put a board across two packing boxes and used it as a typewriter desk. Through the interminably long days, hot and damp in the tropics, I typed out notes, descriptions of incidents, conversations. Somehow it seemed to help me analyze the awful fact of the Pacific War and think about its origins.

In the raw hatred of the first days it seemed that all the weight of responsibility rested on the Japanese . . . If, after the Manchurian Incident, they had let China alone . . . If the rape of Nanking had never been . . . If they hadn't bombed American property and sunk the *Panay* . . . If they had stayed clear of the Axis . . . If the naked threat to Southeast Asia had never been posed . . . Like a prosecuting attorney, I arranged the points in the indictment.

A prisoner yearns first for freedom and then for home. Images of California arose . . . Tar-paper shacks and the "damned Japs" bending over rows of celery . . . Kids throwing stones at them . . . The "Yellow Peril" editorials . . . the California land laws, the Exclusion Act, crude discrimination against them . . . and the eternal chorus, "War with Japan." . . . what issue worth war existed between the United States and Japan in the 1920's . . . politicians playing with dynamite . . . businessmen eyeing an immigrant's profits in flowers and vegetables . . . then the Stimson Notes and the "Quarantine Speech."

Slowly a perspective formed. Factors came into balance. Conclusions began to take shape.

The Japanese had a clear, cold view of Japanese national interest and how they proposed to advance these in China and Southeast Asia. That was aggression. Americans had no clear view of American national interests in that part of the world or whether they were worth fighting for. That was fuzzy and therefore dangerous thinking. The Japanese were only too ready to back words with bullets. That was militarism. Americans insisted on condemning and taking a position, but would not fight for it. That was a folly that could only encourage militarism.

Above all, both violated Human Dignity.

When recognition of human dignity is withheld from a man because of his race or nationality or religion, when he is scorned and persecuted, when his weakness is exploited, then the law of retribution is as sure as fate.

This law is operating today in China. The Chinese are having their revenge on history. Revenge for the years of misery.

Revenge for the lost fruits of the Chinese Revolution. Revenge for the Opium War, the Japanese atrocities, for every ricksha coolie a white man slapped. They will have it in full measure. Then, but not before, we will restore friendship with China as we have with Japan.

Index

A NOTE ABOUT THE AUTHOR

RELMAN MORIN was born in Illinois in 1907, grew up in Los Angeles, and was graduated from Pomona College. In 1930 he studied at two Chinese universities. Since that time he has been a newspaperman, first with the Shanghai *Evening Post-Mercury*, then with the Los Angeles *Record*. In 1934 he joined the Associated Press, holding posts in Los Angeles, as Bureau Chief in Tokyo, and in Southeast Asia, where he was captured and interned by the Japanese in 1942. After he was repatriated, he covered many war fronts, and later was the A.P.'s bureau chief in Paris and Washington. The Korean War took him to a battle front again; for his efforts here he won a Pulitzer Prize (1951). Since then he has been a special correspondent, winning a George Polk Award for a series of articles on Senator McCarthy (1954), a second Pulitzer Prize, and another Polk Award in 1958 for his reports on Little Rock. He is the author of a book dealing with the last days of white supremacy in the Far East, *Circuit of Conquest* (1943).

A NOTE ON THE TYPE

THE TEXT of this book was set in CALEDONIA, a Linotype face designed by W. A. Dwiggins, the man responsible for so much that is good in contemporary book design and typography. Caledonia belongs to the family of printing types called "modern face" by printers—a term used to mark the change in style of type-letters that occurred about 1800. It has all the hard-working, feet-on-the-ground qualities of the Scotch Modern face plus the liveliness and grace that are integral in every Dwiggins "product" whether it be a simple catalogue cover or an almost human puppet. The book was composed, printed, and bound by H. Wolff, New York. Paper manufactured by S. D. Warren Co., Boston. Typography and binding based on designs by W. A. DWIGGINS.